T0283511

Rebel Sounds

Rebel Sounds
Music as Resistance

Joe Mulhall

First published in 2024 by
Footnote Press

www.footnotepress.com

Footnote Press Limited
4th Floor, Victoria House, Bloomsbury Square, London WC1B 4DA

Distributed by Bonnier Books UK, a division of Bonnier Books
Sveavägen 56, Stockholm, Sweden

First printing
1 3 5 7 9 10 8 6 4 2

A CIP catalogue record for this book is available from the British Library.

ISBN (hardback): 978-1-804-44116-9
ISBN (ebook): 978-1-804-44117-6

Printed and bound in Great Britain
by Clays Ltd, Elcograf S.p.A.

MIX
Paper | Supporting
responsible forestry
FSC
www.fsc.org   FSC® C018072

For Dad,
who gave me my love of music and history.

*Art is not a mirror to reflect reality, but a hammer
with which to shape it.*

– Bertolt Brecht

Contents

INTRODUCTION
Music as Resistance

I WAS LATE TO MY appointment with the National Philharmonic of Ukraine because of an air-raid. It was 9am on 22 February 2023, two days before the one-year anniversary of the full-scale Russian invasion. I was climbing into the shower when a picture of a missile in a red circle flashed up on my phone: 'Air Alert: Immediately proceed to the nearest shelter.' Seconds later, the Tannoy in my room popped into life with a looped recorded message, first in English, then in Ukrainian: 'We recommend you proceed to the shelter, take the stairs next to room twenty.' Then came the wailing drone of the sirens, bouncing off the buildings and down the streets of Kyiv.

I hurriedly put on my clothes and followed the arrows that directed a sleepy procession of half-dressed guests down to the shelter. The bottom floor of the underground car park had been transformed: camp beds placed in rows where cars were once parked, tables with chairs, even beanbags along one wall. There was a solitary vending machine, which would repeatedly steal my money as the week progressed, its chocolate bars balanced precariously but stubbornly unobtainable. The set-up was completed by a wicker bowl of tea bags but no milk. Though safe from any rockets, the bitter sub-zero temperatures above ground managed to penetrate the concrete. The collected journalists, aid workers and security consultants around me

1

were hunched over their laptops in thick winter coats and hats, warming their hands around paper cups of black tea. The smell – a mixture of car fumes and tobacco escaping from the designated smoking stairwell – hung dense in the air.

It being my first time hearing an air-raid siren, I had rushed down nervously, not thinking to bring a book, phone or laptop with me. It's amazing how quickly fear can turn to boredom. Upon arriving in Ukraine, I'd been told to expect regular Russian air raids to mark the war's anniversary, so I had no intention of ignoring them, but I was surprised how quickly I came to regard the once-terrifying sound of swirling sirens as an inconvenience. After a few laps of the garage, a quick shake of the vending machine and a little bounce on the camp bed, I'd relaxed enough to begin worrying about missing my interview with the orchestra. But as quickly as it had begun, it was over: the map of Kyiv on my phone, that had flashed red an hour before, returned to black.

I hurried upstairs, grabbed my recording equipment and rushed out into the stinging morning air. At first glance, Kyiv looked and felt relatively normal. The streets, shops and restaurants bustled with people going about their lives. Look a little closer, however, and it became clear how completely transformative and tragic the war has been for the people of Ukraine. Bombed-out tanks, missile-ravaged skyscrapers, checkpoints, sandbags and tank-traps all scar the city. I found a taxi and mumbled 'Lysenko Column Hall' to the driver, who pulled out with a nod.

The grand philharmonic hall is just moments from the vast Dnipro river and steps from the famous glass bridge that traverses the Saint Volodymyr Descent. So close, in fact, that when, in October of the previous year, a Russian missile had struck the bridge, the hall windows shattered. I was warmly greeted by the orchestra's head of marketing, Taras Ostapenko, who waved away my apology for being late. The disruption caused by war had rendered appointments more fluid, with people turning up as and when they could.

When war first broke out, the philharmonic hall was hurriedly converted into a barracks for soldiers. 'They lived in the building and our team was supposed to take care of them,' explained Taras. Unsurprisingly, with Russian tanks closing in and many expecting the city to imminently fall, there wasn't much time for concerts. 'There were no people left to play. Everyone left.' Yet, following the successful defence of the city, the citizens of Kyiv emerged from their shelters and some musicians did the only thing they could think of: play. Gathering an audience was too dangerous, so they recorded their performances online via Facebook and YouTube. 'We just played for streaming so that people understood that we were alive, that everything is OK,' Taras said with well-deserved pride.

Remarkably, despite the constant threat, the falling bombs, the endless power cuts and some of the musicians joining the army, the orchestra managed to carry on. Rehearsals resumed, sometimes by candlelight or torch. 'We don't need special equipment,' he grinned. 'We're just acoustic.' Siren-interrupted concerts were staged, albeit with a severely reduced capacity, in the main hall, and alternative arrangements were made when necessary. 'The room which is downstairs,' Taras said pointing to his feet, 'is multifunctional. It's a bomb shelter and it's a musical concert hall.'

I found it hard to imagine why, with fire falling from the sky, people still felt the need to risk leaving their homes and shelters to see live music. 'I can tell you about myself,' said Taras. 'When you stay in your flat, on the seventh floor, or the twentieth floor, and you have all the channels and all this information – "They are shooting from the Caspian", "from Crimea", whatever – you feel crazy. I think people are looking for an exit from that. And they find somewhere to go just to forget about war. Many of them feel they need it for medicine, to cure their spirit.'

We were joined by Larysa Parkhomyuk, the manager of the orchestra, who waltzed over like a storm of energy, a bundle of paper crushed under her arm. 'A lot of work!' she said, shuffling the pages. 'You see – costs, costs, costs!' I asked her why the orchestra had struggled on in such unimaginable circumstances. 'For everyone, for every person, there are different forms of defiance and resistance. For us, for Philharmonic people, it is a way to go on with life. This is our cultural front. We are fighting here.'

And why do people venture out to watch? 'When the audience come here, they come because of hope. The music gives them hope. The Philharmonic is like a church.' She walked me through to the main hall, where I found an organ-backed stage at one end and a grand balcony on four sides, supported by marble composite columns and all lit by three vast glistening chandeliers. I couldn't think of a worse place to stand if the building was ever struck.

I took a seat in one of the empty rows and quietly watched as the orchestra struck into life. Rehearsing for a series of concerts billed as 'Music of Defiance', they played 'Crying and Prayer' by the Ukrainian composer Valentin Bibik. Not being familiar with the piece, it took me some time to realise that they weren't tuning their instruments but had actually started playing it. Sections of ambling wind instruments were followed by screeching discordant violin strikes that built like a horror-movie soundtrack, before thwacks of the kettle drums and booming horns shook the room. It sounded like chaos, like a legion marching to war. It was exhilarating. I understood, even just a little bit, why some Ukrainians took the risk to leave their homes to attend these concerts. At a time of unimaginable fear and suffering, they decided that playing and listening to music is an act of resistance.

Back in London, I wrestled with how to describe what I felt sat alone in that hall, listening to the orchestra. It was excitement – joy, even – but simultaneously sadness and also fear. That's the thing about music. It has the ability to reach into us, fiddle with our innards, turn up or down particular emotions. Days later, while in the British Library thumbing a copy of the 1905 book *A History of Irish Music* by the wonderfully named musicologist Grattan Flood, I found a description of music's ability to affect our emotions that was more eloquent than anything I could muster. I opened the book's faded blue cover, wiped away the dust, pressed it to my nose and smelt the faint vanilla scent that books of a certain vintage all have. And there it was:

> Music is a universal language, appealing to the very soul of man, and is the outpouring of the heart, whether to express joy or sorrow, to rouse to battle, or soothe to sleep, to give expression of jubilation for the living or of wailing for the dead, to manifest sympathy with society or devotion to the Deity.[1]

Unquestionably, music, in all its glorious diversity, has the remarkable ability to evoke in us any and all emotions. It's why it is so endlessly fascinating. Music is what make us human. There's something about the rumble, pop, clap and thump of organised sound that our bodies find irresistible. Unlike other animals, it compels us to move. We nod our head, tap our feet, fling our arms into the air and gyrate our hips – not always in time, it must be said. The power that music has over us means it can be used by us, or on us. One such way is as an act of resistance.

The genesis of this book came back in 2019, when I stumbled across an exhibition called 'Rebel Sounds' at the Imperial War Museum in London. In a few small rooms, it told the story of people who had risked their lives to play music during conflicts, covering Nazi Germany, Northern Ireland in the 1970s, Serbia in the 1990s and northern Mali under Islamist rule. Naively, I had never really considered the idea of music as form of resistance. Since that day, it has been something of an obsession, taking me around the world to hunt for stories, people and, most importantly, records that contributed to fights against oppression and discrimination.

At first, my understanding of resistance music was narrow, focusing mainly on protest songs with explicitly political lyrics. That all changed after attending a concert-cum-lecture called 'Yiddish Glory: The Lost Songs of World War II'. In a non-descript classroom at Birkbeck University, the musician Pavel Lion (aka Psoy Korolenko) and the academic Anna Shternshis brought back to life a once-lost trove of Yiddish songs. They drew on an archive collected during World War II by a group of Soviet Yiddish scholars led by the ethnomusico-logist Moisei Beregovsky. It included songs of death, but also of survival and resistance to Nazi rule, as well as Jewish wartime service with the Red Army. Tragically, the project was never completed, following Beregovsky's arrest during Stalin's ruth-less antisemitic purges. Their work was sealed and thought lost until librarians at the Vernadsky National Library of Ukraine rediscovered them in the 1990s. Those with preserved melodies were played again for the first time since 1947, while others without were set to new music.

I sat on an uncomfortable seat and listened to Lion play once-lost songs about the massacre of Jews in Zhabokrych – 'Tell the world, every last person, that the town of Zhabokrych was turned into a cemetery' – and of people walking to their death in Pechora – 'Our suffering [and] our sorrows will soon be known to the whole world.' But he also sang about armed resistance: 'He bashed those fascists without a care.' It changed my understanding of not only what music can be used for, but also of what counts as resistance. To the composers and lyricists who scribbled these songs on scraps of paper, perhaps moments before their own deaths, the songs bore witness to a crime. They used a song to document events that might otherwise be lost, using memory as an act of defiance.

Shternshis also explained how one in three of the songs in circulation in ghettos and camps were humorous. Surrounded by death and squalor, laughing, smiling and singing funny songs was a humanising act of resistance. It made me realise that any exploration of this topic had to go beyond traditional protest songs and explore how even those songs that aren't overtly political, or don't address grand themes of opposition, can be used by people to inspire resistance within themselves.

These stories of resistance opened my eyes – and ears – to a part of the Holocaust I was unfamiliar with. My PhD was on the history of fascism, as were my first three books, and I'm now the director of research at the UK's largest anti-fascism organisation, HOPE not hate (HNH). For a decade, I sat on the board of the Holocaust Memorial Day Trust. Despite this, I had failed to consider the role of music, perhaps even dismissing it. But hearing Pavel Lion play those Yiddish resistance songs woke me up to the hidden – or sometimes ignored – role of music in major world events.

It also made me look back at my own activism. Though utterly irrelevant when compared to the remarkable stories of struggle I cover in this book, I realised that music accompanied everything I have done. When sent to monitor and photograph far-right demonstrations for HNH, I would listen to anti-fascist songs in the car to prepare myself. Before going undercover at fascist meetings across Europe and North America, I would always listen to Julio Iglesias' version of 'La Mer' to calm my nerves. At times, my activism, and that of my HNH colleagues, has been funded by benefit concerts by Billy Bragg, Paul Heaton and the Libertines. Looking back now, I'm not sure any of it would have been possible without music.

This book is a collection of these stories and hidden histories about how music has provided light in the darkest of times over the past century. How it steeled souls and inspired resistance to oppression. How, in moments of unimaginable fear and suffering, just playing and listening to music can be an act of resistance. It tells of those rare and brave people who loved a record so much that they risked imprisonment or even death just to listen to it. Those who danced through the night in back rooms and derelict warehouses of bombed-out cities to forget pain and vanquish fear. Those who resisted not with guns and bombs, but with trumpets and drums, guitars and microphones. Those people who remained spiritually free, despite the oppression that surrounded them. Of course, music itself doesn't change the world; it's people who change it. But music can give us hope when we have none. It can heal wounds and force us to our feet when we don't think we have the energy to stand any longer.

The hardest part of writing this book has been deciding what to include and, even more difficult, what not to. I've tried to find a range of stories that best typify the different, complex and nuanced ways in which resistance music has manifested itself. The danger of going beyond traditional protest songs – though plenty are discussed within – is that the result might not include some of the examples that people would expect or perhaps hope for. There will be readers who send this book whistling across the room when they realise there isn't a chapter on Bob Marley, Bob Dylan, Woody Guthrie or a specific one on hip hop or punk. Of course, their absence doesn't mean that music wasn't important or transformative. But many of those stories have been told before in countless other books and documentaries or there are other examples that I think better explain the various ways music has been used to fight for justice.

There will also be exasperated music fans or historians appalled that I have overlooked the staggering impact of their favourite Indian tabla, Ethiopian masenqo or Chilean charango player. No matter how much research I do, there will be remarkable stories I can't include, perhaps because of space or simply because I didn't know about them. Then there will be the anoraks, those obsessives who will email me in horror that I didn't mention that the album sleeve of – insert obscure record here – had a spelling mistake on the label and my failure to notice means I don't know what I'm talking about. To them, I say, 'I think you're missing the point.'

However, one of the joys of writing this book has been the endless recommendations and ideas I've been offered along the way. There are a million artists, genres and records that each changed the world a little bit, even for just one person. Sadly, though, I can't include them all.

The truth is that wherever there is or has been oppression of people, there will be examples of resistance taking on a musical form. It has formed part of every struggle for freedom, be it feminism, anti-racism or LGBTQ+ rights. They all have their own soundtracks. For this reason, despite the stories covered here, there remains fruitful ground that demands further exploration elsewhere. Right now in Iran, music and dance is part of the struggle for women's rights. In West Africa, the desert blues scene continues to operate in the face of Islamist threats. With the war on Gaza, songs continue to be part of the Palestinian resistance movement. I've no doubt that, even in North Korea, people are secretly playing and listening to banned music. The absence of these stories from this book is often explained by it currently being too hard or impractical to safely visit the places where this music is being made. As such, I'll just have to watch in admiration from a distance . . . for now at least.

Finally, there will be historians and experts frustrated by the truncated histories of the various regimes and systems of oppression that are discussed within. I, of course, empathise, but to cover all the complexities of centuries of British rule in Ireland, the rise and fall of the Soviet Union or the minutiae of decades of apartheid in South Africa within single a chapter has demanded I be selective. Particular events might be absent, a little nuance may be lost, but hopefully not accuracy.

I hope you will find some stories you don't know, some songs or artists you haven't heard but go on to fall in love with and, across them all, a better understanding of the transformative power of vibrations in the air.

ONE

The Tri-Coloured Ribbon: Rebel Songs and the Struggle for a Free Ireland

Recommended Listening:
Peadar Kearney – 'Tri-Coloured Ribbon'
Thomas Moore – 'Oh! Breathe Not His Name'
Jim Connell – 'The Red Flag'
Paddy McGuigan – 'The Boys of the Old Brigade'
Peadar Kearney – 'The Soldier's Song'/'Amhrán na bhFiann'
James Connolly – 'A Love Song'
Arthur M. Forrester – 'The Felons of Our Land'
Dominic Behan – 'Come Out Ye Black and Tans!'

–

DUBLIN IS ONE OF the most overrated music cities in the world. If you google 'Best places in the world for live music', Dublin is regularly listed in the top ten. *Lonely Planet*, the backpackers' guide of choice, waxes lyrical about the city on its 'musical metropolises' list, claiming that 'the gig selection is as eclectic as anywhere in the world'. It goes as far as encouraging visitors to 'forget the museums and retracing history; Dublin is about the fleeting thrill of live performance'.[1]

In reality, the city centre is cluttered with endless disappointing pubs packed beyond comfort with American tourists nursing an unwanted Guinness and singing along to 'Summer of '69' by Bryan Adams or 'Don't Stop Believing' by Journey. Hordes of British stag parties descend on its famous Temple Bar area to projectile vomit in unison to the sound of acoustic dad rock. Music, music everywhere, but all of it is rubbish.

However, if you leave the city centre behind, cross over the famous Ha'penny Bridge that elegantly straddles the Liffey, and walk far enough north that the cacophony of competing pop mediocrity finally subsides, you reach the Smithfield area of the city. Just past the Old Jameson Whiskey Distillery, on the corner of North King Street and Red Cow Lane, is a crumbling and frankly unwelcoming-looking pub – dirty black walls, small square windows squinting out from behind white metal bars, a solitary metal pillar unconvincingly holding up the corner of the building. As I approached on a dark and rainy Sunday afternoon in November, the three opaque glass lamps clinging to the external brickwork flickered intermittently, forcing me to read the name in fleeting glimpses: the Cobblestone.

I tentatively entered, forcing the door shut against the howling wind behind me. It was quiet, save for a few elderly regulars resting on the bar, signalling to the barman for another Guinness with a flick of their tired eyes. Inside was an altogether more welcoming prospect than the outside had suggested. Stained, dark wooden floorboards. Deep-garnet-red walls, covered with a clutter of framed pictures of musicians. Stools topped with lush red leather before a deep mahogany bar. And shelves overflowing with whiskey. As I ordered my drink, a low droning noise started, spreading from the corner of the bar like a creeping fog. I looked over and saw two men I'd missed before, sat around a small wooden table covered in

12

instruments. On the wall behind them was a sign that said 'Please Respect Musicians'. It read like a general call to respect *all* musicians, not just the ones in the pub.

The low drone was emanating from a set of uilleann pipes, the national bagpipe of Ireland. It looks like an impossibly complex instrument to grapple with, comprised of bellows, bag, chanter, three drones, seven reeds and three keyed regulators. The player, a rotund middle-aged man with thinning hair and a Confucius beard, inflated the bag using a small set of bellows that he pumped under his right arm and squeezed down on the bag with his left. Each pump forced air to three untouched open pipes that constantly play droning notes an octave apart, while the rest flowed to the chanter, which he played with his fingers like a flute.[2] It sounds nothing like the booming and cracking of the Great Highland bagpipes that instantly conjure up images of marching soldiers. The uilleann pipes are much quieter, more subtle – sweet, even – and thought by some to be the 'woolen bagpipe' referred to by Shylock in Shakespeare's *The Merchant of Venice*.[3]

The player's fingers danced a jig up and down the chanter, making an infectious sound that made me feel like I was finally in 'real' Ireland, years away from Temple Bar. His companion, a bald man wearing more denim than would be advisable, was moved to pull out a fiddle and match the pipes note for note. Together they merged into a repetitive pattern which, after a few minutes, became almost hypnotic. The sound flowed out across Dublin, summoning musicians, and by the time I had finished my drink, the pair had been joined by an accordionist, a flautist and a tin whistle player. Together, they filled the pub, first with sound, then with people. The gathered crowd began to sway, shuffle and then dance, kept in time by the guttural thump of the accordionist's foot on the uneven wooden floor.

This type of Irish music is usually called 'trad' – short for 'traditional' – a type of dance music played on string, wind, and free-reed melody instruments. Some people disregard it as simple and repetitive; 'it all sounds the same' is a common criticism. But this completely misses the point. The repetition is trance-inducing and the subtle nuances and decorative flourishes, the alterations in rhythm and tempo or changes of key become exciting if you're properly locked into the repeating melody. It has a surprising amount in common with electronic dance music, with the excitement and joy that follows subtle alterations and drops. It's no surprise as both are designed to make you move.

While trad music is a fundamental part of Ireland's cultural identity, it isn't overtly political, unlike the linked tradition of so-called 'rebel songs' and political ballads. While trad tends to be purely instrumental, Irish rebel music always features a singer, who often sings and plays guitar alone. However, if accompanied, the band traditionally consists of an Irish frame drum called the bodhrán and a mandolin or tin whistle. 'These latter two instruments make frequent use of tremolos, giving the music a trembling or shivering effect,' explains the historian of Irish rebel music, Stephen R. Millar.[4] This tradition goes back hundreds of years, but the songs often touch on similar themes: peasants desire for land; religious emancipation; discrimination; racism; oppression; colonialism; hunger and starvation; and, of course, the struggle for Irish freedom from British rule. In the words of the Irish author Samuel Beckett, 'When you are in the last ditch, there is nothing to do but to sing.'[5]

Writing in the 1960s, the historian Georges Denis Zimmermann argued that rebel songs weren't merely entertainment but actually had a societal impact: 'In every period before an expected rising, nationalist movements published violent songs which must have helped to raise the public to a high pitch of excitement and to prepare the minds for the coming disturbances.'[6] For this reason, watching rebel music is part gig, part political rally and part ceremony. As the ethnomusicologist Thomas Turino argues, 'the success of a performance is more importantly judged by the degree and intensity of participation than by some abstracted assessment of the musical sound quality'.[7] Remarkably, stood at the bar in the Cobblestone, I was about to witness this for myself.

The band downed instruments, a chance to refill glasses and empty bladders, and an unassuming elderly man who had been watching raised his voice. 'Do you mind if I sing a song?' he asked the musicians, who nonchalantly nodded their approval. 'My grandma was in the Easter Rising,' he continued, speaking of the 1916 insurrection by Irish republicans against the British, 'so this one is for her.' As soon as he started singing, an instant hush fell over the pub. The clinking of glasses, the shuffling of feet, the chatter, all fell silent.

I had a true love if ever a girl had one
I had a true love a brave lad was he
One fine Easter Monday with his gallant comrades
He started away for to make Ireland free

For all around my hat I wear a tri-coloured ribbon, oh
All around my hat until death comes to me
And if anybody's asking me why do I wear it
It's all for my own true love I never more will see

He whispered 'Goodbye love, old Ireland is calling'
High over Dublin our Tri-colour flies
In the streets of the city the foe man is falling
And wee birds are whistling 'Old Ireland arise'

15

Each time he reached the chorus – 'For all around my hat I wear a tri-coloured ribbon' – the whole pub joined in, falling silent again to listen intently to the verses. The Irish writer Thomas Davis declared that 'no enemy speaks slightly of Irish music, and no friend need fear to boast of it. It is without rival.'[8] Sitting in that pub on a bleak November Sunday, I finally understood where that confidence came from, the source of Irish music's power when done properly. He was singing about a rebellion against the British that his own family had taken part in, an event that had reignited his nation. Listening to him sing was a communal experience. It was a history lesson, an injection of identity directly into our ears, and it all happened, as is so often the case, in a pub.

For many people, pubs are life's punctuation; they mark the beginning and end of events. You 'wet the baby's head' after the arrival of a new child. A small gathering with a beige buffet following their christening. A pint on their eighteenth birthday. Lovers are met, lost and met again. The wedding reception. The anniversary parties. And then, finally, the wake. All these can happen in the pub. It's where people celebrate successes and commiserate losses. It's where they go when in a good mood, but also when they're sad. Pubs are transformative spaces, magical even. People enter them lonely but leave with friends. They go from being single into relationships and back again. It's a space where moods can be transformed, for better or worse. And all these experiences are lubricated by an endless array of wonderous brews and potions.

In an age where society's communal spaces disappear by the day – libraries close, factories shut, community centres turn into flats and fewer of us attend church – the pub remains the community living room. For these reasons, pubs can also be the place that people turn to in the darkest of moments, where

16

they gather to drown their sorrows together. Most importantly, however, it's not just local gossip you can pick up across the bar. It can be an education. Pubs can be where the history of a village, a town, a city or a country is kept alive, where macabre stories of murder or triumphant tales of daring rebellion and struggle are passed between generations. More often than not, the keepers of these stories, washed smooth like river stones, are musicians. Gathered around a table in the corner of the pub, they set story to song, the audience imbibing history unnoticed. Nowhere is this truer than in the place I was headed next: Galway.

Galway is a perfectly formed little city in the west of Ireland, where the river Corrib empties into the North Atlantic. Not the most picturesque of places – though not unpleasing – it's the city's cultural scene that really marks it out. I arrived by train from Dublin on a wet evening. Just minutes from the station is the peculiarly named Latin Quarter, a warren of medieval streets packed with pubs, bars and restaurants. The buildings are brightly coloured, with rich yellows, reds and greens reflected in neon streaks across the damp, cobbled road. Though it was only early evening, the sounds of fiddles already danced out of each window and door, while the pavements thronged with waltzing drunkards who had started too early. Galway plays host to a remarkable array of festivals, ranging from visual arts, comedy and drama to the Galway Races and the Galway Arts Festival. On the weekend when I was in town, there were two in full swing: Galway Folk Festival and, rather amusingly, Ukefest, which, as its name suggests, is an international ukulele festival.

I must admit that a town crawling with ukulele players sounded like hell. There's a reason that this funny little instrument is beloved by comedians; it looks amusing and sounds ridiculous.

I was taking refuge from the roaming gangs of players in Tigh Neachtain's, an enchanting old pub littered with wood-panelled nooks and crannies, and walls plastered with faded pictures of long-dead writers. As I walked to the toilet through a leak-drenched passageway, I heard the strum of a ukulele coming from a back room. There was no escaping Ukefest! As if passing an accident on the motorway, I found myself drawn towards the horror and tentatively poked my head through the door. To my utter surprise, what I found was unavoidably joyous: a tiny room packed with twenty people playing 'Sacrifice' by Elton John on their instruments. They enthusiastically strummed away, all belting out the lyrics – and some attempting misjudged harmonies – but all with the biggest smiles I'd ever seen. It was a group of strangers sitting around the table in a pub and singing together, with players eagerly watching the fingers of whomever started a new song so they could copy the chords and join in. It was infectious and, frankly, quite beautiful.

Everyone I asked before my trip told me that the best place to find trad music in Galway was the Crane Bar. A short walk from the Latin Quarter in the west end of the city, it looked exactly as I had hoped. The external walls were painted a deep green, with burgundy skirting along the bottom and up the corner, while Streaks of orange rust dripped from unused flag holders screwed into the facing. A bricked-up doorway showed a painting of an elderly man playing a tin whistle. It all looked very promising. Once inside, it was as expected, a standard pub of the Irish variety, with small groups of American tourists telling uninterested locals about their great-great-great-great grandfather who supposedly hailed from the area. One woman grabbed her three-quarter-poured Guinness as it rested on the bar and made for her table. The alarmed barman ushered her back. 'As I like you, I'll fill this one all the way to the top,' he said with a wink. 'Oh, thank you,' she replied, blushing. Another ordered 'three glasses of European pilsner', only to be met by a blank-faced barman. 'You mean Kronenbourg?' he offered. She shrugged noncommittally, so he began to pour.

As I waited for my drink, I noticed a thumping on the ceiling: the unmistakable sound of feet pounding on the floor. I grabbed my drink, hurrying up the stairs and through the double doors into a packed room of people, all of whom were facing a slightly raised stage along one wall. Despite the wind and rain outside, it was punishingly hot, with beads of sweat dripping from every brow. Leak-ruined plaster peeled from the dank yellow walls, an assortment of bric-a-brac cluttered the top of an unused piano, and candlesticks covered in the wax of long-spent candles sat on tables. It was perfect.

Similar to the Cobblestone in Dublin, all eyes were on the uilleann pipes, this time played by a ruggedly handsome old man with a perfectly formed white beard. His intricate but repetitive melody was replicated by a guitar, flute, banjo and tin whistle. Some stood in awe, while others stomped their feet, clapped and shuffled to the beat. There really is no form of music as infectious as Irish trad. Fortunately, it's difficult to avoid in this part of Ireland. Galway simply drips with music. And not just in the pubs; the streets are cluttered with musicians, playing before an open suitcase on every corner and crossing.

On a day when the weather lifted a little, I travelled an hour and a half south to see the Cliffs of Moher. This fourteen-kilometre stretch of sea cliffs marks the western frontier of Europe, towering over the Atlantic Ocean and looking across to the Aran Islands, distant smudges on the waters of Galway Bay. Their scale is difficult to comprehend, with only grazing cows, gliding seabirds and hikers shrunk to mere dots in the distance offering perspective. These vast sandstone and shale walls rise vertically out of the sea to a staggering height of 700 feet, their tops crested by lush green grass. Unsurprisingly, it thronged with tourists dropped off by a battalion of coaches. Picnic benches, gift shops and a hot-dog stall all eagerly relieved visitors of their money. Yet, even here, music was everywhere. Among the clutter of souvenir shops shifting beer mats and keyrings emblazoned with traditional Irish surnames was a music shop. It's hard to think of another country in the world where a site of natural beauty would be deemed an obvious place to sell instruments and sheet music.

A series of metal plaques ran along the cliff walls, explaining the importance of busking at the site. Musicians have come to the cliffs to play for visitors for generations. One plaque announced that 'the basic features of the music produced at the Cliffs have a close association with aspects of the local area, such as the gentle rolling landscape in this part of the country, the rough seas along the coast and the soaring Cliffs of Moher'. Players held 'pitches' at regular intervals so their music 'would not sonically overlap'. Another sign explained how the strong winds and salty sea air corroded their instruments, forcing them to regularly replace them or, more intriguingly, use 'instruments custom-made for rigorous outdoor environments'. Sadly, no details about how one would modify an accordion, flute or banjo to better withstand a brisk salty wind were offered. As I enthusiastically devoured a surprisingly reasonably priced hot dog, I noticed an elderly couple dancing to the songs of one the buskers, oblivious to the mass of day-trippers wheezing past them up the steps to the cliff's edge. I guess it was testament to trad music's enduring ability to make people forget the present, to remember the past and, of course, to dance.

—

As an Englishman, it is with some measure of trepidation that I dip my toe into Irish history. While not impossible, it's always a sensitive task for anyone to write about the history of another country, something I do throughout this book. Even when undertaken with the greatest care, it's possible to miss the nuances or to filter information through one's own ingrained prejudices and preconceptions. This, of course, becomes even harder when much of the history of that country is stained from oppression by your own. Being British, this is the case with depressingly large portions of the globe.

In Ireland, however, this challenge feels especially acute. After all, war still raged in the north of Ireland in my life-time. As a child, I remember my father being late home from work whenever London's Waterloo station was closed following an Irish Republican Army (IRA) bomb scare. This likely makes any complete objectivity impossible, no matter how hard one tries. But then I think that about all history anyway. There is also an understandable suspicion, and in some cases hostility, in Ireland towards 'the Brits'. Yet, as is so often the case when it comes to Anglo-Irish relations, there is a complexity to this story tied up in the history of my own family.

I once found myself at a pub in Dublin with activists from Sinn Féin, the republican political party with a history of close association with the IRA. We were having drinks after a trade union conference on 'International Solidarity' that we had all attended and I mentioned to them that I had visited the Irish Emigration Museum, a wonderful place which traces 1,500 years of Irish history. It's a sobering sight for an Englishman, with room after room documenting the countless horrors and atrocities committed by the British in Ireland.

'I felt rather ashamed,' I told them honestly.

'Well, at least you've got the grace to feel ashamed,' snapped one of the Sinn Féin activists.

I began to bristle, not least because the person who said it spoke with a thick American accent. I think what most angered me was that much of my family was Irish at the time many of these crimes were committed. My relatives on my father's side moved from Ireland to Liverpool in the immediate wake of the Great Famine, so the painfully moving, emaciated sculptures of the Famine Memorial at Custom House Quay on the banks of the Liffey is as much part of my family history as it likely was hers. My grandfather even sang rebel songs to my father as a boy. Yet, sat in the pub, with my accent, I was expected to feel shame. I'm not saying I shouldn't. After all, I've grown up in a country that has benefitted from its rampant imperialism. I'm just noting that it's complex, and an acceptance of complexity isn't a bad place to start when it comes to any history, especially that of Ireland.

The historian Micheál Ó Siochrú has described the history of Anglo-Irish relations, 'from Henry VIII's Reformation in the 1530s, through the horrors of the Tudor conquest and the wars of the seventeenth century', as a 'seemingly relentless tale of blood, tragic episodes, punctuated by periods of relative peace, which did nothing more than enable both sides to regroup before resuming the struggle once again'.[9] Such sentiments are nothing new, however. As far back as the sixteenth century, an English civil servant wrote: 'It is a proverb of old date, that the pride of France, the treason of England and the war of Ireland, shall never have an end. Which proverb, touching the war of Ireland, is likely always to continue, without God set it in men's breasts to find some new remedy that never was found before.'[10]

Depending on how one defines 'the English', you can argue there was roughly 800 years of English rule in Ireland, starting

with the Anglo-Norman invasion in 1169. Control was solidified following the Nine Years' War between 1594 and 1603
with the defeat of the Ulster Gaelic chieftain Hugh O'Neill
and the subsequent Flight of the Earls in 1607. Around ninety
of O'Neill's followers fled Ireland to mainland Europe, essentially marking the end of the old Gaelic order and clearing the
way for the plantation of Ulster.[11] When King James I became
the first monarch to rule England, Scotland and Ireland, he
set about solidifying his control. From 1609 onwards, English
and Scottish Protestants were encouraged to move to northern
counties of the Ireland with a staggering 1.6 million hectares
being made available. In just three decades, upwards of 40,000
settlers had made the journey across the Irish Sea.[12] The new
arrivals were met with opposition; in 1641, dispossessed
landowners rebelled, killing 4,000 Protestant colonists.

However, what followed has forever scarred Anglo-Irish
relations and stands out in the collective Irish consciousness.
Between 15 August 1649 and 26 May 1650, Oliver Cromwell
campaigned in Ireland. Backed by an army of 20,000 men, a
sizeable navy and a vast artillery train, he 'projected himself as
a providential liberator from Irish barbarism, royalist misrule,
and Catholic hypocrisy'.[13] His time in Ireland was marked by
extraordinary brutality. His infamous storming and sacking of
Drogheda on 11 September 1649, when he put to death 'almost
the entire garrison and such recusant clergy as could be found',
has been described by the historian J. C. Beckett as 'one of
the best-remembered events in Irish history'.[14]

Though he spent just nine months in Ireland, Cromwell 'stands
accused there of war crimes, religious persecution and ethnic
cleansing on a dramatic scale'[15], with Ó Siochrú describing him
as 'unquestionably the most ruthless exponent of his country's
uncompromising policy of conquest and colonisation'. For this

reason, Cromwell remains a viscerally hated figure in Ireland and, for many, exemplifies the cost of British brutality. 'Throughout the island, people blame him for every ruined castle or tower house, while local folklore is replete with stories of terrible acts committed by his troops against the native population.'[16]

For Ireland's beleaguered and oppressed Catholics, a brief glimmer of hope followed the accession of the Catholic James II to the throne in 1685 – even if much of the Gaelic Irish populace only fought for him due to the promise of land. Even this far back, music was a means by which Irish people expressed their politics. 'It was stated that soon after the accession of James II in 1685, ballads written by hired scribblers were bawled about the streets in Ireland, "to inflame the spirit of the common people".'[17]

Any respite was short-lived, though, with James's defeat at the Battle of the Boyne in 1690 at the hands of William of Orange, a date that, despite the paucity of English awareness of Irish history, is often still marked on British calendars. However, despite centuries of war, oppression, rebellion and uprisings, it was not until the 1790s that militant republicanism as we think of it today properly emerged.[18] The Irish historian Thomas Bartlett called this period 'the crucible of modern Ireland when separatism, republicanism, unionism and Orangeism captured the Irish political agenda for generations to come'.[19] There is not space here to touch on the endless manifestations and machinations of the Irish republican movement from the end of the eighteenth century until the Irish Revolution and Independence in 1921, but there are several people and events too important not to touch upon briefly, many of which involve music.

Influenced by the intoxicating revolutionary spirit in France and the newly minted United States, Ireland rose in 1798. The United Irish Society had been founded in Belfast and Dublin in 1791 to work towards parliamentary reform and Catholic emancipation. Drafted by Theobald Wolfe Tone, their October 1791 declaration called for 'a complete and radical reform of the representation of the people in parliament'.[20] Frustrated by the lack of progress resulting from a constitutional approach and influenced by increasingly revolutionary ideas, they led a genuinely mass uprising in May of 1798. Motivated by what Alvin Jackson calls a combination of 'an intellectually coherent, and indeed accessible, ideology of liberation with ancient historical resentments and religious prejudices', they managed to convince at least 27,000 people to fight in Ulster alone.[21]

However, the rebellion was brutally put down with various levels of resistance, while the French forces that came to aid the Irish arrived too late. The death toll ran into the tens of thousands (estimated to be around 30,000) and Wolfe Tone was captured, arrested and sent to Dublin, where he committed suicide. Despite the failure of the uprising, however, the events of 1798 and Tone's defiance became legend and inspired future generations of republicans and Irish radicals.

More than any other country I can think of, music plays an important role in so many major events in Irish history, the 1798 uprising included. The author of *Sounding Dissent*, Stephen R. Millar, has shown how the United Irishmen used music 'to shore up shared notions of Irishness, activating people to mobilise against Britain'.[22] Writing in the early nineteenth century, the novelist James McHenry argued that the songs produced by the United Irishmen 'did more to increase the numbers of the conspirators than all the efforts of the French emissaries, or the writings and harangues of all the political philosophers and age-of-reason men of the times'.[23]

Wolfe Tone himself was a proficient flautist well versed in Irish traditional music, while its co-founder, Thomas Russell, played the harp.[24] Another, Edward Fitzgerald, was a very talented uilleann piper. They even produced a songbook titled *Paddy's Resource: Being a Select Collection of Original and Modern Patriotic Songs, Toasts and Sentiments*, and supported the 1792 Belfast Harp Festival, which was an example 'of how Irish musical prowess could be used to push the notion of Irish exceptionalism, while promoting a cultural unity among those living on the island'.[25] To mark the third anniversary of the storming of the Bastille in France, they organised a vast outdoor meeting in Belfast where French and Irish revolutionary songs were sang, including one penned by Wolfe Tone that finished:

Then let us remember our madness no more,
What we lost by division, let Union restore,
Let us firmly unite, and our covenant be,
Together to fall, or together be free.[26]

Remarkably, Tone was by no means the only leader of an uprising to also compose resistance songs. Following the failed uprising, Britain's prime minister, Pitt the Younger, passed the 1801 Act of Union, resulting in direct rule from Westminster. If Pitt had hoped the move would pacify Ireland, he was mistaken and, in 1803, Robert Emmet led an abortive rebellion, which was to be the last action of the United Irishmen and essentially spelled the end of the group – although its ideology lived on long afterwards.

Having returned from hiding in France, Emmet gathered the remaining United Irishmen and launched a premature, doomed and short-lived uprising on 23 July. He was captured, tried and executed. Once again, however, his failure entered the legend of Irish resistance, inspiring future generations of radicals. He is now best remembered for his defiant speech from the dock where he declared: 'Let no man write my epitaph ... When my country takes her place among the nations of the earth, then shall my character be vindicated, then may my epitaph be written.'[27]

His words inspired the song 'Oh! Breathe Not His Name' by the Irish songwriter Thomas Moore.[28] However, similar to Wolfe Tone, Robert Emmet wrote his own songs and poetry. His song 'Lines' finishes with the stirring call:

Erin's sons, awake!-awake!
Oh! Too long, too long, you sleep;
Awake! arise! Your fetters break,
Nor let your country bleed and weep.[29]

This tradition of songs being at the heart of the struggle for emancipation continued for the rest of the century. Just as the United Irish Society had before them, the Irish Republican Brotherhood – founded in the United States in 1858 and more commonly known as the Fenian Brotherhood (or simply the Fenians) – also produced a songbook to accompany their struggle for independence. In New York in 1866, they published *Stephens' Fenian Songster, Containing All the Heart-Stirring and Patriotic Ballads and Songs, as Sung at the Meetings of the Fenian Brotherhood.* Being penned and published by Irish emigres unsurprisingly affected the lyrics, which sought to stir support for their oppressed homeland and join the fight for an independent future.

Writing in the 1960s but looking back at the 1800s, the influential author of *Irish Political Ballads and Rebel Songs* Georges Denis Zimmermann explained that 'Ireland is one of the countries where patriotic and political songs have been for a long time peculiarly popular, and perhaps influential'.[30]

He identified two main trends within the lyrics of political songs from the period, namely the struggle of the peasantry for land and middle-class nationalist aspirations, often combined with the desire to throw off the religious persecution imposed by the minority community.[31] Importantly, Zimmermann argued, these songs weren't merely an articulation of people's angers and hopes, but also a form of propaganda that could bind people together and shape their understanding of events.[32]

The centrality and influence of music on the struggle is exemplified by a note by the editor of the nationalist journal *The Nation* who, on 14 January 1843, wrote:

> We receive at least twenty songs every week, full of bitter complaints of the fallen condition of our country, or hopes of her speedy resurrection. Every one of these we recon of more value, as an evidence of the condition of the popular mind, than a dozen speeches or a score of petitions.[33]

For this reason, Thomas Osbourne Davis – the Protestant son of a Welshman who had enlisted in the British Army and been stationed in Mallow, County Cork – who became founder of the nationalist Young Ireland movement and editor of *The Nation*, said:

> Music is the first faculty of the Irish, and scarcely any thing has such power for good over them. The use of this faculty and this power, publicly and constantly, to keep up their spirits, refine their tastes, warm their courage, increase their union, and renew their zeal, is the duty of every patriot.[34]

Not everyone agreed with these sentiments, however; some complained that singing songs was a poor substitute for actual radical action. In 1848, John Mitchel's revolutionary paper *The United Irishman* 'complained that too much energy had been wasted in songs', while the *United Ireland* reminded its readers in 1881 that 'singing songs is by no means the highest kind of service to Ireland'.[35] Few would disagree, of course. Songs alone can't break chains or bring down empires, but they can inspire those determined to do so. However, despite centuries of rebellion and songs that inspired and commemorated them, the nineteenth century ended with Ireland still occupied and oppressed. Yet the dawn of a new century, together with Europe's slide into a cataclysmic world war, offered new opportunities for those who dreamed of a free Ireland.

—

Perhaps what's the most enchanting thing about Ireland is the spontaneity with which live music occurs. More than in any other country I've visited, live music just seems to materialise. There's a strong chance that, anywhere where people have gathered, someone will pull out an instrument and begin playing. As if magicked from the air, fiddles, accordions, banjos, pipes and bodhrans just strike up unannounced. And if an instrument isn't to hand, someone will just start singing.

In the summer of 2023, I was at an anti-racism conference held at a golf club in Trim in County Meath. That evening, while having drinks on the terrace, I was sat next to a pleasant elderly lady who I didn't recognise. We made engaging-enough small talk for some time. Then, as the sun finally set, she quietened down the whole group with a wave of her arm. 'I'm going to sing a song,' she said. A hush instantly fell across the group as she began.

The people's flag is deepest red,
It shrouded oft our martyred dead
And ere their limbs grew stiff and cold,
Their hearts' blood dyed its every fold.

So raise the scarlet standard high,
Beneath its shade we'll live and die,
Though cowards flinch and traitors sneer,
We'll keep the red flag flying here.

She sang quietly and her voice had a warm warble to it. When she finished, people clapped before carrying on their conversations as though what just happened was completely normal.

'You know who that is?' asked the person to my right.

'No idea,' I shrugged.

It turned out the woman singing was Bernadette Devlin McAliskey, the famous Irish civil rights leader. A stalwart of the movement since the 1960s, she spent time with the Black Panthers in the United States, even appearing on *The Tonight Show Starring Johnny Carson*. She represented Mid-Ulster as an MP in Westminster and famously crossed the floor to attack the Home Secretary, Reginald Maudling, after British soldiers shot twenty-six unarmed civilians in 1972. Then, in 1981 Devlin McAliskey was seriously wounded in an assassination attempt carried out by the Ulster Freedom Fighters. I couldn't quite believe I was sat next to her as she sang socialist songs. A few minutes passed and the murmuring settled, so she sang again, before expectedly looking around the group for someone else to take the stage.

'Aren't you going to sing?' asked Bernadette.

'I've not got a voice,' I replied, aware that I can't sing and that I was the only Englishman in a group primarily made up of passionate Irish republicans. However strong my sympathies for a united Ireland, it still felt like an easy situation to get wrong.

'I could sing the British national anthem?' I quipped and was relieved when they responded in good humour.

'Come on,' she said, 'you must know a song.'

'I really can't sing,' I offered again.

'It's not about the singer, it's about the song,' Bernadette replied, taking away my final excuse. I rapidly scanned my head for any songs I knew the lyrics to, then scanned the lyrics to make sure there was no mention of Britain 'ruling the waves' or conquering the world. I settled on Billy Bragg's version of Leon Rosselson's 'Diggers' Song'.

'In 1649 / To St George's Hill / A ragged band they called the Diggers / Came to show the people's will . . .'

To my relief, someone joined in and I made it through unscathed. This went on for hours. At one point, the woman behind the bar came out and sang with a staggeringly beautiful voice. 'Is this normal?' I asked the barman, while filling my arms with whiskies for the table. 'Yes,' he replied, as though I'd asked a silly question. But to me it was extraordinary – the way an ordinary drink turned into a chance to communally remember their heroes, toast their victories and lament their losses; the way people from different countries, religions, races and sexualities each told their own histories through song. What seemed ordinary to those sitting around the table was totally magical to me.

Back in Dublin city centre with a thick head, I walked the sodden roads that hug the river Liffey before turning up O'Connell Street, where I was greeted by the blackened bronze

31

face of former MP Daniel O'Connell. The statue, erected in 1882 to memorialise his work passing the Catholic Emancipation of 1829, glares down from a vast granite plinth. You wouldn't notice at first glance, but if you get close enough, you can see it is peppered with around thirty small bullet holes, wounds inflicted by British guns in 1916. Just moments up the road is the likely original target of those bullets, the General Post Office. Six imposing, fluted ionic columns hewn from Portland stone make up the portico of a grand Greek revival building. It was here, in April 1916, that Irish republicans rose once more against British rule in what is now understood to be one of, if not the, seminal moment of Irish history: the Easter Uprising.

At the start of the twentieth century, there was qualified optimism from British quarters that centuries of Anglo-Irish antagonism had settled down. In 1900, Queen Victoria was greeted by more than 50,000 Dubliners waving Union Jack flags in Phoenix Park. Then, in July 1911, King George V visited and was greeted by a rapturous welcome from thousands who lined the streets of the second city of empire. 'There has been no royal progress in Ireland in our memory witnessed by such mammoth crowds as those of Saturday,' read *the Irish Independent*, 'and no British sovereign coming to our shores has had such a reception as that accorded our royal visitors on Saturday.'[36] 'Half the great fog of misunderstanding and suspicion that has brooded so long over the relations between England and Ireland has been cleared away in the seven mile roar of welcome,' the *Daily Telegraph* optimistically declared.[37] However, the events of 1916 and its aftermath meant that no British monarch would return to Dublin for 100 years.

The outbreak of World War I in 1914 meant that the steady progress towards home rule in Ireland was halted. Luckily for

the British prime minister, Herbert Asquith, the leaders of the
two main Irish parties, John Redmand and Edward Carson,
both promised their support to the war effort.[38] Many thousands of Irishmen joined the British army and were sent to the
blood-soaked fields of the Western Front. For others, however,
the commencement of hostilities on the continent offered an
opportunity, a chance to go well beyond the offer of home rule
and to strive for a fully independent Ireland. According to the
historian J. C. Beckett, 'within a few weeks of the outbreak of
war, they had resolved that before it ended the independence
of Ireland should be asserted in arms; and, in making their
resolve, they were moved less by any calculation of the prospect
of success than by a feeling that, if such an opportunity were
allowed to pass, the reality of Irish national aspirations might
be called in question'.[39]

These differing attitudes towards the war can be seen
through the famous wartime song 'It's a Long Way to
Tipperary'. Written by Jack Judge and Harry Williams in
1912, two years before the outbreak, the lyrics tell of an
Irishman in the British army longing for his sweetheart back
in Tipperary. The song became hugely popular during the
war, being sung by soldiers and selling millions of copies,
to the point where it remains a well-known song associated
with the war to this day. I remember singing it at an assembly
while at primary school. However, for those opposed to
Irishmen fighting and dying for Britain, the song was seen
as an insult. An Irish-American songbook from the period,
*Songs and Poems of the Rebels Who Fought and Died For
Ireland in Easter Week*, stated that 'Irish-Americans consider
the so-called song entitled "It's a Long Way to Tipperary"
as a vile, vulgar caricature of their race, a product of the
cheap London Music Halls, which manufacture filthy

red-light literature'.[40] As an act of defiance, they satirically remade the song offering alternative lyrics:

Tis the wrong way to Tipperary – 'tis the wrong way you know;
Tis the wrong way to Tipperary, when recruiting you must go.
Good-bye English army, farewell friend and fie;
Tis the wrong way to Tipperary, for our boys won't go.

This refusal to fight for Britain led some republicans to back her enemy, Germany, a move also reflected in the songbook, with one song, 'Ireland Over All', being set to the tune of 'Deutschland Über Alles':

Ireland! Ireland! 'fore the wide world,
Ireland! Ireland! Over all;
When we fight we'll fight for Ireland –
Answer only Ireland's call:
Plain and mountain, rock and ocean;
Ireland! Ireland! 'fore the wide world,
Ireland one and Ireland free.

Despite the propaganda efforts of songsmiths such as this, 200,000 Irishmen fought, and some 35,000 died, on the muddy battlefields of Europe. However, with Britain's gaze turned to the continent, republicans readied themselves to strike at the Empire from behind. There were many individuals and movements that contributed to the events of April 1916, but the primary planning of the final stages was carried out by the Irish Republican Brotherhood. The men and women who rose came from the Patrick Pearse-led Irish Volunteers, the

Irish Citizen Army led by James Connolly, and women from the all-female paramilitary unit Cumann na mBan.

The morning of 24 April 1916 was warm and sunny, a sleepy city rising for Easter Monday. Yet the peace of that crisp day was soon to be shattered by the chaotic sounds of revolution. As one contemporary ballad went:

It was on Easter Morning the boys got the call
To join their battalions in park, glen and hall,
In less than an hour they were out on parade;
They were true men tho' few in the Dublin Brigade.[41]

By 10am, members of the Irish Citizen Army had mustered below a sign reading 'We serve neither King nor Kaiser but Ireland' hung from Liberty Hall. A countermand had been issued following the disastrous interception of 20,000 rifles destined for the Irish Volunteers, meaning the number of people who mustered come the day was a fraction of what had originally been planned. Just 2,000 men and women assembled throughout the capital. At midday, Pearse and Connolly headed a group of 150 men and women, and made their way to the General Post Office (GPO), the planned main garrison for the rebel forces. It had begun. The organisers of the uprising issued the Proclamation of the Republic, a staggering poetic and powerful scream for freedom. On the steps of the GPO, underneath the flag of the Irish Republic, Patrick Pearse read it allowed: 'In the name of God and of the dead generations from which she receives her old tradition of nationhood, Ireland, through us, summons her children to her flag and strikes for her freedom.' The document was signed on behalf of the provisional government by Thomas J. Clarke, Seán Mac Diarmada,

Patrick H. Pearse, James Connolly, Thomas MacDonagh, Éamonn Ceannt and Joseph Plunkett.

Inevitably, however, with their superior numbers and supplies, the British suppressed the uprising within just six days. When the guns finally fell silent, 485 people were dead: eighty-two Irish rebels, 260 civilians and 143 British military personnel.[42] A staggering 2,600 were injured, many by the heavy bombardment of the city by British gunboats firing from the Liffey. Large sections of the second city of empire had been turned to rubble. As the surviving volunteers fled the burning GPO, they defiantly sang 'The Soldier's Song'/'Amhrán na bhFiann'.[43]

> Soldiers are we
> whose lives are pledged to Ireland
> Some have come
> from a land beyond the wave
> Sworn to be free
> No more our ancient sire land
> Shall shelter the despot or the slave
> Tonight we man the Béarna Baol
> In Erin's cause, come woe or weal
> 'Mid cannons' roar and rifles peal
> We'll chant a soldier's song.

The lyrics were written by Peadar Kearney, who took part in the rising and the song later became the Irish National Anthem.

In the days that followed the crushing of the uprising, those who survived were arrested, including all seven signatories of the Proclamation. Eventually, in a move that would backfire catastrophically for the British, they were executed by firing squad at Kilmainham Gaol. In total, sixteen people were executed, fourteen in Dublin, one in Cork and another in

London. The uprising was over, as were the lives of its key architects, yet the legend of their martyrdom had only just been born. Remarkably, of the seven men who signed the proclamation, five were songwriters.

Today, the best-remembered of this illustrious group is James Connolly. Born in Edinburgh in 1868 and executed by the British in 1916, his truncated life remains an inspiration to socialists, trade unionists and 'agitators' all over the world ('agitator' being the word he used to describe his occupation when applying to join the Socialist Labour Party of Great Britain in 1903).[44] Connolly took part in the famous Dublin Lock-Out of 1913, before co-founding the Irish Citizen Army and becoming one of the key leaders of the 1916 Uprising. As with many of his rebel forebears, he passionately believed that music was an essential weapon in the armoury of a revolutionary. In 1907, he edited *Songs of Freedom*, a collection of eighteen songs published for the working class in the United States, nine of which were penned by Connolly himself. His short but passionate preface declared:

No revolutionary movement is complete without its poetical expression. If such a movement has caught hold of the imagination of the masses, they will seek a vent in song for the aspirations, the fears and the hopes, the loves and the hatreds engendered by the struggle. Until the movement is marked by the joyous, defiant singing of revolutionary songs, it lacks the most distinctive marks of a popular revolutionary movement, it is the dogma of a few and not the faith of the multitude.[45]

The collection includes 'The Red Flag', the song I had heard Bernadette Devlin McAliskey sing; 'The Marseillaise', a hat-tip to the enduring influence of the French Revolution on Irish republicanism; and 'The Rights of Man', a song that previously appeared in *Paddy's Resource*, the songbook produced by the United Irishmen previously discussed. My favourite, however, is Connolly's own achingly beautiful 'A Love Song':

Yes, Freedom, I love you, my soul thou hast fired
With the flame that redeems from the clay,
Thou hast given to me, as to Moses inspired,
A glimpse of that land bright as day,
Whither Labor must journey, tho' each foot of the road
Sweat blood from the graves of its best,
Where, built upon justice and truth, the abode
Thou preparest awaits the opprest.[46]

The song drips with pain and longing, stirring yet gentle, a love song to freedom. Sadly, Connolly never lived to see a free Ireland, being executed for his role in the 1916 uprising. Heartbreakingly, Nora Connolly, his daughter who had taught people her father's songs, later wrote that 'after 1916, I never did any more singing'.[47] Thankfully, many others managed to sing on and James Connolly's role in the Easter Uprising, together with his many songs, inspired his comrades to continue, and others to join, the fight for freedom he so eloquently demanded.

–

The Irish Free State was established in December 1922. Though the Easter Uprising of 1916 had ostensibly been a failure, it had contributed to a profound shift in Irish public opinion to the point where the republican Sinn Féin party won the general election of 1918. With republicanism on the rise, the British were rather sensitive about the singing of what they understood to be seditious songs and, in 1918, nine individuals were imprisoned for it.[48] Jack O'Sheehan was sentenced to two years' hard labour for singing 'The Soldiers Song' and 'The Felons of Our Land'. Police seized songbooks and ballad sheets from Sinn Féin in both 1917 and 1918. In August 1918, a shop on Mary Steet in Dublin was raided by the police and a collection of songbooks confiscated. These crackdowns did little to stop these songs becoming anthems of resistance, but did serve to demonstrate to an already embittered Irish public the lengths that the British state would go to censor Irish free expression.[49]

Rather than taking up their seats in parliament in London, Sinn Féin founded their own, the Dáil Éireann, which subsequently led to the outbreak of the Anglo-Irish War – or the War of Independence – in January 1919. This guerrilla conflict between Britain and the IRA rumbled on for two years and five months before the signing of the Anglo-Irish Treaty of 1921, which founded the Irish Free State, a self-governing dominion of the British empire comprising twenty-six of the thirty-two counties. Not everyone saw this as the final victory they had fought so hard for. A civil war between the Irish Free State and the anti-treaty IRA broke out in June 1922 before the pro-treaty national army was victorious in May 1923. It wasn't until 1949 that Ireland left the Commonwealth and became a republic. The six north-eastern counties remain part of the United Kingdom to this day.

Rebel songs by no means stopped with the creation of the Free State in 1921, with many of the most popular songs, which look back at this period, being written in the subsequent decades. Rebel songs were also popular during the Troubles, the conflict between unionists and Irish nationalists that raged in Northern

Ireland for more than thirty years between the late 1960s until 1998. For some in Ireland and Northern Ireland, the struggle for a single united Ireland goes on; there are plenty of songs still to be sung and perhaps a few more to be written.

Today, however, the issue of rebel songs remains a controversial topic in Irish society. 'Whether a song is dangerous or insulting depends on who you ask, their ideological affiliations, and the political character of the present,' explained a 2023 article in the *Irish Times*.[50] The historical battles of the last 100 years remain live issues, with contemporary political parties often tracing their birth back to the period of the civil war. Which side your party was on then can affect how you feel about a certain rebel song about that period now. Also, with the passing of the Good Friday agreement in 1998 bringing an end to the Troubles, many are understandably cautious, or even hostile, towards the continued singing of songs which venerate violence. 'Rebel songs can become unacceptable to more people the closer the events they describe are to the present. The same song can be, at different times and to different people, a source of community strength, an anodyne historical curiosity or a live and dangerous incitement to violence.'[51]

Historical context and distance is important here, with songs about the IRA during the War of Independence and songs about them now being very different beasts. Is a packed pub raucously singing 'The Rifles of the IRA' a harmless historical exercise or a dangerous endorsement of contemporary violence? It depends who you ask. Recently Pádraig Mac Lochlainn, a member of the Irish parliament for Sinn Féin, tweeted: 'The sickening hypocrisy of some on this space who are lecturing our young people on their history. These hypocrites invite us to celebrate the Irish Republican men and women from 1916 and from 1919 to 1923, but to criminalise the Irish Republican men and women from the 1960s to the 1990s.'[52]

These debates have flared up again recently thanks in large part to the continuing success of the Irish rebel band the Wolfe Tones. Formed in 1963 and, of course, taking their name from one of the leaders of the Irish rebellion of 1798, the band has shocked many with their recent success. In 2020, in response to the Irish government's plans to commemorate the controversial Royal Irish Constabulary (RIC), the Wolfe Tones' 1972 version of 'Come Out Ye Black n Tans' shot to number one in both the UK and Irish iTunes charts.[53]

'Come out ye' black and tans! Come out and fight me like a man . . .'

The song, technically about a row between republican and loyalist neighbours in inner-city Dublin in the 1920s, is understood by many today as a rebuke to the Black and Tans, the British soldiers from World War I who subsequently fought in the Irish War of Independence.[54] Then, in 2022, their song 'Celtic Symphony' – which includes the lyrics 'Ooh ahh, up the 'Ra', a reference to the IRA – also topped the charts following controversy over players in the Republic's women's football team chanting 'Ooh, ahh, up the 'Ra' after a World Cup qualifying match.[55] However, despite some criticism in the media, the band's popularity continues to explode with younger audiences, despite having a combined age of more than 230. They managed to draw the biggest-ever crowd at the 2023 Electric Picnic festival in Ireland and are now set to celebrate their sixtieth anniversary at the huge Dublin 3Arena in 2024. Their renewed success has surprised many, reigniting debates about the acceptability of rebel songs today.

Among this furore, I managed to get tickets to see the Wolfe Tones in London and headed along to decide for myself. I was a little sceptical after talking with the Irish Republican historian Pádraig Óg Ó Ruairc about the band. 'I'm an Irish Republican,' he told me, 'but I'm definitely not a fan of the Wolfe Tones.

To me, there is something really superficial about their concerts and their fans compared to Irish folk singer Christy Moore and his fanbase, who are very engaged and active in politics.

'My experience is that most Wolfe Tones fans like to act the "big man" wearing a Glasgow Celtic jersey, and drunkenly shouting slogans about the North, but few of them have ever been there.' He finished by adamantly saying, 'I wouldn't cross the road to see the Wolfe Tones!' So, I arrived in a rainy Camden Town on a dank and wet Thursday evening wondering if I would agree with him.

What I experienced was one of the oddest live music experiences I've ever had. As Pádraig had suggested, inside the venue was a sea of men in Celtic shirts or Irish rugby tops. Whole groups wore tri-colour headbands and people packed around the merchandise stand to buy flags. Before the gig even started, the boisterous crowd sang 'The Fields of Athenry', a song written by Pete St. John in 1979 about the Great Famine. It was more akin to the atmosphere of a football match, fans drinking and chanting before kick-off.

When the Wolfe Tones finally graced the stage, things got even weirder. Three elderly men – two with guitars, one on tin whistle – began to play. Yet I could hear bodhráns, accordions, maybe even the odd fiddle. They were playing to a backing track – and an oddly '80s-sounding one, with poppy keyboards, at that. It reminded me of the ill-judged '80s reissues that some '60s Motown singers made. For me, it lacked much of what I love about Irish music: its authenticity, the beauty of the playing, its literateness, subtlety and power. It was Rebel Karaoke.

Much of the crowd didn't seem to be actually watching, with whole clumps of people just stood around talking, as you would in a pub with a band in the corner. It was more Temple Bar than the Cobblestones. The real enthusiasm was saved for chants of 'Ooh ahh, up the 'Ra', which broke out in between and during songs, signalling an opportunity to throw flags into the air. But which period of the IRA did they mean? The IRA of the Irish War of Independence, the Official, Provisional, Continuity or Real? Maybe even the New IRA? I got the feeling many didn't know; it was more a general chant of resistance. Perhaps even a little subversive thrill. There was certainly an unsettling contrast between the gravity of the themes in the songs – war, oppression, famine, resistance – and the seeming flippancy of the football chants from the crowd.

I popped to the toilet mid-show to find an Irishman asking trivia questions about history to a collection of urinating cockneys who didn't know any of the answers. But maybe none of this matters? Perhaps it's unfair to expect gig-goers to have brushed up on the *Selected Writings of James Connolly* before a night of live music.

For many, it was more about expressing a collective identity, a general declaration of opposition to British oppression; shorthand for resistance. For many of those with British accents, it was a chance to robustly express their Irish heritage, to be proud and feel part of something. The scenes I saw in Camden could be found in Irish pubs all over the world. There are an estimated 6,500 Irish-themed bars gracing every corner of the world. Their quality varies enormously, but at their best they provide hubs where the country's vast diaspora can find a corner of home, an outpost of the Emerald Isle. And in the very best ones, no matter how distant or remote, you will find musicians gathering around a table and playing songs that tell stories of their history and the Irish struggle for freedom. To an extent, that is the whole point of live rebel music: it is part gig, part political rally and part ceremony.

TWO

A Change is Gonna Come: Music and the American Civil Rights Struggle

Recommended Listening:
Frederick Douglass – 'My Bondage and My Freedom'
W. C. Handy – 'Beale Street Blues'
Preservation Hall Jazz Band – 'That's It!'
Billie Holiday – 'Strange Fruit'
Sam Cooke – 'A Change is Gonna Come'
Aretha Franklin – 'Respect'
B. B. King – 'The Thrill is Gone'
Nina Simone – 'Why? (The King of Love is Dead)'
The Staple Singers – 'I'll Take You There'
James Brown – 'Say It Loud – I'm Black and I'm Proud'
Gil Scott-Heron – 'The Revolution Will Not Be Televised'
The Last Poets – 'Wake Up, Niggers'

—

I WAS STOOD ON the spot where jazz was born. It was a typic-ally close and humid Sunday morning in Congo Square. Louis Armstrong Park, in which it sits, borders New Orleans' French Quarter, one mile of colonial-era buildings with ornate metal balconies that appear to be holding back the crumbling front-ages from collapsing onto the sidewalk below.

Music pours out of every pore of New Orleans. After noon on any day of the week, jazz, blues, rock and hip hop boom out of every car, house and bar window, creating a magical caco-phony. But I was standing here before midday and the undulating cobbled square was deserted, save for the odd bench-loiterer hiding from the already punishing heat. For the first time in days, I heard birds, as the confused mangle of overlapping live bands had yet to start and the bead-clad revellers were still pressed against their air-conditioning units after a night spent rapaciously consuming Hurricane cocktails on Bourbon Street.

New Orleans holds a special place in the imagination of any real music fan. My visit was part of a dream trip crisscrossing the Deep South, drinking in every sweaty drop of its rich and varied musical history, along with plenty of sweet tea. I had visited parts of the South before, reporting from Alabama in the months that preceded Donald Trump's disastrous election victory in 2016. I had experienced its famous hospitality first hand and had long been obsessed with the jazz, blues and soul music that emerged from the region. Yet I had also been shocked by the inequality, the continuing and often open racism, and the way in which the legacies of slavery and the Jim Crow era continue to infect everyday life like a festering wound. Now was a chance to return to the South and explore the role that the music played in the civil rights struggle – an opportunity to better understand the music I love, the motiv-ations of the people who made it and the impact it had at the time. Standing in Congo Square, where it all began, I was tingling with excitement.

During the colonial period of the eighteenth century, Spanish and French colonial law allowed enslaved people to meet, drum and dance in Congo Square, often joined by indigenous and free people of colour. The square became an artery through which African rhythms flowed into the continent, along with the shackled humans who brought them. The tradition continued through the antebellum period and into the post-Civil War years. Slaves enjoyed their solitary day of rest by congregating, socialising and dancing to the hypnotic syncopated rhythm of the bamboula drum, a rudimentary instrument of goat's skin stretched over a barrel or other similar hollow wooden shell.

But enslaved people's music was far more than just hypnotic rhythms. In the last few decades of the eighteenth century, right through to the abolition of slavery in the 1860s, so-called spirituals (often called Negro-spirituals) constituted 'one of the largest and most significant forms of American folksong'.[1] Typically sung in a call-and-response pattern which slaves brought with them from Africa, spirituals reflected a full range of emotions, from joyful, fast and rhythmic 'jubilees', through to slower melancholic laments; pain given voice. As the famous author and civil rights activist W. E. B. Du Bois put it, 'they that walked in darkness sang songs in the olden days – Sorrow Songs – for they were weary at heart'.[2] Spirituals could also be a form of protest, such as the abolitionist Frederick Douglass's 1853 song 'My Bondage and My Freedom':

We raise de wheat,
Dey gib us de corn:
We bake de bread,
Dey gib us de crust;
We sif de meal,
De gib us de huss;
We peel de meat,

Dey gib us de skin;
And dat's de way
Dey take us in;
We skim de pot,
Dey gib us de liquor,
And say dat's good enough for a nigger . . .

Enslaved people's music, then, in the words of the historian Lawrence Levine, 'confronts us with the evidence that however seriously the slave system may have diminished the sense of community that had bound Africans together, it never totally destroyed it or left the individual atomised and emotionally and physically defenceless before his white masters'.[3]

In the decades that followed the blood-soaked Civil War of 1861–1865, something transcendent happened. The pain and suffering – along with the love and hope of African-American communities in the Deep South – emerged once more as music that would capture the imagination of the world. Writing in his 1964 book *Shadow and Act*, the African-American author Ralph Ellison argued that instead of 'social or political freedom . . . the arts – the blues, the spirituals, the jazz, the dance – was what we had in place of freedom'.[4]

First came the painful birth of the blues. The home of W. C. Handy – the 'Father of the Blues' – is in Florence, Alabama, where a tiny wooden log cabin still stands with a view down to the Tennessee river. Later in my trip, I visited this spot of pilgrimage in the Delta to see where it all began. But while an important figure, the true 'father' of the genre is likely an unknown Black sharecropper who put angst to music, building on the field hollers and work songs sung by slaves in the fields of the South.

Many of the genre's first performers and earliest innovators were men exempt from picking cotton or other manual labour due to disability, which explains why so many of the early greats were blind: Blind Lemon Jefferson, Blind Willie Johnson and Blind Boy Fuller, among a surprisingly long list of visually impaired greats.[5] Blues was cathartic, melancholia in twelve bars, a release of pain and struggle in musical form but with a healing purpose. 'Blues is a tonic for whatever ails you,' explained the great B. B. King. 'I could play the blues and then not be blue anymore.'

Then, in the melting pot of the Louisiana bayous, blues was mixed with traditional African rhythms, church spirituals and ragtime. Though you wouldn't think it on that quiet morning, Congo Square in New Orleans played a fundamental role in the birth of jazz. In the early years of the twentieth century, a new form of Black expression emerged, the first two decades of which were never recorded. It wasn't until the early 1920s that the first African-American bands were captured on wax.

Jazz is a diverse genre, with endless tributaries and subcategories all typified by complex harmonies, syncopated drum patterns and a penchant for improvisation. From the very start, jazz artists 'were realigning attitudes towards race and culture, proving to anyone paying attention that jazz could spur integration and cooperation,' explains the jazz pianist and music historian Ted Gioia. 'It celebrated human agency and personal autonomy to a rare degree, but also channelled the creative expression of an ostracized underclass ... turning it into a powerful engine for social change.'[6]

The keeper of this flame in New Orleans is the famous Preservation Hall. I nearly didn't bother going after having dinner at Jacques-Imo's on Oak Street in the Uptown district, made famous by the chef and TV presenter Anthony Bourdain. After trying their (frankly overrated) shrimp and alligator sausage cheesecake – part of the American tradition of combining ingredients that don't go together – the barman said not to bother. 'It's a tourist trap and not worth it.' He couldn't have been more wrong.

Nestled in the heart of the French Quarter on St Peter's Street, just a spilt drink away from the thumping bars and mediocre rock bands of Bourbon Street, is a rusted metal gate. The building is shabby, even by the low standards around it, with rotting wooden shutters covering the windows and walls drained of their colour by years of humidity. A man stood on the street and explained the rules before I entered: the toilets are only for the band (if you need to go, hold it); absolutely no phones, not even for pictures; and if you get too hot, and it will get too hot, leave and stand in the court-yard. I was then ushered through the gates and into 1920s New Orleans. There is no stage, the band set up on the floor before four rows of low, wooden benches. A collection of much-needed fans move too slowly to create a breeze, perhaps explaining the mouldy walls, stained yellow by decades of tobacco smoke.

The venue hosts the Preservation Hall All Stars, a collection of more than fifty master musicians from which a small band assembles each evening. I was lucky enough to be there on a night when the legendary ragtime percussionist Shannon Powell was leading the band. Earlier that day, I'd learnt from the Drumsville exhibition at the Jazz Museum that New Orleans gave birth to the drum kit as we think of it today. Powell ambled behind the kit and introduced himself as 'playing the boom boom' – and he didn't disappoint. For forty-five minutes, they played traditional old-style New Orleans jazz with its roots firmly in the 1920s. It was a world away from the effortlessly cool sound that took over the world in the late 1950s. This was a bouncing and swinging form that reminded me more of

Louis Prima's 'I Wan'na Be Like You' from *The Jungle Book* than anything by Miles Davis or John Coltrane.

Unlike later jazz with virtuoso soloists taking turns, this style relies more on all the horns dancing together into a sumptuous blend where the individual solos and the collective sound merge together effortlessly.[7] The booming trombone languidly provides the lower tones, the trumpet the middle and the clarinet the high with its bright feel, together combining into an undeniably joyous sound. The band appeared to be having as much fun as the audience, Powell's toothy grin beaming out infectiously. They finished with a delicate and touching version of Louis Armstrong's classic 'What a Wonderful World' and I floated out to the street, feeling it might just have been the happiest forty-five minutes of my life. And I thought to myself, Louis was right.

–

In order to understand the birth of jazz and blues, you have to understand the birth of the American nation. The roots of musical genres that spread all around the world can be traced back to the dark history of the country from which they emerged. Between 1525 and 1866, an estimated 12.5 million Africans were transported in shackles across the Atlantic. Due to the unimaginably barbaric conditions, just 10.7 million survived the journey. Six per cent of the enslaved people (roughly 388,747) landed in British North America, with the rest sent further south to the Caribbean and South America.[8]

While Portugal controlled the early years of the trade and transported the most slaves, Britain came to dominate the trade with its colonial vessels purchasing an estimated 3,415,500 Africans between 1662 and 1807. Between 1791 and 1800, around 1,340 slaving voyages left British ports, with cities such as London, Bristol and Liverpool benefiting hugely from the trade of humans. In 1798 alone, almost 150 ships left the city of Liverpool for west Africa, a stain on the history of a city that today is known as one of the music capitals of the world.[9]

The treatment of enslaved people once they had arrived in North America is hard to describe in its inhumanity: violence, sexual abuse, dehumanising conditions and the splitting-up of families, all compounding their total absence of basic freedom. The British finally passed the Abolition of the Slave Trade Act in 1807, outlawing the British Atlantic trade and then later, in 1833, passed the Abolition of Slavery Act, which ordered the gradual abolition of slavery within its colonies. However, there was a vast difference between stopping the trade and ending slavery.

America secured its independence from Britain in 1776, issuing the perhaps unsurpassed piece of political poetry known as the Declaration of Independence. Yet its bold and powerful statement 'that all men are created equal, that they are endowed by their creator with certain unalienable rights' was never extended to enslaved people. It was a hypocrisy that has haunted the nation ever since. Slavery wasn't officially abolished in the United States until 31 January 1865, with the Thirteenth Amendment to the US Constitution declaring that 'neither slavery nor involuntary servitude, except as a punishment for crime whereof the party shall have been duly convicted, shall exist within the United States, or any place subject to their jurisdiction'.[10]

The actual end of slavery came after the remarkably bloody Civil War that dragged on between 1861 and 1865 with the death of possibly as many as 850,000 people.[11] The war started as a means to keep the United States as a whole entity, rather than an explicit war to abolish slavery – initially at least. Yet the Southern states seceded to protect their rights, foremost their right to keep people as chattel. Victory for the Union brought the war to an end, but certainly failed to destroy the notion of white supremacy in the States. Lincoln was assassinated in 1865 in what the historian Peter Kolchin has described as the first casualty of 'a long civil rights movement that is not yet over'.[12]

What followed was known as Reconstruction, a tumultuous period where the seceded southern states and its millions of newly freed slaves were to be reintegrated into a united country. Yet the end of Civil War and legal slavery was by no means the end of racism and oppression. Before the ink had even dried on the Thirteenth Amendment, laws and practices were introduced that ensured the preservation of white rule and power. The so-called Black Codes limited freedoms for African-Americans and ensured continued cheap labour for white land-owners.[13] In the years that followed, the United States saw the emergence of Jim Crow, the name given to a system of racial segregation, operated primarily, though not exclusively, in the southern and border states from 1877 onwards.[14] Under a plethora of draconian laws, African-Americans were systematically relegated to second-class citizens with racism and white supremacy being entrenched.

An exemplar of this fanatical desire to segregate Black people was the raft of anti-miscegenation laws. The first to ban marriage between races was passed in Maryland as early as 1661 and, by the 1960s, twenty-one primarily southern states still had similar legislation in place. The last to repeal the ban on interracial marriage was Alabama, which remarkably didn't do so until the year 2000.[15]

Where laws weren't deemed sufficient, locals used violence and terror to ensure the maintenance of white supremacy. The Ku Klux Klan (KKK) was originally founded as a social club between late 1865 and the summer of 1866 by six former Confederate officers in the town of Pulaski, Tennessee. The members soon found that their night-time 'horseplay' in town caused fear among former slaves in the area. The group rapidly expanded, which resulted in a meeting in April 1867, at which the organisation's rules and structure were decided. Standing in direct opposition to the extension of rights for those recently freed, the Klan engaged in a campaign of violence and murder against former slaves and African-American leaders.

However, following law enforcement suppression and internal fighting, Nathan Bedford Forrest, Grand Wizard of the KKK, officially disbanded the organisation in the early 1870s. Nearly forty-five years later, the Klan was revived in 1915 by William J. Simmons in Atlanta, following the film release of *The Birth of a Nation*, a racist picture which glorified the first incarnation of the KKK. This new reincarnation had a wider programme than its predecessor and added an extreme nativism, anti-Catholicism and antisemitism to its traditional white supremacism.

By 1921, the ranks of the Klan had swollen, with some estimates placing the group's membership as high as between 4 and 5 million, though in reality it was likely much smaller. At its peak in 1925, 30,000 uniformed Klansmen famously marched through the streets of Washington DC By the end of the decade, membership had shrunk to 30,000 as it broke into dozens of fragments, faced pressure from law enforcement and garnered a bad reputation for its violence and extremism. Despite its decline, however, its reign of terror had long-lasting ramifications still felt to this day. The civil rights struggle emerged in the face of this toxic combination of structural and legally entrenched white supremacy, combined with the ever-present threat of extreme racist violence and murder.

It was in this tumultuous and violent period, prior to World War II, when the KKK roamed the streets, that one of the greatest and most mournful protest songs of the whole struggle was released: 'Strange Fruit'. Billie Holiday doesn't start singing until one minute and nine seconds into the song. It opens with a haunting muted trumpet played by Frankie Newton, followed by an ambling piano line by Sonny White that thickens the air and transports you to the American South. Then, in her unmistakable style, Holiday begins to sing: 'Southern trees bear a strange fruit / Blood on the leaves and blood at the root . . .'

The lyrics were written by the communist poet Abel Meeropol after seeing the infamous photograph of Thomas Shipp and Abram Smith being lynched in Indiana in 1930. The photo is horrifying. Shipp and Smith, rope around their necks, hang from a tree before a gathered crowd of white onlookers, some grinning at the camera. Holiday later recorded the song in 1939. I first heard it when travelling to report on a far-right demonstration happening in the UK back in 2011. A colleague played me a homemade CD of what he called 'anti-fascist music'. When I asked what the song was, he turned to me shocked, before enthusiastically explaining its history and significance.

Later that day, I stood and watched a crowd of baying far-right extremists, soundtracked in my head by the dulcet tones of Billie Holiday. The jazz musician and writer Leonard Feather called it 'the first significant protest in words and music, the first unmuted cry against racism'.[16] Whether or not it was the first is disputed, but as we will see, it was certainly not the last time that the suffering, pain and demand for civil rights was put to music.

–

Nashville is a fun town. It pulsates with drunk people; bachelor and bachelorette parties mingle with tourists and music pilgrims, dancing at all hours of the day and night. Broadway, the city's major thoroughfare, is a neon stripe running through the heart of the city. Almost every building has three or four floors of bars, each one hosting a band. Live country music starts in some places as early as 9:30 in the morning and finishes long after I had been defeated. The bands overwhelmingly play modern country rock – think rotund bearded men in ten-gallon hats singing about Budweiser beer and their peculiarly close affinity with their truck.

But scattered among the Frat Boy megabars are some old honky-tonk staples, perhaps most famous among them being Tootsie's Orchid Lounge. There, a gauche purple exterior gives way to a dingy wooden-floored bar, with tobacco-stained walls covered with hundreds of peeling pictures of country music legends. In its early years, Tootsie's was the drinking den of choice for Kris Kristofferson, Willie Nelson, Hank Cochran and Patsy Cline.[17] Here, you can still hear steel guitars, and fiddles twang away over a two-beat rhythm: boom-chick, boom-chick, boom-chick. Gone are the songs about trucks. It's all about railways, bourbon and loss in here.

It's because of places like Tootsie's, the Country Music Hall of Fame and the nearby Ryman Auditorium, home of the Grand Ole Opry, that Nashville is known as Music City. But like almost everywhere in the American South, it has a complex history, forever marred by the scars of segregation and injustice.

Major sites of musical significance are just moments away from civil rights landmarks.

If you turn off Broadway and onto Fifth Avenue North, walking for long enough that the mangled thumping of bands falls silent, you get to number 221. Here, at 12:30pm on 13 February 1960, 124 students, most of them Black, entered a branch of Woolworths and the neighbouring S. H. Kress and McLellan stores, and asked to be served lunch at the counter. When refused, they defiantly took a seat anyway. Coordinated by the Nashville Student Movement and the Nashville Christian Leadership Council, these protests against segregation were part of the sit-in movement that was spreading across the American South. Brave protestors were often met with vile racist taunts and the inevitable violence that was a tragic reality for Black people at the time.

When I visited the building, it was derelict, a staged lunch counter in the front window gathering dust. A nearby metal sign, erected by the Tennessee Historical Commission, one of countless such plaques that helpfully dot the South, offered a succinct overview of the site's historical significance: 'The student protestors experienced no violence until February 27. On that day at Woolworth's and McClellan's, white resisters threw the students from their seats, punched, kicked, and spat upon them. Nashville police only arrested the student protestors.'

The term 'white resisters' made me feel uncomfortable. To me, resistance is something one does against oppression, not to maintain it. Despite the arrests – and the subsequent bombing of the home of Zephaniah Alexander Looby, the lawyer representing the students – the protests continued until on 10 May 1960. On that day, Nashville became the first major city to begin desegregating its public facilities.

The victory in Nashville was not the start of the civil rights struggle, and it was far from the end, but trying to define the scope of the movement isn't as easy as one might expect. The civil rights leader Julian Bond, co-founder of the Southern Poverty Law Centre, has argued that the popular understanding is that 'Rosa sat down, Martin stood up, and the white kids came down and saved the day'.[18] This would date the start of the struggle in 1955 with the Montgomery bus boycott and end with the death of Martin Luther King Jr in 1968.

Of course, it's more complex than that. It's possible to argue that it started with emancipation and the Civil War, or the resistance to the Black Codes, the founding of the NAACP in 1909, Congressman Leonidas Dyer's fight to make lynching a federal crime in the 1920s, or Harry Truman's 1948 executive order desegregating the US armed forces.[19] For most, however, it's the events of the 1950s and 1960s, starting in 1954 with the Supreme Court ruling in the Brown vs Board of Education case, which overturned the pernicious 'separate but equal' doctrine that had subjugated African-Americans since the 1800s.

Over the next fourteen years, in the face of institutionalised oppression and widespread violence, African-American communities and their white allies put their lives on the line in the fight for racial equality. In 1955, Rosa Parks refused to give up her seat to a white man on a bus in Montgomery, Alabama. In 1957, the 'Little Rock Nine' fought for integration in education at Central High School in the Arkansas state capital.

In 1961, the courage of the freedom riders, who took trips across the American South protesting segregated bus terminals, shocked the world. In 1963, 250,000 people gathered in Washington to hear Martin Luther King talk of his dream that his 'four little children will one day live in a nation where they will not be judged by the colour of their skin but by the content of their character'. Along the way, there were huge victories, such as the Civil Rights Act signed by President Eisenhower in 1957, the 1964 Civil Rights Act, the 1965 Voting Rights Act and the 1968 Fair Housing Act, the last three all signed by Lyndon B. Johnson.

Yet there was also unimaginable suffering, with each step forward taken over broken bottles and in the face of swinging truncheons. The murder of fourteen-year-old Emmett Till in Mississippi in 1955, the bombing at Sixteenth Street Baptist Church in Birmingham, Alabama, that killed four young girls in 1963, and the assassination of Malcolm X in 1965 were just a few of the countless painful episodes in the struggle for freedom. As King said on the steps of the Alabama State Capitol after the completion of the bloody Selma to Montgomery march in 1965, 'the arc of the moral universe is long, but it bends toward justice'. For many, the bend towards justice must have felt unbearably slow.

The end date of the struggle is as contested as the start. In the popular imagination, what most people think of as the civil rights movement drew to a close in 1968 with the murder of Martin Luther King and the passing of legislation designed to provide equal housing opportunities. However, many rightly argue that equality before the law is not equality in practice, meaning the struggle for civil rights in the United States continues to this day. I've reported from around the country over the past ten years and it certainly feels that way, especially in the wake of the murder of George Floyd and the subsequent rise of the Black Lives Matter movement.

—

The slow and painful victories of the civil rights movement came as a result of the bravery and dedication of thousands of people, some of whom sacrificed their lives in the struggle. Whether it was the towering figures like Martin Luther King, Rosa Parks, Philip Randolph, James Farmer, Whitney Young and John Lewis or the millions of ordinary Black people who maintained their dignity and engaged in small but no less important acts of daily resistance, the credit for the arrival of civil rights should be widely spread.

Among those deserving is a group of musicians, songwriters, producers, label owners and music fanatics who soundtracked the movement. In the 1960s, soul music unquestionably became inseparable from the struggle for equality in the United States. Along the way, some of the greatest records of the century came into being. This music has always been something of an obsession for me. As a child, I enjoyed it when my parents' parties got raucous enough that one of their drunk friends would wobble over to the CD player and put on a Motown compilation. Everyone jumped to their feet and began to dance. It was instantaneous; the music demanded it. Later, I presented a soul show on university radio and briefly DJ'ed at a tiny club in London's Soho, unimaginatively called the Bar. As have many before me, I started with Motown before falling in love with the harder, angrier sound of Southern soul.

According to the Rock & Roll Hall of Fame, soul is 'music that arose out of the Black experience in America through the transmutation of gospel and rhythm & blues into a form of funky, secular testifying'. The American music critic Peter Guralnick argues it 'can be seen largely as the story of the introduction of the gospel strain into the secular world of rhythm and blues'.[20] To me, it's more of a feeling. Soul music can be rage that makes you dance or it can be sadness that makes you cry, It can be heartbreak set to lush strings or jubilation in a hip thrust. It can feel like being doused in molasses or being woken up with a pail of water to the face. Soul music reaches inside you and twists.

Guralnick dates soul music as starting in the mid-1950s, coming into its own in 1960, crossing over to the mainstream in 1965 or 1966 and being a spent force by the early 1970s, a lifespan that closely tracks with the popular understanding of the civil rights era. 'Certainly, it can be seen as paralleling the civil rights movement stylistically as well as chronologically,' he argues, 'emerging with stealth at first, slowly gathering strength, then learning to assert itself without apology or fear, until forced to retrench in the face of a series of traumatic events and jarring disappointments.'[21]

The racial turmoil of the South was central to the development of the music. 'Ultimately,' Guralnick writes, 'soul music derives, I believe, from the Southern dream of freedom.'[22] But music didn't just emerge out of the struggle for freedom. It also inspired it. Martin Luther King described songs as 'the soul of the movement' in his 1964 book *Why We Can't Wait*. Civil rights activists 'sing the freedom songs today for the same reason the slaves sang them,' wrote King, 'because we too are in bondage and the songs add hope to our determination.'[23]

Among the many soul artists of the period who turned pain into music, Sam Cooke stands out. Born in Clarksdale, Mississippi, in 1931, he was, like so many stars of the era, the son of a preacher. Cooke's family soon moved to Chicago where he became a professional gospel singer while still a child. He began releasing pop records under the alias Dale Cook before finding success under his own name in the second half of the 1950s. Like all Black artists at the time, he saw the horrors of segregation when touring the South. Refused service at hotels and restaurants, he was forced to make sandwiches in the car and wash in rest-stop bathrooms.

In 1961, Cooke refused to play to a segregated audience at Ellis Auditorium in Memphis, a stand similarly made in March that year by Ray Charles in Augusta, Georgia. Then in 1963, he heard Bob Dylan's 'Blowin' in the Wind'. Speaking to the BBC years later, Cooke's younger brother, a singer in his own right, said 'Sam always said a Black man should've wrote "Blowin' in the Wind", it was unfair, so he said "Nah, if he can write a song like that, surely I can come up with something equally as good", so he sat down to write "A Change is Gonna Come".'[24]

The final catalyst for writing his most famous song came on 8 October 1962, when he was turned away from a whites-only motel in Louisiana. When he refused to leave, he was arrested. The words came to him in a dream: 'It's been a long, a long time coming / But I know a change gonna come / Oh yes it will.' With its lush string arrangement and powerful lyrics that mixed foreboding with hope, the song became the anthem of the civil rights movement. Later, in 1968, when Rosa Parks heard of the death of Martin Luther King, she described the song as like 'medicine to the soul'.

In the years that followed, Cooke became an increasingly prominent figure in the movement, famously becoming friends with Malcolm X and appearing ringside alongside Cassius Clay for his 1964 fight with Sonny Liston. Sadly, that same year, the singer was shot dead in confusing circumstances by Bertha Franklin, manager of the Hacienda Motel where he was staying in Los Angeles. He was just thirty-three. Franklin admitted the shooting, but claimed it was self-defence after Cooke had threatened her life. She reported that Cooke had attempted to rape a young woman, who was also residing at the hotel and, following her escape, he attempted to attack Franklin. In the years since the event, Cooke's friends and family have questioned the official account, noting his badly beaten body or claiming he was executed for his civil rights work.[25]

If Billie Holiday gave voice to the experience of racist violence, and Sam Cooke sang of imminent change, Aretha Franklin demanded respect. Born in Memphis, Tennessee in 1942, Franklin conquered the world with her booming and soulful vocals on timeless records like 'Think', 'I Say a Little Prayer' and '(You Make Me Feel Like) A Natural Woman'. However, in 1967, she travelled to New York to record a cover version of the Otis Redding song 'Respect'.

While ostensibly a song about demanding respect from her partner, it soon became a feminist and civil rights classic. In her memoir, *From These Roots*, Aretha explained how the song reflected 'the need of a nation, the need of the average man and woman in the street, the businessman, the mother, the fireman, the teacher—everyone wanted respect'. 'Respect' went beyond the personal, too. 'It was also one of the battle cries of the civil rights movement. The song took on monumental significance.'[26]

Martin Luther King's daughter, Dr Bernice King, later explained that Franklin, 'as a daughter of the movement ... not only used her voice to entertain but to uplift and inspire generations through songs that have become anthems'. However, Franklin's support for the struggle went well beyond providing inspiration. After her death, the civil rights activist Jesse Jackson revealed that Franklin had anonymously supported and funded all manner of activism. 'When Dr King was alive,' said Jackson, 'several times she helped us make payroll. On one occasion, we took an eleven-city tour with her as Aretha

Franklin and Harry Belafonte . . . and they put gas in the vans. She did eleven concerts for free and hosted us at her home and did a fundraiser for my campaign.'[27] Whether it was providing funds or inspiration through music, Aretha Franklin perhaps best personifies the importance of soul music to the civil rights movement.

—

The Lorraine Motel is a squat, two-storey, sand-coloured building on Mulberry Street in downtown Memphis. Its turquoise doors add a pop of colour, though strangely they are numbered from 200 on the ground floor and 300 on the first. At first glance, it looks like one of the countless motels that cover every off-ramp and highway across the United States, with their ramshackle charm, '60s movie kitsch and, often, a slight air of menace.

Yet the Lorraine Motel is unique. On a dripping Tennessee evening, with a slight breeze in the right direction, you can hear the muffled sound of the world-famous Beale Street just a few minutes' walk away. In the words of B. B. King, who arrived in Memphis after World War II, 'when I got to Beale Street, it was like a fantasy come true. I didn't think of Memphis as Memphis. I thought of Beale Street as Memphis.'[28]

Sadly, the years haven't been kind to the street. Once the bustling hub of the local African-American community, serving humdrum needs by day and sparkling with some of the best blues music by night, it now feels more like a movie set. Where once you might stumble across B. B. King or, from an earlier time, W. C. Handy, I heard a series of bog-standard, twelve-bar cover bands in what felt like themed restaurants, rather than the authentic juke joints and bars where the sound was born. The music historian Francis Davis is scathing about what Beale Street has become, describing it as a 'blues theme park, a tourist lure, several blocks of clubs, takeout windows, and souvenir shops for suburban and out-of-town white boys on the prowl'.[29]

He is correct, of course, but as one of those out-of-town white boys from suburban England who had dreamt of hearing the blues on Beale Street, I couldn't help but feel a giddy excitement. I blocked out the souvenir shops, ignored the T-shirts and bumper stickers for sale in every bar, and transformed the uninspired chugging cover bands into the cathartic beauty of the true blues. I can see why the old-timers and originals might walk Beale Street today mumbling the words to B. B. King's hit 'The Thrill is Gone', but for this white boy on the prowl, it was like a fantasy come true.

The Lorraine Motel was listed in the *Negro Motorist Green Book*, a guide to all manner of businesses available to African-Americans during the Jim Crow era. This, coupled with its proximity to Beale Street – and, a little further out on East McLemore Avenue, the unsurpassable soul music hit factory Stax Records – the Lorraine Motel welcomed everyone from Otis Redding, Cab Calloway and Louis Armstrong to Aretha Franklin and Nat King Cole. Remarkably, it was where Wilson Pickett wrote 'In the Midnight Hour' and Eddie Floyd and Steve Cropper co-wrote 'Knock on Wood', both smash-hit records in the mid-1960s.[30] This alone would be enough to make it among the most historically important motels in the United States. Sadly, though, that's not what the Lorraine Motel is now known for.

On 4 April 1968, Martin Luther King Jr was in Memphis to support striking African-American sanitation workers. On the evening of 3 April, he attended the Mason Temple and delivered his now-famous 'I've Been to the Mountaintop' speech:

> Well, I don't know what will happen now. We've got some difficult days ahead. But it really doesn't matter with me now, because I've been to the mountaintop. And I don't mind. Like anybody, I would like to live a long life. Longevity has its place. But I'm not concerned about that now. I just want to do God's will. And He's allowed me to go up to the mountain. And I've looked over. And I've seen the Promised Land. I may not get there with you. But I want you to know tonight, that we, as a people, will get to the promised land!

The next evening, King stepped out of his room on the second floor of the Lorraine Motel to greet his friends on the walkway that overlooked the car park. In a house across the street, holding a Remington rifle, was James Earl Ray. At precisely 6:01pm, as King turned to go back inside, a shot was fired. The bullet pierced through King's jaw and he crumpled to the ground. At 7:05pm, he died and, with him, the most eloquent, powerful and dignified voice of the civil rights struggle.

When news broke of King's assassination, a recording session was in progress at Stax. Al Bell, co-owner of the label, recalls being in the studio that day with the little-known artist Shirley Walton. 'She couldn't get into the song – the passion wasn't there. Then, on the sixteenth take, Homer Banks came in the studio and said, "Hey, Dr. King just got killed." This was as the tape was rolling. Shirley started singing, and tears just poured from her eyes.' Aptly, the song Walton recorded that day was titled 'Send Peace and Harmony Home'. 'We did a limited-edition release on that,' explained Bell, 'and gave copies to Mrs Coretta King and the family and had it read into the Congressional Record. Afterwards we destroyed the master, because the idea wasn't to exploit the song.'[31]

Also in the studio that day were Issac Hayes, a driving force behind the Southern soul sound, and his songwriting partner David Porter. Hayes is best known for his 1971 number-one smash hit 'Theme From Shaft', but together with Hayes wrote some of the most famous soul songs of all time, not least 'Soul Man', a huge hit for Sam and Dave in 1967. Also present was the singer William Bell, who scored a UK top-ten hit that year with 'Private Number' and co-wrote the blues classic 'Born Under a Bad Sign'. As news spread of King's assassination, the streets of Memphis erupted into widespread rioting, with African-American musicians escorting their white colleagues Steve Cropper and Duck Dunn to their cars for safety.[32]

King's assassination only served to widen the chasm between Black and white in the United States. 'That was the turning point,' said Booker T. Jones, leader of the seminal Southern soul band Booker T. & the M.G.'s. 'The turning point for relations between races in the South. And it happened in Memphis.'[33] Similarly, Isaac Hayes later described how he 'went blank. . . . I couldn't write for about a year – I was filled with so much bitterness and anguish, 'til I couldn't deal with it.'[34]

If Hayes 'went blank', others channelled their anger and pain into music with staggering speed. Just three days after King's assassination, the 'High Priestess of Soul', Nina Simone, played the Westbury Music Fair on New York's Long Island. Softly tinkling the keys of her piano, she addressed the audience. 'We want to do a tune written for today, for this hour, for Dr Martin Luther King. We stated earlier that this whole programme is dedicated to his memory, but this tune is written about him, and for him. We had yesterday to learn it, so we will see.'

What followed was an unparalleled articulation of rage and heartbreak put to music, a new soundtrack for a country burning as she played. 'But he had seen the mountaintop,' she rasped with a voice broken by emotion. 'And he knew he could not stop / Always living with the threat of death ahead.' The song, 'Why? (The King of Love is Dead)', thankfully recorded live and released on Simone's *'Nuff Said!* album later the same year, has been described as 'the saddest song ever written'.[35] Her performance of it finished with an impassioned monologue set to sporadic piano chords. 'We can't afford anymore losses. They are shooting us down one by one,' she raged before kicking back into the song with a final conquering chorus of 'Folks you'd better stop and think / Everybody knows we're on the brink / What will happen, now that the King is dead?'

The effect of King's assassination on race relations across the United States was sadly reflected within the music industry as well. One of the remarkable qualities of soul music was that many of the greatest hits were created through the collaboration of Black and white artists. Peter Guralnick describes this racial mix as an 'irreducible component of Southern soul music', and that 'idealistically, of course, it did bear out the promise of integration, and one participant after another – Black *and* white – has credited the partnership as evidence that the American dream can work, has laid the success of soul music to "blacks and whites working as a team".'[36]

Not all have agreed, of course, with some arguing this has been overstated, but the fact that many classic soul records emerged out of these collaborations between artists is a fact. This was one of the central ingredients in the success of Stax Records. The guitarist Steve Cropper, the bassist Lewie

Steinberg, and the drummer Donald 'Duck' Dunn were part of the rotating Stax house band, between them playing on records by landmark artists such as Otis Redding, Sam and Dave, Rufus Thomas, Albert King and Carla Thomas. Stax's African-American co-owner Al Bell described the harmonious atmosphere at work:

> I was amazed to sit in the same room with this white guy [Stax co-owner Jim Stewart] who had been a country fiddle player ... We had separate water fountains in Memphis and throughout the South. And if we wanted to go to a restaurant, we had to go to the back door – but to sit in that office with this white man, sharing the same telephone, sharing the same thoughts, and being treated like an equal human being – was really a phenomenon during that period of time. The spirit that came from Jim and his sister Estelle Axton allowed all of us, Black and white, to come off the streets, where you had segregation and the negative attitude, and come into the doors of Stax, where you had freedom, you had harmony, you had people working together. It grew into what became really an oasis for all of us.[37]

Meanwhile, around the corner from Stax, was the American Sound Studio with their backing band the Memphis Boys, who plied their trade on tracks by Joe Tex and Wilson Pickett among many others. However, the most famous example of white musicians contributing to soul classics is the famous Muscle Shoals rhythm section, better known as the Swampers, working out of Muscle Shoals, Alabama. In the 1960s, this small collection of white musicians played on some of the greatest records of all time, many of which became part of the soundtrack of the civil rights struggle. These were Black and white musicians collaborating years before the forced horror of Paul McCartney and Stevie Wonder's 'Ebony and Ivory.' In addition to playing on timeless records by Aretha Franklin, they played with, or engineered or produced hits by, an unbelievable roster of artists, including Paul Simon, Bob Dylan, Etta James, Wilson Pickett and later Lynyrd Skynyrd.

The song that unquestionably captures their sound is 'I'll Take You There' by the Staple Singers, a chart-topper in 1971. A song isn't merely a collection of notes played in a particular order. If that were the case, there wouldn't be as many bad tribute bands as there are. 'I'll Take You There' is definitive proof of this. I've been in numerous bands over the years who have all tried to cover the song and never managed to land it – or even get close. There's something about the way it plods and swings at the same time that makes it so hard to replicate.

The obvious reason why all my bands failed to recreate its sound would be that we were a group of white boys from England. Then you realise that the Staples Singers' version was made by a group of white boys from Alabama. The funky repetitive bassline that demands you walk with a little extra swagger was played by David Hood, and the crisp rimshot snare cracks by Roger Hawkins. Along with Barry Beckett and Jimmy Johnson, they made up one the most important bands in all of music: the Swampers. Even if you haven't heard of them, you've unquestionably heard their music. Their home for much of the 1960s and 1970s was a remote and unremarkable corner of Alabama.

I left Memphis and took Highway 72 east along the Tennessee–Mississippi border until I crossed into the northwest corner of Alabama. The music on the radio switched from B. B. King to Lynyrd Skynyrd to let me know I'd crossed the state line. 'Sweet home Alabama / Where the skies are so blue' – and blue they were, not a cloud in the sky. Emerging out of an expanse of cotton fields, and nestled on the banks of the mighty Tennessee river, is the nondescript town of Muscle Shoals.

There are few better ways to spend time than with an articulate music obsessive. Terrill Benton, a tour guide at the Muscle Shoals Sound Studio, is just that. The building is an unassuming, stone-clad box that sits on its own at 3614 Jackson Highway. When you park up next to the painted sign that reads 'Welcome To City of Muscle Shoals: Hit Recording Capital of the World', it doesn't seem possible that this is the place where a wildly improbable number of classic songs were recorded – including a three-day visit by the Rolling Stones in December 1969, during which time they recorded 'You Gotta Move', 'Brown Sugar' and 'Wild Horses'. The building is Tardis-like, inexplicably larger on the inside than it looks from the outside. It's also a time machine to transport you back to the 1960s.

Terrell is a short man of late middle age with a shock of white hair that grows into a neatly trimmed white beard framing a welcoming smile. He tells stories with an infectious reverence for the music and musicians, and all delivered in a friendly, lilting Southern drawl. It's impossible not to be charmed. He met me in a cramped entrance room and led me through a door into the recording studio, a single room with a sound booth at the far-end, a drum room to the right and a piano sat proudly in the middle.

When you enter, the air is dense, like just before the first crack of a thunderstorm. Maybe it's the humid Alabama summer creeping through the breezeblock walls or maybe, just maybe, that's the magic in the air that so many music legends claim to have felt while recording there. I stood in awe as Terrell enthusiastically listed off an unimaginable list of famous records put to tape in that tiny room. He nonchalantly pointed at the instruments played by mega stars. The tour even included the toilet where Keith Richards allegedly wrote 'Wild Horses'. I stumbled out of the studio in shock, pinching myself that I had visited this holy place.

Before setting up their own studio, the Swampers' home was FAME Studios just down the road. It's another nondescript building, this one with ugly brown frontage that makes it look like a branch of the Waffle House chain. Run by Rich Hall, the studio cut a roster of soul classics, such as Etta James' *Tell Mama* album and Wilson Pickett songs like 'Mustang Sally' and 'Land of 1000 Dances'.

However, it was the story of a fateful session in 1967 that really excited me. A relatively unknown Aretha Franklin had been struggling to find her sound, singing on poppy releases for Columbia Records. But after moving to Atlantic, she was sent down to FAME in Muscle Shoals, where she was paired up with the Swampers. They proved to be the perfect foundation for Aretha's powerful and emotive singing. The outcome of that session was 'I Never Loved a Man (The Way I Love You)' and 'Do Right Woman, Do Right Man', hits which catapulted Franklin into the stars. To stand in the very room where she had recorded was all a bit much. I rushed out into the car park before the tour guide could see me welling up.

For many of the musicians, Black and white, operating out of these studios in the 1960s, their work was a testament to the possibility of racial harmony. The soundproofed studio walls blocked out the noise of the raging storm beyond, allowing them to create beauty inside, together. However, just as the assassination of Martin Luther King was a turning point for race relations across the United States, so too was it within these musical oases. 'It was just that one shot that stopped everything,' said the producer and songwriter Dan Penn, who operated out of America Studios in Memphis. 'Their man got assassinated and it ruined the business I loved.'[38]

Stax's white co-owner Jim Stewart highlighted the ramifications of the assassination. 'It had a tremendous impact. It kind of put a wedge, or at least opened up that suspicious element, [within] the company. Although we tried to bond together and continue to work together, from that point on it changed considerably. There wasn't that happy feeling of creating together.' His business partner Al Bell agreed:

It heightened internally the racial sensitivity amongst those of us at Stax. . . . Dr King's death had a tremendous impact at Stax. We were there in the middle of the Black community and here we were an integrated organisation existing in a city where integration was an issue. Dr King's death caused [some] African-American people in the community to react negatively toward the white people that worked for Stax Records.[39]

While some remarkable soul records emerged out of continued inter-racial musical collaboration over the following decade, it seems that the wonderful if perhaps naïve belief that the raging inequality and struggle outside the studios wouldn't affect the harmony within slowly ebbed away.

—

Following the death of Martin Luther King, the civil rights movement fragmented. But, as always, African-American music adapted to give voice to however the struggle manifested itself. As much as music inspired and soundtracked the civil rights struggle, it also reflected it – and, by the end of the 1960s, the Black Power movement was in full swing. It called for economic empowerment, the development of African-American-led institutions and emphasised racial pride. In 1965, Stokely Carmichael, a former freedom rider and chairman of the Student Nonviolent Coordinating Committee (SNCC), rallied the crowd in Mississippi to chant 'We want Black Power'.[40]

For some African-Americans, particularly the young, protesting segregation fell short of what was required for real liberation. Often inspired by the work of Malcolm X and anti-colonial liberation movements around the world, they wanted economic and political power of their own.[41] If soul music at the start of the 1960s had provided a balm for open wounds, it took on a more confident and confrontational edge by the end of the decade, to reflect the emergence of the Black Power movement.

In 1968, for example, James Brown released the funk classic 'Say It Loud – I'm Black and I'm Proud'. 'Some people say we got a lot of malice,' Brown sang. 'Some say it's a lotta nerve / But I say we won't quit movin' / Until we get what we deserve.' Released shortly after violence had erupted in Washington DC, Chicago and Baltimore, the 'Godfather of Soul' wasn't asking for change, he was *demanding* it. And this demand contributed to the ongoing process of African-Americans re-defining themselves. The open and angry demands articulated by Brown became an increasing staple of African-American music over the next decade in the wake of King's death.

Just weeks after the assassination, on 19 May 1968, the Original Last Poets were founded. Stood in Mount Morris Park in East Harlem, New York, on what would have been the forty-third birthday of Malcolm X, the group uttered their first poems in public. The audience didn't know it then and there, but this was hip hop's Big Bang.

In 1970, the group released its remarkable self-titled album, which combined politically charged lyrics with African-inspired instrumentations typified by their track, 'Wake Up, Niggers'. The trio would later be sampled by hip hop royalty, such as NWA, A Tribe Called Quest and Public Enemy. That same year, Gil Scott-Heron released his live album, *A New Black Poet – Small Talk at 125th and Lenox*, which included the landmark song 'The Revolution Will Not Be Televised'. 'There will be no pictures of pigs shooting down brothers on the instant replay,' barked Scott-Heron over a funky, flute-based backing track. The mixture of powerful spoken-word poetry over funky beats was the genesis of the genre. It was 'King's assassination [that] provided the necessary conditions for hip hop to spring forth from the blood of generations that had spilled in street after street,' argues the American journalist Vann R. Newkirk II. 'The final irony in all this is that, in its deeply held fear of a Black "Messiah" arising, the government missed that Black youth were creating their own.'[42]

My trip around the American South was drawing to an end and, just as this story about the role of music in the civil rights struggle of the 1950s and 1960s ends with the birth of hip hop, so too did my trip. All roads led north to New York. I woke with a hangover that could peel paint, one of those shockers that makes every slight movement feel like someone is prodding your brain with a sharp pencil. I'd spent the night before on Bleecker Street in Greenwich Village, trying to sample a taste of the magic that had made it so special in the 1950s and '60s. Whether it was jazz players like John Coltrane, Dizzy Gillespie and Sonny Rollins, poets and writers such as Allen Ginsberg and Jack Kerouac, political folk singers like Phil Ochs, or civil rights activists and writers including Maya Angelou and James Baldwin, the Village vibrated with art and music that explored and challenged the injustices of the time.

It was famously described as the village of low rents and high arts. Sadly, whatever energy that fizzed around those streets then has long since dissipated. You can still see brilliant jazz players at Blue Note or Smalls, some of the old venues like the Village Vanguard and Café Wha? still remain, and the Stonewall Bar, birthplace of the modern LGBTQ+ struggle, still sits proudly on Christopher Street, but the place has long since been gentrified with bougie loft apartments rented for extortionate prices by city boys, with the bars filled with insufferable tourists like me listening to cover bands. The village of high rents and low arts.

Waking in a fog, I got the Lexington Avenue Express train, which trundles and bangs its way up Manhattan and into the Bronx. The New York Subway system is simultaneously disgusting and wonderful. The stations are filthy, with rats picking over piles of litter for their daily meal. The rusted pillars that precariously hold up the roofs seem to drip with water, even in the summer, and the graffiti-covered trains jolt into the stations with an ear-splitting screech that makes you lose all faith in their brakes. Yet it's also exciting, a feast for the senses, with all manner of strange stories playing out before your eyes.

I arrived at 149th Street–Grand Concourse station and walked down to the new Universal Hip Hop Museum. The main museum won't open for several years, but there was a small temporary exhibition titled [R]Evolution of Hip Hop: The Golden Era 1968–1990. I had booked a ticket for a specific time, but when I arrived, the door was locked.

'You here for the tour?' asked a man smoking by the door.

'Erm, for the museum,' I responded.

'Yeah, just wait behind that,' he said, pointing at the sort of velvet rope that cordons off VIP areas in bad nightclubs.

'Tour?' I was sure I had booked to look around a museum. I was in no state to be out of bed, let alone to be walked around a museum by a tour guide. I made to leave and the door swung open.

'Joe?'

'Yes,' I replied, resigned to my fate.

I was ushered into a small room with a large TV screen on the wall and given a short talk about the birth of hip hop. The guide explained its emergence in New York during a time of oppressive police brutality. He then switched on the TV and played a short film featuring fascinating clips of early hip hop pioneers.

When it finished, he asked: 'What did you think of that?'

'Great,' I sheepishly replied.

'No, what did you *really* think of it?'

I wiped away the hangover-induced waterfall of sweat that was pouring down my forehead and tried again.

'It was great,' I offered again.

'No, I want you to really tell me how that made you feel.'

For a moment, I genuinely considered darting for the door. I just wasn't in a fit state for this. I tried again. 'Very interesting. Really, very interesting.'

The guide stared at me unimpressed and, realising that was all he was getting, pointed me the direction of a black door. 'OK, head into the Time Tunnel.'

I opened the door, hoping it was only the start of my visit that involved a guide and that I would be ushered into the museum to browse the collection alone. I couldn't have been more wrong. The Time Tunnel was a long, thin black room. I entered to find a woman stood there staring at me.

'Are you ready to go back in time?' she announced enthusiastically.

'I'd love to go back two hours to when I was still in bed,' I mumbled inaudibly under my breath. 'Can't wait,' I said unconvincingly.

At that moment, the room started flashing and hip hop began to play at an ear-splitting volume. It climbed into my ears and began shaking my brain.

'Come on, DANCE!' she screamed.

I tapped my foot as ordered.

'No, DANCE!' she bellowed again, throwing her hands in the air and gesturing for me to follow suit. I managed to raise my left arm into the air and stood there petrified. A combination of the loud music, the flashing lights, her enthusiasm and my hangover made me want to cry. I finally realised that, with me stood statue-still, left arm raised high, it looked an awful lot like I had walked into the Time Tunnel, refused to dance and then given the Sieg Heil salute. I hurriedly lowered my arm and mustered every ounce of energy I had left to dance with enough gusto to ensure her I wasn't a Nazi.

'That's more like it!' she yelled. 'You can try rapping if you want . . .'

'Absolutely not,' I instantly replied and made for the door, which thankfully led to a wonderful, unaccompanied exhibition about the birth of hip hop. A series of corridors were plastered with memorabilia from early Run DMC and Beastie Boys concerts, archive footage of breakdancing, graffitied walls and a Public Enemy custom leather tour jacket that was so gorgeous I would happily have worn it home in New York's baking heat.

The Last Poets' debut album opens with the line 'I understand time is running out' and that was the case for my trip through African-American music and its role in the civil rights struggle. I had travelled hundreds of sweltering miles through the Deep South and seen sites I had dreamt of my whole adult life. I had visited Congo Square, drunk in bars once graced by B. B. King and stood on the spot where Aretha Franklin recorded 'I Never Loved a Man (The Way I Love You)' and where Sam and Dave sang 'Hold On, I'm Comin". I had treasured seven-inch singles of these songs and many more, but to enter the rooms where they were made had felt almost overwhelming. From the spirituals of the 1800s, to blues, the emergence of jazz and the inspiring sounds of Southern soul, through to the birth of hip hop, I'd had the tiniest glimpse of the transformative power of this music.

Yet the trip was about more than just music. It swung between moments of joy and excitement to periods of sadness and heartbreak. Whether I was staring up at the balcony of the Lorraine Motel where Dr King drew his last breath or waiting at Rosa Parks' bus stop, the history I saw didn't feel all that long ago in the South. Ambling through the lush backroads of Alabama, Mississippi and Louisiana, I regularly passed houses proudly displaying the Confederate flag, just as they have done for more than 100 years. Hung limp in the thick evening air, they were a constant reminder that the struggle against racism and discrimination isn't merely something to look back on. The Black Lives Matter movement, which received renewed global attention following the murder of George Floyd, and the continuing spectre of Donald Trump are reminders of that.

As I sat on the plane home to London, I listened to songs I had heard countless times before, but this time, they sounded different. Seeing what they meant to people, and the role they had played in the fight for justice, meant they sounded a little more soulful, a little angrier, a little more painful and a lot more important.

THREE

Tropicália: Bossa Nova and Brazil

Recommended Listening:
João Gilberto – 'Chega de Saudade'
Stan Getz and Astrud Gilberto – 'The Girl From Ipanema'
Nara Leão – 'Opinião'
Stan Getz and João Gilberto – 'Desafinado'
Carlos Lyra – 'Maria Moita'
Caetano Veloso – 'Tropicália'
Os Mutantes – 'A Minha Menina'
Gal Costa – 'Tuareg'
Tom Zé – 'Jimmy, Renda-Se'
Jorge Ben Jor – 'Take it Easy My Brother Charles'

—

'Do you want to see a magic trick? You flew to one Brazil, but I'm going to show you that there is two.'

The main roads look like anywhere else. Bustling traffic zips past shop-lined streets selling all manner of goods. Busy bars play the highlights of the latest Vasco da Gama match. Long queues outside barbershops are entertained by booming radios. But turn off the street into any one of a thousand cramped alleyways and you enter a different Brazil. Tiny houses hang together with labyrinthine stairways winding above and below. In the heart of the favela, the sun does not rise, the rays unable to penetrate through the mosaic of slanted roofs and the thick tangle of overhead wires. The stagnant, humid air and constantly damp floors make it feel like a subterranean tunnel, the darkness only lifted by colourful wall paintings and bright red election stickers plastered on every other pillar and wall.

Carlos was my guide around Rocinha, Brazil's biggest favela. He has lived here his whole life. 'This is a social experience,' he insisted. 'People come to Rocinha and drive around in tour buses and are too scared to get out. It's not a safari. We aren't animals.' There was bite in his voice.

There are more than 600 favelas in Rio alone, mostly to the north and west, though Rocinha is in the south of the city, just moments from the white sand and postcard views of Ipanema. These favelas are cities within cities, each a unique community – within Rio de Janeiro but not part of it. They don't even look like the rest of the city, with square terracotta-coloured buildings stacked on top of each other like a pixelated image. Looking down from Sugarloaf Mountain, the favelas dot the horizon like glaciers of brick, sliding down crevices and valleys.

'What about the elections?' I asked Carlos. It was just days before the first round of the 2022 presidential elections. Luiz Inácio Lula da Silva, the former centre-left president, was running against the incumbent fascist Jair Bolsonaro.

'Most poor people support Lula,' he replied, but he wasn't completely convinced. 'They vote for him because he gives them food.'

'Food's important,' I offered in response.

'We don't want to be given food. We want to be able to buy it ourselves.'

We stopped in a roadside bar for a plastic cup of caipirinha, a sweet cocktail made with the Brazilian spirit cachaça and handfuls of lime and sugar, and spoke with a much younger resident of the area. 'Bolsonaro is crazy, but Lula is corrupt,' he said, a refrain I would hear regularly over the week. He lived on what they affectionately called 'Snoop Dog Alley', a street known for the dealing of drugs.

'On a Saturday and Sunday, this road will have 400 guns on it,' he said with a laugh. It was hard to imagine that as we sat on a bustling main road, sipping a cold drink, but clearly there is more than just one favela. Carlos, a wiry man in his fifties who taught himself English with a second-hand dictionary, was passionate about his community and outspoken about the problems it faces. Many leave the favela each morning for work in the city and return each evening. 'Some families survive on as little as $15 a week,' he explained. 'It's modern slavery.' Yet, walk five minutes down the hill and you'll find swanky houses with dramatic sea views over Ipanema Beach that cost millions of dollars. This is what Carlos meant when he told me there were two Brazils.

With dusk fast approaching, I headed back down the winding road towards the beach, each bend taking me further away from Rocinha and back into the Brazil of guidebooks and postcards. The cramped, dank and humid shelters of the favela stopped abruptly, replaced by wide boulevards flanked by palatial apartment buildings. Different cars, different shops, different homes, different Brazil.

It took no more than ten minutes before I reached Ipanema beach, 2.6 kilometres of pristine golden sand being hungrily lapped at by thundering waves. Despite the inclement weather, the beach was still dotted with small clusters of impossibly attractive people playing volleyball under the ever-watchful eye of the Dois Irmãos (the Two Brothers), a pair of bare stone hills that dramatically jut upwards from the sea. I took a seat at one of the countless waterfront bars and, before my drink had even arrived, I heard it.

'Dim-dum-dum, pling-gung-gung, pling-gung-gung,' sung in a whisper by João Gilberto over a subtle and soft guitar opening. The sporadic and sparkling plink and plonk of piano and a creamy smooth tenor sax played by Stan Getz join in before Astrud Gilberto steals the show with her subtle vibrato-less vocals in English:

> Tall and tan and young and lovely
> The girl from Ipanema goes walking
> And when she passes, each one she passes goes 'Ah!'

'The Girl From Ipanema' is the most famous record ever to come out of Brazil. It is regularly claimed to be the second most-covered song in all of pop music, behind only 'Yesterday' by the Beatles. Written in 1962 by Antônio Carlos Jobim and Vinícius de Moraes, the version by Getz and Gilberto became an international hit in the spring of 1964, putting Brazilian bossa nova on the musical map. Ironically, at the exact moment that this beautiful song, with its graceful syncopation and subtle lyricism about love and longing, reached the top of the charts around the world, tanks rolled down the sea road next to Ipanema Beach, announcing the start of the brutal military dictatorship that went on to oppress Brazilians for the next twenty-one years.[1]

—

The road to the military coup of 1964 was a long one. Brazil was claimed by the Portuguese in 1500 and remained a colony until 1822. The Napoleonic wars made an anomaly of the country: it was the only colony to serve as the seat of government for its mother country when, in 1807, the royal court fled from Napoleon's invasion of Portugal and resettled in Rio de Janeiro. The Portuguese prince regent Dom João elevated Brazil as co-equal with Portugal in 1815 and then proclaimed its independence in 1822, humbly crowning himself as emperor on 1 December.[2]

Slavery wasn't abolished there until 1888 and the monarchy was overthrown a year later, a result of 'a restive military, a brooding landed aristocracy, and a resentful clergy', as well as a growing divide between the elites in the countryside and more progressive city dwellers.[3] The resulting republic was ruled by a succession of civil 'coffee presidents', who offered a modicum of democracy, though with a tiny suffrage and fraudulent elections.

A military coup attempt in 1922 ushered in a prolonged period of instability and unrest until 1930 when the defeated presidential election candidate, Getúlio Vargas, came to power via a revolt. It would place him at the centre of Brazilian national life for decades to come. With the backing of the military, he ruled as a dictator until he too was ousted by a coup in 1945, only to be re-elected as president in 1951. This period of rule came to a dramatic end in 1954 when, following an ultimatum from the military to resign or be overthrown, he took his own life.

On 24 August, he shot himself through the heart, leaving an impassioned and histrionic suicide note: 'Nothing remains except my blood. I gave you my life, now I give you my death. I choose this way to defend you, for my soul will be with you, my name shall be a flag for your struggle.' It ended: 'I take the first step to eternity. I leave life to enter history.'[4] The subsequent election saw the victory of Juscelino Kubitschek de Oliveira, a president who would transform the country.

Brazilian conservatives feared Kubitschek and his radical proposals, concerned by the unsolicited support provided by the illegal Communist Party. While in power, he oversaw an expansive programme of modernisation that crisscrossed the country with new highways, powered it with hydroelectric projects and expanded coal, steel and petroleum production. He is best known for the creation of the new federal capital of Brasília, a remarkable modernist edifice emerging out of the great interior of Brazil. However, politics is brutal and Kubitschek was replaced by Jânio Quadros in the elections of 1960, before a swift constitutional crisis saw the left-wing vice-president João Goulart take the reins just months later.

The ascension of Goulart, leader of the Brazilian Labour Party, further aggravated the existing political and social conflicts that divided the country.[5] What followed was a package of reforms that were, in practice, relatively moderate, with economic measures designed to more equitably distribute property, modernise institutions and expand suffrage to more people, yet the entrenched conservative elements of Brazilian society balked at the changes.[6] Scared by recent events in Cuba, the US government also became nervous, a misplaced fear at the thought of another of their relative neighbours falling to Communism, which saw them help to destabilise the Brazilian regime. Documents released more recently have shown Britain also played a covert role in the events.[7] Ideological polarisation, endless political crisis, reactionary fear of moderate reforms, economic turmoil and 80 per cent inflation all contributed to what followed. On 31 March 1964, as 'The Girl From Ipanema' was climbing the charts around the world, a coup d'état took place that subsumed Brazil under a bloody military dictatorship.

The legacy of the military dictatorship still affects Brazilian society today, a spectre that haunts contemporary politics – and a historical alternative that some on the right still believe to be better than the current democracy. In the cafés and bars of Copacabana, I found it surprisingly easy to find people who openly rejected democracy – a worrying situation considering the forthcoming elections and the widespread talk of a possible military coup in the event of a left-wing victory.

—

The first thing I did when I got to Copacabana was to buy an umbrella. An unseasonably torrential rainstorm was battering the city. The beach was near deserted, save for the odd hardy jogger battling against the wind and disappointed staff watching the thunderous white waves just beyond their empty bars. People playing beach football had been replaced by intrepid dog walkers in raincoats, while the horizon was dotted with vast cargo ships and oil tankers carrying away black gold. Just a few weeks before, this very beach had been drenched in sun and packed with tens of thousands of Bolsonaro supporters dressed in green and yellow in what the *Guardian* called 'a thumping display of political strength on his country's most famous beach in a bid to energise his stagnant re-election campaign'.[8]

Despite the rain, the area was still pulsating with politics. Every street corner was occupied, with people waving flags adorned with the faces of candidates. The streets were littered with party leaflets and every other person was proudly wearing a sticker, some for Lula, others for Bolsonaro. I spotted a small group of Bolsonaro supporters wearing Brazil football shirts covered in political stickers and drinking in a beachfront bar. Sadly, it seems that they have captured the Brazilian flag and even the iconic national football shirt. 'It's got to the point where anti-Bolsonaro supporters are even debating whether to support the football team,' the journalist Luís Costa told me over a coffee just back from the beach – something previously inconceivable in this soccer-obsessed country.

A man in a Brazil football shirt waved a huge green and yellow flag and pointed to a group sat in the bar. 'Very good people!' he shouted enthusiastically. I went over and was introduced to Valdinei Martins, a candidate standing to be state deputy in Rio for the Brazilian Labour Party and a fervent Bolsonaro supporter. Bolsonaro's face dominated the flags, his grinning visage occupying the bottom right corner.

'Foda-se Lula' (Fuck Lula) was the first thing Martins said to me, whispering it quietly in my ear. Using a translation app, I asked about his hopes for the presidential election. He explained that it would be close-run, which was surprising considering the polling suggested that Lula would win, perhaps even in the first round of voting.

'That's not what the polls suggest,' I replied.

'Fake news,' he snapped back in English.

'So who supports Bolsonaro?'

'Everyone!' He then jabbed his finger at each of his friends around the table. 'Taxi driver, public servant, businessman. Everyone!'

'And will Bolsonaro leave office if he loses?' I continued, very aware I had just invited myself onto their table. But it was the question on everyone's mind: would there be a coup and the reimposition of a dictatorship?

'Bolsonaro is a democrat,' explained Valdinei. I could feel a 'but' coming. 'But people have to trust the election.' Bolsonaro had spent recent months purposefully seeking to undermine trust in the electoral process, mimicking the Trumpian tactic.

'And what about his views on women and LGBT people?' I asked, pushing a little harder than was perhaps wise. All I got back was a shrug. It seemed our discussion was over. He asked me to pose for a picture with his flag, but I politely declined and made for the exit. As I left the bar, I asked one of the men enthusiastically waving a Bolsonaro flag why he supported the president.

'I don't', he replied. 'Bolsonaro supports the rich, Lula the poor. They pay me thirty reals [approximately £4.50] to wave the flag. It's my son's birthday today and I want to buy him a cake.'

One bar over, I sat down to eavesdrop on the conversation, but was quickly invited to join a family that was merrily drinking and singing along to a thumping samba band. They instantly asked what I thought would happen in the election; politics seemed to be the only topic of conversation in Brazil.

'What do you think will happen?' I replied.

'We all support Lula,' said the only English speaker, pointing to her mother and aunt. 'But he supports Bolsonaro,' raising an eyebrow in the direction of her uncle.

'Do you think Bolsonaro will leave office if he loses?' I asked in his direction.

After a short pause for the question to be translated, he replied, 'I hope not!' He went on to explain his support for the military dictatorship that ran Brazil between 1964 and 1985. 'It was safer and there was less corruption.'

'He doesn't like democracy,' added his niece with a smirk.

—

As the drizzly day turned to a drizzly evening, I jumped in a cab and headed to the Lapa district of Rio. Stepping out the car, my ears filled with a cacophony of competing percussive claps spilling from a jumble of bars. I joined the queue for the busiest – usually, but not always, a safe bet – received my wrist stamp and took a seat on the sole remaining bar stool. It faced towards a low, raised stage that was overflowing with instruments eagerly awaiting their players. A jaw-clenchingly strong caipirinha arrived on my table – unordered but welcome – and the evening began.

The musicians filed onto the stage and, after a moment of tapping and tuning, a percussive roar engulfed the bar. As if attached by strings to the drummers' flailing arms, the audience rose from its seats and burst into a hurricane of legs. The *surdos* drum provided a booming beat that underpins everything, while the *caixas*, a sort of snare drum, and the *tamborins*, a small cymbal-less tambourine struck with sticks, popped and clapped the higher tones. Then came the unmistakable scraping sound of the *reco-reco*, a sawtooth notched piece of wood, and the screech of the *cuica*, a tension drum that wails like an exotic bird. The drums danced in complex and infectious polyrhythms, often below a lead singer called a *puxador*, who provided the melody. 'He who doesn't like samba isn't a good guy,' goes the famous song, 'Samba da Minha Terra' (Samba of My Land). 'He's rotten in the head or sick in the feet.'[9] Sat alone in that bar, people gyrating and grinding around me, I couldn't have agreed more.

Samba emerged into a distinct genre in the early twentieth century, its roots and genesis being complex, disputed and sometimes mythical. Just as with Congo Square in New Orleans and the birth of jazz, samba has its origins 'in the traditional religious ceremonies brought to Brazil by African slaves'.[10]

Likely emerging in the part of the Brazilian region of Bahia known as 'Little Africa', many of these communities headed to Rio following the abolition of slavery in 1888.

Escolas de samba (samba schools) emerged as an artistic outlet for poorer communities and, by the 1920s, the genre had gained increasing popularity. From 1930 onwards, under the presidency of Getúlio Vargas, escolas de samba began to receive government subsidy as part of a wider project to forge a new Brazilian national identity. So, while Afro-Brazilian in origin, samba came to represent the newly created national identity of the 'mestizo', meaning culturally mixed Brazilian.[11] In the decades since, samba – or often a fruited-headed caricature of it – has spread around the world and, for many, has become indivisible from people's image of the country.

However, just as there is more than one Brazil, there is much more than one samba. What most people, me included, first think of as samba is the booming, rattling, clanging and raucous sound of carnival known as samba-de-enredo, an explosion of audible colour followed by infectious blast waves that demand you dance. Yet, the varieties and subgenres are seemingly endless and, to the non-expert, can sound only loosely related. There is samba de roda, samba carnavalesco, partido alto, samba exaltação, samba de gafiera, samba de breque, samba-lanço, samba pagoda and samba reggae, with even more blends and permutations in between.

This is confused further by the way many Brazilians discuss samba as something almost spiritual, ritualistic and deeply personal. I asked a Brazilian friend what she understood samba to be and the response made no mention of the actual music. Instead, I was met with poetic gushing about the soul of Brazil.

With the pounding of the surdos drum still reverberating in my ears, I jumped in a cab back towards Copacabana in search

91

of a nightcap. The dank weather had cleared the streets and the few remaining open bars looked uninviting. I shuffled up and down the roads that run perpendicular to the beach, diving into empty restaurants and bars during especially heavy downpours.

Conceding defeat, I headed back towards my hotel to call it a night and to watch the televised presidential debate between Lula and Bolsonaro. That's when I saw it: between a row of shuttered shop fronts was a tiny bar with its lights on. As I approached, I first heard the intricate syncopated tapping of a tambourine, then the gentle and sparce plucking of a nylon-string acoustic guitar. When I reached the entrance, I was greeted by an indifferent nod from a portly man with a mop of greying hair swept to one side and an imposing musketeer beard. He exuded cool. Uninterested but not unfriendly, he sat watching the election debate on his phone, wrote my name down and gestured to a fridge at the back where I was to get my own drink.

The bar was cramped, only around eighteen metres square, and every inch of its walls packed with framed pictures of famous Brazilian musicians slotted together like a jigsaw. There was only one table, around which sat seven musicians quietly playing bossa nova music with enchanting skill. Two guitars, a tambourine-like instrument called a pandeiro, where the cymbalettes around the edge are cupped to create a crisper and less sustained ring, a flute, a violin and an elderly man tapping gently on what looked like a tiny homemade xylophone with a mallet, all merged to create a gentle but complex music. It was the sound of a lover whispering in your ear; subtle, personal, sexy, a lyrical longing. Occasionally, the D'Artagnan-like proprietor hobbled to his feet and waved for the musicians to play quieter. I was never sure whether this was to placate the neighbours or to ensure they kept loyal to the authentic quiet style of bossa nova. I liked to think the latter.

Trying to track down the moment a new genre is born is an impossibility; one invariably flows from others. The moment a new idea emerges is usually untraceable and often fiercely contested in contradictory accounts by those involved. Bossa nova is no different. It has been argued that it started in a Copacabana flat owned by the parents of the singer and actress Nara Leão, where a small group of musicians, who came to typify the new genre, would meet regularly.[12]

Amusingly, the British music newspaper *Melody Maker* ran an article in 1962 titled, 'The bossa's not so nova', in which the Spanish bandleader Xavier Cugat claimed that it 'originated in Hollywood. It was a combination of boys playing jazz and boys playing samba, and they created a new mixture.'[13] An article the following month, however, was more accurate, with the American jazz guitarist Charlie Byrd mercifully confirming that 'IT *IS* BRAZILIAN'.[14] Its origins are perhaps best summed up by the musician Tom Jobin who, in 1966, argued that 'bossa doesn't have an owner. We are all part of a movement that comes from way back. It was being defined and rehearsed long before it was baptised.'[15]

Almost universally accepted, however, is the identity of the first bossa nova record cut to vinyl. The three giants of the new genre were João Gilberto, Vinicius de Moraes and Antônio Carlos Jobim and, in July 1958, Gilberto released 'Chega de Saudade', with music by Jobim and lyrics by Moraes. The song has been described as 'ground zero for modern Brazilian music'.[16] Running to just more than two minutes, it's effortlessly cool, with a sweet flute hook and near-whispered lyrics dangled suggestively first in a minor key, then major. It's all accompanied by guitar playing that mimicked the rhythmic patterns of the pandeiro, in what became the hallmark of bossa nova music.

Despite its subtle sound, the record had an explosive effect on those who heard it. For Caetano Veloso, later to become the central figure in the Tropicália movement discussed later, 'Chega de Saudade' was 'the manifesto and the masterpiece of a movement: the mother ship'.[17] As he explained in his auto-biography *Tropical Truth*, 'bossa nova overwhelmed us. And it delighted my intelligence to follow closely this radical process of cultural transformation, which led us to re-evaluate our tastes, our heritage and – even more important – our possibilities.'

As with so many genres, bossa nova was a development, not a wholly new break. The innovative sound centred around João Gilberto's transference of a samba beat to a guitar rhythm. The DJ and Brazilian music aficionado Gilles Peterson has described the centrality of this shift. 'The musical landscape of bossa nova was the samba beat distilled down the rhythm of just one instrument – the guitar – on which were overlaid complex harmonic structures and post-bop intervals. Clean, angular musical lines, off-kilter rhythms and sophisticated lyrics, a far cry from the samba of the day which now sounded dated.'[18]

Dated, maybe, but bossa nova was an adaptation of samba, not a wholesale rejection. Veloso described Gilberto's music as 'a deeply penetrating and highly personal interpretation of the spirit of samba. He did this through a mechanically simple but musically challenging guitar beat that suggested an infinite variety of subtle ways to make the vocal phrasing swing over a harmony of chords progressing in a fluent equilibrium.'[19]

The immense variety of samba allowed for musicians to pull on whichever thread most interested them. By the time Gilberto invented the guitar beat that launched bossa nova, the dominant form was samba-canção; while maintaining a samba beat, it was a slower, quieter form of the genre, typified by ballads 'in which the samba rhythm is perceptible only to a Brazilian ear trained to recognise it in all its variations of stress and tempo'.[20] The leap from samba-canção to bossa nova is far less daunting than from the booming carnival sound we first think of as 'samba'.

Bossa nova emerged as a middle-class art form, reflecting at first a modernising Brazil. By the end of the 1950s, Rio had emerged as the centre of modernity, a bubbling melting pot scene of young, affluent, beautiful people determined to make the most of a changing Brazil. For this set, the subtle, guitar-led bossa nova was replacing the bombastic carnival dancing and samba singing, and it encapsulated a new, cooler Brazil.[21] It is unsurprising, then, that early bossa nova generally ignored the political, economic and social conditions of the time, focusing instead on love and the country's natural beauty.[22] However, this optimism was short lived, with the military coup of 1964 changing everything.

The subtle tones of bossa nova soon reverberated beyond Brazil and found an enthusiastic and willing audience in the US and Europe. The 1959 film *Black Orpheus*, which has a beautiful bossa nova score, won the Cannes Film Festival Grand Prize and the Academy Award for Best Foreign Film, introducing the music to an international audience. 'I'd heard some music in the *Black Orpheus* film, which I liked very much, and I had the idea of doing something similar,' explained the jazz superstar Paul Desmond, alto saxophonist in the Dave Brubeck Quartet, to *Melody Maker*.[23]

Three years later, in 1962, two landmark events built on the success of *Black Orpheus* and catapulted bossa nova onto the wider international scene. The first was Stan Getz's *Jazz Samba* album, recorded in 1962 with guitarist Charlie Byrd. Released on 20 April 1962, it sold half a million copies in eighteen months and stayed on the charts for seventy weeks.[24] It remains the only jazz album to ever top the US Billboard pop chart. Its break-out song, 'Desafinado', written by Antônio Carlos Jobim, respectively reached number fifteen and number four on *Billboard*'s pop and easy-listening charts, and number eleven in the UK. The song was quickly covered by Ella Fitzgerald.

The second landmark event was a transformative concert at Carnegie Hall in New York on 21 November 1962. João Gilberto, Luiz Bonfá and Sérgio Mendes were among the many performers who enthralled a crowd of interested music fans, including Dizzy Gillespie and Miles Davis. The following month, the headline on *Melody Maker*'s cover screamed 'Bossa nova's here!'[25] By 1962, this subtle Brazilian genre, born within earshot of the lapping waves of Copacabana beach, was taking over the world.

Decades later, sitting in the tiny bar listening to these remarkable players, I completely understood the enchanting magic of bossa nova. It was mesmerising, genuinely beautiful, and I sat there transfixed for hours. Called Bip Bip, I later found out that the bar was an institution, a keeper of the authentic flame of Brazilian bossa nova.

Suitably inebriated, I pulled up a chair and began merrily tapping along on the table as they sang softly in unison. While having a smoke a touch later, a Portuguese man pulled me to one side to explain that the musicians around the table were virtuoso players. He had travelled to Brazil and come to the bar every night for three months to learn to properly play the pandeiro by watching and listening. That could explain why my enthusiastic but unskilled table thumping raised a few eyebrows from the other players.

'How was the debate?' I asked the musketeer on the door as I paid up.

'Lula win,' he assured me.

Another man in a Lula T-shirt interjected. 'But it's whether Bolsonaro leaves if he loses.' Just as they had during the military dictatorship, people had gathered at Bip Bip to listen, play and sing together, hoping for better times ahead.

–

As the 1960s got underway, some musicians began to understand the need for bossa nova to better reflect the realities of Brazilian life. What had primarily been a middle-class music that sung of love and longing developed a new, more politically conscious wing with artists such as Carlos Lyra, Nara Leão, Marcos Valle and Paulo Sérgio Valle increasingly singing about social injustice.[26] Central to their politicisation were collaborations with musicians from beyond the coastal neighbourhoods of Rio. They began to be inspired by, and play with, less affluent samba and folk musicians from shantytowns in the north-east of the country. This exposure 'led protest bossa singers back and forth between unearthing the roots of Brazilian music and building the communicative potential for their work for political ends'.[27]

In 1961, a group of young artists and intellectuals came together to form the 'Centro Popular de Cultura' (CPC), a left-wing cultural group connected to the National Union of Students. The CPC sought to align music with an overt left-wing political agenda and to create democratic art that spoke to the needs and struggles of ordinary Brazilians.[28] For CPC's music director, Carlos Lyra, that meant finding ways to break bossa nova out of its middle-class bubble, highlighting injustice and making it more relevant to working-class people.

'I started to realise the importance of lyrics that delivered a social message,' Lyra said.[29] 'After I joined the political movement, my lyrics gained new layers. What I do, until this day, is bossa nova, but neither my lyrics nor myself are alienated.'[30] Examples of this more politicised style are songs like 'Influência do Jazz' and 'Maria Moita', which explored the topic of class and gender inequality in Brazil.[31]

The CPC had an important effect on politicising Brazil's music scene; Caetano Veloso later credited it with 'establishing a political art'.[32] However, the life of the CPC was brought to an abrupt end in 1964 when, on 31 March, the coup d'état that would bring the Fourth Brazilian Republic to an end was launched, ushering in an age of repressive military dictatorship. With the government tightening its grip on Brazil, Nara Leão, the 'muse of bossa nova', returned from a tour of Japan. Getting to grips with the new societal reality, she declared 'enough bossa nova'. In essence, the advent of the military regime made traditional bossa nova anachronistic and blind to the experiences of people living under it. Leão's 1964 album *Opinião,* released just eight months after the creation of the Fifth Republic, reflected her shift towards more political music.

She was by no means alone in being radicalised by the onset of the dictatorship and feeling that bossa nova, at least in its traditional form, was dead. Veloso later explained that 'everything was heightened by the instinctive rejection of the military dictatorship, which seemed to unify the whole of the artistic class around a common objective: to oppose it'.[33] As the sleevenotes of a later compilation explained, 'the introspective lyrics of bossa nova changed into calls for the masses to rise up'.[34] Bossa nova redefined itself as MPB (Música Popular Brasileira), an amorphous term used by some to

98

describe any late-'60s Brazilian music, but more narrowly as the post-bossa nova scene that emerged under the dictatorship in the middle of the decade. Like the CPC before it, 'artists saw MPB as an important way of discussing and disseminating ideas of national affirmation and social justice, and of criticising the dictatorship'.[35]

As the decade progressed, the smouldering embers of cultural rebellion ignited into another artistic and musical movement. Tropicália emerged around 1967, but lasted for little more than a year as a coherent scene. In the liner notes of the retrospective album *Grandes Nomes: Caetano*, the music critic Tárik de Souza traces its birth to a Caetano Veloso performance of 'Alegria Alegria (Joy Joy)' at the 1967 TV Festival. 'The introduction of electric instruments to Brazilian popular music, until then unplugged, the new costumes, made of plastic, the bristling hair of the performers and the aggressive stage performances, making a stark contrast with the acoustic guitar and the quietude of bossa nova, were elements that changed definitely the course of Brazilian popular music'.[36]

It all sounds very reminiscent of Bob Dylan going electric. The following year, as the world exploded in historic conniptions – the Prague Spring in Czechoslovakia, the Tet Offensive in Vietnam, the assassinations of Martin Luther King and Robert F. Kennedy, and a wave of student protests that spread around the globe – Brazil had its own moment of cultural rebellion.

I first heard of Tropicália late one evening about a decade ago. I found myself deep down a YouTube rabbit hole, endlessly clicking from one music video to the next, unclear exactly what I was looking for but certain I hadn't found it. I eventually landed on a clip titled 'Paul Weller – What's in My Bag?'[37] The video showed the English musician walking around

Amoeba Music, a record store in Hollywood, selecting albums he liked.

'I've picked two records that every home should have,' he said, before reaching into the basket and pulling out a CD titled *Tropicália: A Brazilian Revolution in Sound*. 'Late '60s Brazilian music that kind of took over from bossa nova. Every track is great on this, I'd say.' The white sleeve had an image of three police officers, batons drawn, painted in red, and the word *Tropicália* doodled in multicolour marker pen. This cover, the five-second clip of a song and my implicit trust in Weller's taste was enough to convince me to buy it unheard.

A few days later, the album arrived and, to my relief, every track was great. As the record turned, filling my room with an electric energy, both familiar yet alien, I read the extensive sleevenotes written by Stuart Baker. He described Tropicália as a mix of 'American and British psychedelic rock and pop with Brazilian roots and European avant-garde and experimental music' that 'was both distinctly Brazilian and truly international ... Tropicália created musical and cultural anarchy under a military dictatorship and ultimately paid the price. And they created a Brazilian revolution in sound ... The chaos and anti-authoritarianism that seemed to be sweeping the world was beautifully recreated in the music of Tropicália.'[38] The compilation, released by Soul Jazz Records in 2006, remains one of my favourites, planting a seed that would eventually grow into this book.

The challenge with trying to describe the sound of Tropicália is its diversity. The musical architects of the scene were Caetano Veloso, Gilberto Gil, Gal Costa, Tom Zé and the band Os Mutantes, with associated acts such as Jorge Ben, Nãra Leao and Maria Bethânia. More than just a musical scene, it also included poets such as José Capinan, Torquato

Neto, Augusto and Haraldo de Campos and visual artists like Hélio Oiticica.[39] In fact, the name Tropicália was first coined by Oiticica before being used as the opening track on Veloso's 1968 self-titled album.

While there are certain common musical references, perhaps most notably the Beatles song 'Strawberry Fields Forever', each artist associated with Tropicália had a unique and often very different sound. Jorge Ben fused rhythm and blues with samba, Tim Maia mixed soul with the northeastern Brazilian genre of baiao, while Roberto Carlos mixed pop-rock with bossa nova.[40] As the music historians Chris McGowan and Richard Pessanha correctly state, 'in Tropicália, anything went: rock and samba, berimbaus and electronic instruments, folk music and urban noise, the erudite and the kitsch'.[41] The historian Christopher Dunn described it as 'a rereading of the tradition of Brazilian popular song in light of international pop music and vanguard experimentation'.[42]

Looking back on the movement that he helped give birth to, Veloso explained what allowed for this diversity of sound to emerge from a semi-coherent artistic movement. 'The tropicálistas decided that a genuine blend of the ridiculous aspirations of Americanophiles, the naïve good intentions of the nationalists, traditional Brazilian "backwardness", the Brazilian avant-garde – absolutely everything in Brazil's real cultural life would be our raw material. Genuine creativity could redeem any aspect of it and make it transparent.'[43]

From the start, however, the movement had a mission beyond the creation of music. For Veloso, Tropicália saw American mass culture as potentially liberating while simultaneously being a rejection of domination by powerful groups at home and abroad. 'It was also an attempt to face up to the apparent coincidence, in this tropical country, of a countercultural wave emerging at the same time as the vogue in authoritarian regimes,' he explained.[44] Perhaps this is what he meant when, in 1967, he told a journalist: 'I am Bahian and I am a foreigner.'[45] The line was later used by Tom Zé in his song *2001*.

The movement's musical manifesto, the compilation record *Tropicália: ou Panis et Circencis*, was released in 1968 on the Philips label. Unashamedly echoing the artwork of the *Sgt Pepper's Lonely Hearts Club Band* sleeve, the cover features the scene's key players: Gilberto Gil, Rogério Duprat, Gal Costa, Torquato Neto, Caetano Veloso, Nara Leão, Tom Zé and Arnaldo Baptista, Rita Lee and Sérgio Dias from Os Mutantes. Despite the oppressive regime around them, the musicians still sought to sneak rebellious sentiments past the watchful censors. Songs by both Gil and Costa mention spilled blood, while Veloso's contribution 'Soy Loco Por Tí, América', pays subtle homage to Che Guevara.[46]

Despite being generally uplifting and upbeat, the musicians sought to convey 'an atmosphere of violence and official repression'.[47] Tropicália reflected – and sought to undermine – a Brazil where democracy had been extinguished, demonstrations were forbidden and torture, death, disappearances and executions all happened at the hands of a terrorist state. It was these smaller acts, rather than more overt or confrontational forms of opposition, that typified Tropicália, with its musicians forced to operate within the censorious framework laid down by the regime.

'Half the songs that we sent to the censors returned marked up and mutilated,'[48] explained Tom Zé. Yet this didn't necessarily stop them. 'Since the censors did not have a set standard, and offices were located in different cities, we sent all of our songs to each office. One office would censor one and let pass another. The next office did the same with two others. And you ended up having, at times, the whole album "liberated" for release.'[49]

Through subtle lyrical nods and subversive and satirical aesthetic choices, they critiqued not only the visceral nationalism of the regime, but also what they saw as the dogmatic and narrow approach of the organised left-wing opposition.[50] It's unsurprising, then, that for many on the Marxist left, these more subtle acts of rebellion were deemed far from adequate and were brandished as apolitical or 'obsessed with superfluous Western pop music rather than traditional Brazilian sounds'.[51] Whatever the Marxists felt, it soon became clear that the far-right military dictatorship deemed Tropicália subversive enough to act.

On the morning of 27 December 1968, military police arrived at the São Paulo apartments of Caetano Veloso and Gilberto Gil. The exact cause of their eventual arrest remains unclear, though it seems that the scene's irreverent output eventually became too troublesome for the regime to ignore, especially when broadcast on TV during a series of shows throughout the year. Veloso described his understanding of the situation, believing that 'they didn't know whether it was a political movement or not – but they saw it as anarchic, and they feared it'.[52] He described how, during interrogations, military officers claimed that Tropicália music was more subversive than normal protest songs because it 'undermined the structures' of Brazilian society – a likely reference to its embrace of international culture and its modern outlook being a challenge to the traditionalism and nativism of the new state.[53] Gil and Veloso were subsequently exiled to swinging London, essentially bringing an end to Tropicália as a coherent musical movement.

Just a fortnight before their arrest, on 13 December, the regime had passed its infamous Institutional Act Number Five

(AI-5), which outlawed political opposition, suspended habeas corpus and instituted restrictive censorship over all press.[54] The effect, as intended, was to crush opposition to the regime. On the day it was passed, the magazine *O Cruzeiro* published an article by Marisa Alves de Lima titled 'Marginália: Arte e cultura na idade de pedrada (Art and Culture in the Stone-Throwing Age), accompanied by a picture of Veloso. It drew on many of the themes present in the various artistic manifestations of Tropicália and reads like an epitaph for a movement about to be crushed by AI-5:

> What is new today might be dead tomorrow. Down with prejudice. Art and culture as a totality. A new aesthetic. A new moral. Communicate through polemics. We're no longer in the Stone Age. We're in the 'Stone-throwing Age.' Which world is this? Fission. Fossil. Down with elite culture. 'Art is suspended etiquette.' No more swallowing of finished works. Participate. Culture without gods. From the bottom up. Everything has changed. Imagination in power. Third World. Art, chewing gum. Artist, Quixote. Marginal, marginalia. The rebels think so.[55]

With such onerous state oppression, two of the key protagonists in exile and numerous others arrested, Tropicália was snuffed out after barely more than a year. Yet while a regime may be able to crush a musical movement, they can't vanquish the ideas it espoused, a point best made by Tom Zé:

> What the military regime could not imagine was that, in the deepest recesses, in the conduits of subversion of cerebral connections, and especially in that soil reshaped

by the tornado of Tropicália, new ideas emerged that allowed Brazil to survive. Just as fear is the father of dreams, cowardice is the mother of courage.[56]

–

On 13 December 1968, as the people of Brazil felt the shackles tighten with the signing of Institutional Act Number Five (AI-5), a small bar called Bip Bip, just back from Copacabana beach, opened its doors for the first time, the bossa nova mecca I would spend a transformative evening in more than fifty years later.[57] With the first round of the Brazilian presidential elections that day, and talk of a possible military coup, not dissimilar to the regime of the 1960s, I decided to try and spend another evening in Bip Bip, but the bar wasn't yet open, so I meandered around the surrounding streets looking for an alternative. The sun finally broke through the clouds, painting Rio in a light that matched the postcards. There was an uneasy tension hanging in the air and a noticeably large police presence – walking in large groups, sparkling revolvers strapped to their thighs, some carrying long wooden poles like chair legs. They looked more like a gang than law enforcement. Police helicopters flew low over the beach, their side doors open like a scene from a Vietnam war movie. Then, as the evening deepened, the military made an appearance, with large lorries of heavily armed and helmeted soldiers driving up and down the beach.

In Brazil, people vote on computers rather than paper, meaning the results begin to trickle in soon after the polls close. The side street bars began to fill with excited supporters huddled around TV screens. I grabbed a drink in a small restaurant which was already thronged by Lula supporters, who greeted each result with a groan or cheer, depending on who it favoured. A group of middle-aged women entered the bar, dressed all in red and covered in Lula stickers. One proudly sporting a T-shirt emblazoned with the words 'Lula Inocente', a reference to his spell in prison for corruption. She cheered results with such gusto that her voice was already hoarse by 6pm. One especially large victory for Lula flashed on the screen and she pulled up her dress to reveal Lula's face emblazoned on her underwear.

For the first few hours, Bolsonaro remained in the lead, not unsurprising due to the early results coming in from the northern and southern regions where he was always expected to do well. But, as the hours progressed and he remained in front, people became increasingly nervous. An anti-fascist writer from Brazil texted me: 'I'm very distressed . . . In the last four years, I have been studying and warning that the extreme right was establishing itself here.'

It wasn't until 70 per cent of the vote had been counted that Lula finally took the lead. The street I was on erupted with cheers and chants of 'Olé, Olé, Olé, Olé! LULA, LULA!'

I walked a few streets down to another bar where there was a bigger TV screen and a more mixed group – half Lula supporters, half Bolsonaro. As I sat down, a drunk Bolsonaro supporter in a Brazil football shirt walked past and took aim at a young gay couple stood by the bar. Passions flared and a brief scuffle broke out between supporters of both political sides before being separated by bar staff. A woman involved in the scrap spotted me sat at the table and walked over. 'I'm Black, I'm a woman and I'm a lesbian. I'm everything they hate.' She clasped her hands around her neck, 'These people have been stood on my neck for four years.' She introduced herself as Marilia, a chef who had worked in New York for many years, before joining me at my table. 'Watch my dog,' she said. 'She's a total bitch.'

We watched the last 10 per cent of votes being counted together as she threw back her drink with enthusiasm. 'If Bolsonaro loses tonight, we're going to get so fucking drunk!' Marilia shouted, waving to the waiter to bring more drinks. I asked what the fight had been about. 'He was a bully. I can't stand bullies.' I believed her. She proudly sported a rainbow sticker that read 'Amar os Amigos: Desarmar os Inimigos', which she translated as 'Love your friends, disembowel your enemy' – although it seems 'disarm your enemy' may be a more accurate translation.

Another strong result for Lula flashed up on the screen and Marilia jumped out of her seat to face a group of Bolsonaro supporters celebrating a birthday on the table behind us. 'You're not celebrating any more, are you?' she fearlessly said before sitting down with a broad grin and a cackle. 'We're going to get so drunk tonight,' she said again, smashing her hand down on the table. In Brazil, the winner must obtain more than 50 per cent of the vote, which means a presidential election is usually held over two rounds, with the two highest-placed winners from the first going to head to head in the second.

When the results had finally all been counted, Lula had failed to make it across the line. He was painfully close to winning in the first round, but with 48.4 per cent, he fell just short. 'We'll beat him next time,' Marilia optimistically declared as we parted ways (a prediction that was proved true with Lula's second-round victory four weeks later). However, Bolsonaro had performed much better than most people had expected, securing 43.2 per cent of the vote in the first round. This was despite some pre-election polls estimating Lula would emerge with a thirteen- or fourteen-point margin of victory, leading many to ask serious questions about the accuracy of the polling.

With the last of the sun now extinguished, I made for Bip Bip one last time to taste the mood. As with my first visit, a group of musicians sat around the only table, quietly playing bossa nova with consummate skill. But the mood on the street in front of the bar was sombre. Not only had Bolsonaro far exceeded what was expected, the far right had performed well in congressional and governors' races as well. Bolsonaro's Liberal Party (PL) became the largest party in the lower house of Congress, with dangerous and extreme allies of Bolsonaro doing well. One Lula supporter in a rainbow shirt dejectedly shook my hand. 'I had no idea just how strong the far right really are,' he said, on the edge of tears. He raised his can of Heineken. 'To the death of our democracy,' he toasted.

Another Lula supporter came over. 'I don't want to be here drinking. I want to be at home crying. But a friend said it's better to be around friends who can hug you.' In that moment, unaware that Bolsonaro would later lose the second round of the election and despite his supporters storming the capitol, no coup would materialise, these people saw the pillars of their democracy wobble once more. They feared the return of a dictatorial regime, the sort that had oppressed their country before. Yet rather than staying at home, they chose to come to Bip Bip, to gather in a bar that opened on the very day that AI-5 was passed, and to listen to music, to find strength and hope in the very same songs that their parents and grandparents had sung in the 1960s.

FOUR

Zombies!:
Fela Kuti and Afrobeat in Nigeria

Recommended Listening:

Fela Kuti and His Koola Lobitos – 'It's Highlife Time'
Fela Ransome Kuti – 'Viva Nigeria'
Fela Kuti with Ginger Baker – 'Black Man's Cry'
Fela Kuti – 'Expensive Shit'
Fela Kuti – 'Question Jam Answer'
Fela Kuti – 'Coffin for Head of State'
Fela Kuti – 'Zombie'
Fela Kuti – 'Water No Get Enemy'
Tony Allen and Hugh Masekela – 'Never (Lagos Never Gonna be the Same)'
Femi Kuti – 'Truth Don Die'
Seun Kuti – 'Black Times'
Ezra Collective – 'Welcome to My World'

–

'GET BACK OR WE'LL SHOOT!' shouted the young officer guarding the presidential residence at Dodan Barracks in Lagos. Reports vary as to whether Funmilayo Ransome-Kuti's body was actually in the coffin her son was carrying towards the gates that day. On 1 October 1979, Nigerian Independence Day, Olusegun Obasanjo was due to step down as head of state, ending thirteen years of military rule in Nigeria.

'I just couldn't let him get away like that,' Fela Kuti later explained. 'Obasanjo's soldiers had killed my mother. That man will have to answer to that one-o!' The coffin had been on the roof of his new home emblazoned with a banner that read: 'This is where justice was murdered.'[1] The day before the transition of power, Fela took the coffin down and placed it in the back of his van. 'Vrrrrroooooooom! We were off for Lagos. Coffin inside bus, man.' The plan was no secret. In fact, he had told anyone who would listen. He shouted it from the stage at the Shrine, his legendary music venue, told the press and spread it around the streets. 'I knew I might get killed trying to do it. But I knew I would do it. That's the least I could do for my mama, man! So I said, "Fuck it!"'

They sped towards the barracks, dodging the roadblocks set out to stop him. Recognising the vehicle, the armed soldiers – Zombies! – frantically waved for him to pull over. Then, 'Bam! Bam! Bam! Bullets hit the bus.' No one was injured, so Fela drove on with the soldiers giving chase behind them. 'Man, I don't know how they didn't kill us that day.'

He got out the bus and along with a selection of his wives – he had twenty-eight – he carried the coffin towards the gates of the president's residence. 'Oh, my wives, those women are courageous-o!' The sentries pointed their machine guns at them and threatened to shoot. 'My brothers, will you also shoot my women?', responded Fela, before lowering the coffin to the floor.[2]

The pictures taken that day later adorned the sleeve of Fela's 1981 record 'Coffin for Head of State', a hypnotic, rage-induced twenty-three-minute song with powerful horn lines over a repetitive groove that lulls you into a menacing trance. 'Them steal all the money,' says Fela over the top of the track. 'Them kill many students / Them burn many houses / Them burn my house too / Them kill my mama / So I carry the coffin.'

In the song, he accuses head of state Olusegun Obasanjo and Brigadier Musa Yar'Adua of corruption. Fela's criticisms were well founded. The regime he railed against had failed to halt the endemic corruption that was crippling the country and impoverishing its people, and was willing to use its military might to crush those who fought back.[3] Fela's protest that day at the Dodan Barracks was a near-suicidal act of defiance carried out by a man engulfed by grief and fury. 'Seeing my mother die has made death very unimportant to me now,' he said just a few months after her death in 1978. 'I swore on the day I first saw her dying that I would put my struggle into top gear.'[4]

—

As I approached passport control at Lagos airport, I realised something wasn't quite right. There was a wall of men in military uniforms allowing locals past, but stopping anyone with a British passport.

'Where is your escort?' asked one of the soldiers.

'What's an escort?' I replied earnestly.

'Is it your first time in Nigeria?'

'Yes.'

'Then you need to have arranged an escort to take you through.'

I looked around and, sure enough, there was a bank of people with official-looking lanyards greeting people and ushering them towards the immigration officers.

'Erm, well, I haven't got one,' I said, starting to sweat a little.

'Why are you in Nigeria?' he asked with a menacing look. 'Passport!'

I sheepishly handed it over and began to wonder if this trip was going to be rather shorter than I had expected. 'I'm here for a music festival,' I offered, 'Felabration.'

'You like Fela Kuti?' asked another of the soldiers.

'Love him,' I replied. His face cracked into a broad smile.

'I'll take you through!' he bellowed, grabbing my passport out of the other soldier's hand. And, with that, I was in. Fela Kuti was evidently a name that still carried weight in Nigeria, even with stony-faced customs officers.

When I finally reached the baggage carrousel, there was the usual mass of annoyed passengers growing ever more agitated at the punishingly slow and sporadic arrival of our battered cases. Losing hope that mine had made it, I looked around to see who else was still waiting and, to my total surprise, I saw the most exciting jazz band to come out of the UK in a generation – Ezra Collective. Just weeks before, they had won the coveted Mercury Prize for their album *Where I'm Meant to Be*. I rushed over for a quick chat, told them how much I love them, went into too much detail about seeing them support Kamasi Washington at the Troxy in London and then asked for an interview. Their keyboard player Joe Armon-Jones gave me their manager's number and told me to set something up through her.

I headed off through customs where I was stopped by three different guards who all asked for money – 'What have you got for me?' each asked in turn – before stepping out into the sticky and thick Lagos night. My taxi driver had a relaxed attitude to road safety, weaving between packed minivans and lorries of live goats, bouncing over canyon-esque potholes and treating traffic lights as mere suggestions. But I made it to my hotel unscathed, if a little crumpled.

–

On Friday, 1 October 1960, Nigeria became an independent country at an opulent ceremony at Lagos racecourse. As the red, white and blue Union flag was lowered and a green and white Nigerian one raised in its place, the federal prime minister, Alhaji Abubakar Tafawa Balewa, announced: 'This great country, which has now emerged without bitterness or bloodshed, finds that she must at once be ready to deal with grave international issues.'[5]

Sadly, in the years that followed, that absence of bloodshed marking the transition to independence wasn't to last. The subsequent decades were as complex and diverse as the people who called Nigeria their home. With its wealth of natural resources, the country soon became the 'Giant of Africa' and was recognised as being at the forefront of the battle against both imperialism and the continued racist domination of southern Africa. In the words of the historians Toyin Falola and Matthew M. Heaton, Nigeria saw itself 'as a beacon of hope and progress for other colonised people emerging from the yoke of alien rule'.[6] Yet, it was also to experience one of the most traumatic civil wars of the twentieth century and be plagued by coups, corruption and an extended period of military rule.

However, just as the early 1960s was a period of exciting artistic exploration in Europe and the Americas, Nigeria bloomed culturally, with writers and artists drawing on indigenous and historical imagery and music to help forge the future of a new nation.[7] Fela Kuti returned to Nigeria in 1963 with his band Koola Lobitos, having been living in London since 1958. He had travelled to Britain for his musical education and studied at the prestigious Trinity College of Music in Greenwich (now known as the Trinity Laban Conservatoire of Music and Dance), though arguably he learned more from the clubs and bars of the city than he ever did in the classrooms. He returned to a Nigeria that was wrought by tensions and began to develop Afrobeat, a new musical style that was to change African music forever.

Afrobeat is a complex and electrifying mix of jazz, funk, soul and highlife, infused with traditional west African musical styles like yoruba and igbo. Central to the musical tradition on which it drew is percussion, especially the gongon drum. It's an hourglass-shaped instrument with two leather drumheads tuned by tension cords, struck by a stick in the shape of a shepherd's crook. It's sometimes called the 'talking drum', because the player can change the tone by manipulating the cords to mimic a voice. Others claim it got its name because the drum was used to communicate between villages. Whatever the etymology, it lets off an almighty clap when struck.

For me, Afrobeat is all about the drumming, the funky and hypnotic groove that underpinned Fela Kuti's records. Its innovator was Tony Allen, who was inspired by the structural innovations of modal jazz and funk.[8] Michael E. Veal, co-author of Allen's autobiography, described him as being 'like a great boxer. He knows when to jab with his bass drum in order to punctuate a soloist's line, when to momentarily scatter and reconsolidate the flow with a high-hat flourish, when to stoke the tension by laying deeply into the groove, and when to break and restart that tension by interjecting a crackling snare accent on the downbeat.'[9] Allen's drumming sat within a percussion section including clefs (claves), congas and a beaded rattle known as a shekere. On top of this heady percussive brew was Fela on saxophone or keyboards, with his highly politicised and aggressive lyrics sung in a mix of English and Yoruba. The songs were long and repetitive, much like Irish trad music or later dance music; the repetition becomes hypnotic, making the small shifts or changes exciting.

While Fela was developing the genre that became known globally as Afrobeat, Nigeria was in turmoil. The Nigerian Civil War (or Biafran War), exploded in 1967. Its roots are complex, but in part they lay in the fact that Nigeria as a country was a creation of the British Empire, an amalgamation that brought together a host of ethnic and religious groups. The people within its borders were known as Nigerians, but most people remained more attached to local communities and tribal ties that predated the creation of the state by centuries.[10]

At the time of independence, Nigeria was essentially comprised of three semi-autonomous regions, which all pushed back against the centralisation of authority.[11] A series of ethnic and religious differences added to the complex picture. The majority of northern people were Muslim, while the south was made up of a fragmented collection of tribes, alongside the Yoruba kingdoms in the west, the Benin kingdom of the mid-west and the Ibos of the east. Add to this a series of destabilising coups in January and July of 1966 and the scene for conflict was set. The final trigger was the attempted secession of the south-eastern provinces of Nigeria as the new Republic of Biafra. On 30 May 1967, Emeka Ojukwu declared independence and, on 6 July 1967, the federal army entered the region, beginning the war. According to the historian Richard Bourne, the simplest explanation for the war is that 'in Nigeria, where the slogan was "One Nigeria", it was simply about preserving the country as a single entity'.[12]

The suffering that ensued made it one of the worst conflicts of the entire post-war period. At first, the world was slow to wake up to the horror of the conflict, in part because its eyes were turned to the Six-Day War in the Middle East and the ongoing conflict in Vietnam. But shocking images of emaciated and dying Biafrans were soon beamed around the world causing widespread alarm. Biafra ultimately collapsed and, on 11 January 1970, Ojukwu fled to the Ivory Coast, with his army commander surrendering the next day.

By the time the federal forces won, the combined military casualties were estimated to be around 100,000, while civilian deaths, mainly from starvation, totalled between a staggering 500,000 and 2 million. On top of these were 4.6 million Biafran refugees. While it has been argued that there was a surprising lack of desire for vengeance, one issue was the staggering size of the military after the war.[13] Prior to the conflict, it numbered just 10,000 men but, by 1970, it had swelled to 250,000.[14] A military of that size was perhaps always unlikely to hand back power to civilian authorities with much haste.

As Nigeria emerged from the war, it underwent dramatic economic changes that were to add the opportunity to grab enormous wealth to the military's motivation to hold onto power. At the time of independence, Nigeria was an overwhelmingly agriculture-based economy, in part because industrialisation had been discouraged by the British colonial regime. This changed as the 1970s progressed with sizeable growth in various industries, such as a textiles, pharmaceuticals, beer and soap. Most dramatic was the arrival of car manufacturing, with six plants springing up to build Volkswagens, Peugeots, Leyland trucks, Steyrs, Fiats and Daimler-Benzes.[15]

However, what truly changed the country was the arrival of oil, and lots of it. In 1960, cocoa, groundnuts and palm products accounted for 80 per cent of exports, but from 1974 onwards, crude petroleum dominated, making up 80 per cent of exports and fundamentally altering the nature of the Nigerian economy and thus the country's place in the world.[16] With oil came remarkable wealth which, in turn, came with systemic corruption and a growing frustration that the oil dollars were failing to trickle through the economy and substantively improve the life of many ordinary Nigerians.

Following the war, the military government originally set 1976 as the date for a return to civilian rule. However, on 1 October 1974, the head of state, General Yakubu Gowon, announced that the military would not be handing back power as promised. The failure to return to a democracy was partly due to continuing constitutional disagreements among those in power and in part due to a 'substantial number of leading soldiers who were in no sense ready to hand over power to the civilians'.[17]

Nigeria was not alone in this. As the 1970s progressed Africa saw the emergence of a number of military dictatorships that postponed the dream of democracy for millions of people. 'As elsewhere in Africa, the military had acquired a taste for power,' explains the historian Guy Arnold, 'and were ready to persuade themselves that they could rule as well or better than the civilians.'

Despite military rule, the 1970s wasn't a particularly stable period for Nigeria. While it became an African giant, with influence across the continent, it continued to experience political instability at home. In 1975, Gowon was ousted in a coup and replaced by Murtala Muhammed, whose Supreme Military

Council set 1979 as the new date for a return to civilian rule. However, Muhammed was soon assassinated during a failed coup attempt in February 1976 led by Lt-Col Bukar Dimka. With Muhammed dead, Lt-Gen Olusegun Obasanjo rose to become the next head of state and, in September 1978, the new constitution was accepted and the state of emergency, which had been in place since 1966, was finally lifted.

The plan was to have elections the following year and, on 1 October 1979, Nigeria ended thirteen years of military rule, returning to a civilian government with Shehu Shagari becoming its first executive president. This interregnum lasted until 1983, when military rule returned. Many have sought to point out that, as far as military dictatorships go, this one wasn't too brutal and that in the words of the Nigerian lawyer Mr Justice Bello, the country 'enjoyed the most liberal military democracy in modern history'.[18] However, despite its questionably benign reputation, it did remain a military dictatorship, dogged by corruption and, when needed, happy to brutally crush opposition and dissent. It was this brutality that Fela Kuti set out to challenge.

—

Today, Lagos is a pulsing mass of crumbling buildings held together by red or green corrugated metal roofing. Densely packed houses stretch to the horizon below a halo of visible pollution. The city is bordered to the east by a vast brown lagoon and to the south by the Gulf of Guinea. As it reaches the sea, Lagos tears into a complex array of islands divided by winding creeks that work their way towards the Atlantic. International companies hide in glass towers, while fishermen occupy stilted homes at the water's edge.

There isn't much in terms of sights to see, but the city has its own frenetic energy. The streets are busy at all hours and life is lived in the open with people grouped by the road eating, drinking, talking, getting haircuts and buying and selling anything you might need – and if they don't have it, they will certainly find you someone who does. But the poverty is unavoidable and heartbreaking, the result of rampant corruption, which has led to an understandable seething anger. Many citizens live in densely populated shanty towns where small shacks are crushed together and children go without shoes. I saw a naked homeless man lying in the dust beneath a punishing sun. I didn't speak to a single person who wasn't angry about the state of the country; neither did I find anyone who wasn't convinced the elections earlier in 2023 had been rigged. Poverty and corruption – the exact things Fela Kuti railed against – still blight Nigerian society today.

I jumped in a cab near my hotel on Victoria Island in the south of the city and headed 45 minutes north to Ikeja, home of the Kalakuta Museum. We drove over the Third Mainland Bridge, a remarkable twelve-kilometre motorway over the Lagos Lagoon that hugs the city's flank. Huge barges sat idle, while tiny wooden fishing boats spluttered around like water striders. As we neared the museum, the roads became cramped by businesses in tiny shacks. I spotted a large metal sculpture of Fela Kuti's head sat atop a metal fence and pointed it out to my driver.

On arrival, I passed through the unmanned gate and walked in the entrance to find a surprised-looking lady sat in the dark behind the desk.

'Can I help you?' she asked.

'I'm here to see the museum,' I replied. Clearly not accustomed to visitors, she explained that I would have to wait while they switched on the generator so the lights could be turned on. I was pointed in the direction of some rusting metal steps at the back of the building and told there was a bar on the roof where I could wait. From the top, I saw a man hurrying towards the museum with a jerry can of petrol for the generator. Ten minutes later the lights flickered on.

The museum is located in the three-storey building that was home to Fela Kuti from the late 1970s until his death in 1997. However, this was actually the second fabled Kalakuta Republic, the original being in the Lagos suburb of Surulere until its dramatic destruction by the state. On the afternoon of 18 February 1977, more than 1,000 armed soldiers stormed Fela's compound. Located at 14 Agege Motor Road in Lagos, the sprawling complex was the headquarters of his world, housing much of his family, as well as providing shelter to a shifting coterie of musicians, friends, outcasts, lovers and hangers-on. It had a free health clinic, a recording studio and rehearsal space – and even farm animals in an attempt to make the compound as self-sufficient as possible.

The Kalakuta Republic had been a target of the authorities for years. Back in April 1974, the commune was raided by fifty armed police reportedly looking for drugs and underage women. Fela was arrested, along with sixty other occupants. According to Fela's biographer, Michael E. Veal, the police planted a block of incriminating hemp – possession at that time came with a decade in prison – but he was able to grab and swallow it. After being arrested anyway, Fela secretly used the communal toilet at night while the guards slept and ate smuggled-in vegetables so that, by the time the authorities finally got hold of a sample, the incriminating evidence had all disappeared into the sewers of Lagos.[19] The episode was later immortalised in song as 'Expensive Shit'.

In the wake of the raid, Fela erected electrified barbed wire and renamed the compound the Kalakuta Republic – a reference to the name of the police cell he had been held in – and proceeded to declare it an autonomous homeland, free from the laws and control of Nigeria. With the blood barely dried from the secessionist Biafran war, the military rulers didn't take Fela's declaration lightly, however far it was from a genuine breakaway. 'The government couldn't stand this "republic within a republic" thing,' explained Fela's drummer, Tony Allen, 'especially because they themselves had critics all over the world because of all the craziness that Nigeria was going through at the time.'[20]

The police raided again in November 1974, with Fela ending up in hospital for seventeen days with injuries sustained during the brutal rampage.[21] He once again put his pain and anger to music, telling the story of the raid on his best-selling 1975 *Kalakuta Show* LP, the sleeve of which showed club-wielding officers storming the compound. 'So the government kept trying to break him down,' explained Allen in his autobiography. 'The raids started following each other, one after another . . . And it never stopped . . . Between 1974 and 1977, it was a hot, hot time. It was like we were caught up in a war zone.'

The brutal state opposition to Fela and the Kalakuta Republic came to a fiery climax in 1977. It was a year of radical music around the world. Back in London, the former imperial motherland, punk was exploding onto the streets. The Sex Pistols topped the UK charts with their phlegm-covered album *Never Mind the Bollocks*, while the Clash released their debut, the highlight of which was the call-to-arms punk classic 'White Riot'. Also released that year was Bob Marley and the Wailers' *Exodus* album, recorded in London after a failed assassination attempt on Marley back in Jamaica. To this 1977 triptych of revolt was added Fela Kuti's album *Zombie*, released in Nigeria on Coconut Records.

While there was little musical crossover, there was a commonality of spirit and rebellion in what they were all doing. Fela's album was to become a classic, a scathing musical assault on the Nigerian military that labelled its obedient soldiers 'Zombies': 'Go and kill (joro, jaro, joro) / Go and die (joro, jaro, joro).' The record's popularity only served to anger the regime further, with youths taunting soldiers in the street by singing the song, dancing and mockingly impersonating their mindless marching, with sticks as rifles.[22] The next chance the authorities got, they exacted their revenge.

'Let me tell you how the thing went-o!'[23] explained Fela years later when recalling the events of that bloody day. On 18 February 1977, soldiers arrived at the Kalakuta Republic searching for Segun, one of Fela's drivers, who either merely disobeyed a traffic cop or beat one up, depending on whose story you believe. When the officers arrived at the compound to arrest him, Fela refused them entry and instead taunted them by playing *Zombie* over a loudspeaker.[24] He claims to have told the police, 'You can come with bazookas, rifles and bombs'[25] – and they did just as he suggested. A thousand soldiers soon arrived carrying FN-1 automatic rifles, batons, horsewhips and jerry cans filled to the brim with petrol.[26] Prior to that day, Fela had bought a 65 kW generator, put it on the back of a Ford truck and electrified the perimeter fence. While it delayed the invading soldiers, they soon dealt with it by covering the generator in petrol and setting it alight.

What followed was an attack of staggering brutality, as Fela later recalled. 'They came in, busted the gate open, broke the door down . . . went everywhere in the house . . . beating . . . flogging . . . kicking ass with their boots . . . hitting with rifle butts.'[27] The attack was relentless. 'Oooooooooh!! It was too much, man. They were flogging away, beating everybody, cutting, using bayonets, broken bottles . . . raping the women! It was terrible! Oooooooooh!! Terrible!!'[28]

A number of the men had their testicles smashed while the woman had their nipples ripped by stones. They were beaten, stripped and raped, while some, in an act of staggeringly sadistic torture, had broken bottles forced into their vaginas by the frenzied soldiers.[29] Fela's brother, Dr Beko Ransome-Kuti, was left with a fractured leg and arm after a ferocious beating that left him in a wheelchair for several weeks. Not even the brothers' elderly mother was left alone. 'Then they grabbed my mother,' explained Fela. 'And you know what they did to this seventy-seven-year-old woman, man? They threw her out the window of the first floor.'[30] It was from the lasting injuries sustained that day that she would later die.

Once the beatings subsided, the complex was doused in petrol, set alight and burned to the ground. Gone was the recording studio, Fela's recordings and the instruments with which he made them. The unreleased soundtrack to his forth-coming autobiographical film *The Black President* was turned to ashes before the world could hear it. The Zombies had done as they were ordered and silenced Fela Kuti . . . Or so they thought.

Undeterred, he rebuilt his republic, and after years of neglect following his death in 1997, it was finally reborn as the Kalakuta Museum, opening in 2012.[31] It's a remarkable place, despite there not actually being much to see. There are paintings of Fela, which are pleasant enough, and the stairs are lined with pictures of his wives and children, of which there are plenty. There are a couple of his saxophones, a battered piano keyboard hung on the wall, and his bedroom, left untouched. It's strikingly basic: a mattress on the floor in one corner and dozens of his colourful jackets on hangers along each wall. There's one room that has nothing but a collection of his shoes – silken slippers nailed to the wall. A colourful mosaic reads, 'If a man wants to enslave you forever, he will never tell you the truth about your forefathers.' Fela's typewriter is also on display in the so-called 'Manifesto Room', where he wrote his treatise for his short-lived political party, Movement for the People.

However, the real magic happened outside. As I stood out the front having a beer, two men approached me and asked for a picture, surprised to see a random white boy from England making a pilgrimage to the home of Fela Kuti. It transpired that they both play in the second band of Fela's son, Seun Kuti: trumpeter Elijah Ameh and bass player Aduragbemi Emmanuel. I asked them their thoughts on Fela's music.

'Fela Kuti is a legend,' said Emmanuel. 'When it comes to Afro-music, he's a legend. Even after his departure, we still celebrate him. He's a legend all over the world.'

'But do young people still listen to him?' I asked.

'We are still young!' joked Elijah, his face breaking into a mischievous smile. 'People still listen, because it's very good music. It's music with a message. A message about the country.'

But can music actually change the world?

Emmanuel answered. 'The way I think music can change the world is the way it gives you a chance to talk to people when they don't want to give you the chance to talk. You can use music to pass a message and, when they hear the music, they definitely have to listen to what you are saying.

'Music is life,' he said, as we shook hands and parted.

While I waited for my taxi, an elderly man in a striking red shirt and black trilby on his head was looking over. He oozed cool, nonchalantly leaning on his walking stick, his right eye glazed completely white. 'You like Fela?' he said. 'Of course,' I replied.

'I used to play with him!' he said, as though it was obvious.

'Pardon?' I said with enough disbelief to make him laugh. It turned out I had randomly bumped into Rilwan 'Showboy' Fagbemi, baritone saxophonist in Fela's imperious band Egypt 80. He recorded with him in London, New York, Paris and, of course, here in Nigeria. He asked how I got into Fela's music and I explained I first heard the 1971 album *Live!*, which has two songs with Ginger Baker from Cream, a musical monster and my favourite drummer.

'I know Ginger,' he said, laughing again as my mouth fell open. 'I played with him. I went out to Los Angeles to stay with him.' I didn't know what to say. Baker was an awful person by many accounts, but a musical genius. I saw him play at the Jazz Café in London shortly before his death in 2019, but left at the interval. Time had ravaged him and he could barely play; it was too sad to watch. I had a million questions for Showboy, but my taxi had arrived and the driver was growing inpatient, so I settled for photo, shook Showboy's hand and thanked him. 'Nice to meet you,' he said, still clearly amused by my excitement.

My taxi got bogged down in traffic just behind the museum. I looked out of my window and a goat bolted towards it. A man grabbed it by its beard and pulled it to the ground, causing it to release an ear-splitting yelp. He then did something I've never seen before; he punched it in the head. The goat looked as shocked as I did. He wrestled it to the ground just inches from the car, tightly tied its legs and stepped on the goat's head. More curdling screams rattled the car windows. Then, without warning, he pulled out a machete and sliced the goat's throat open, violently yanking back its head as he slid the knife across. Blood spurted into the gutter; a crimson pool instantly painted the dusty road. The goat spasmed and yelped again so he forced the knife up into the brain with a brutal punch. It fell silent and my taxi drove on. I felt a very long way from home.

—

In the northern suburb of Ikeja, tucked away among warehouses and factories, is the world-famous New Afrika Shrine. I first decided to visit it after reading about Paul McCartney's difficult though fruitful trip to Lagos in 1973 to record the Wings album *Band on the Run*. In McCartney's telling, his encounter with Fela Kuti was frosty, with Fela wary of a famous British musician exploiting African music and musicians:

> We started off thinking of doing a track with an African feel, or maybe a few tracks, or maybe even the whole album, using the local conga players and African fellows. But when we got there, and we were looking round and watching the local bands, one of the fellows, Fela Ransome Kuti, came up to us after a day or two, and said, 'You're trying to steal the Black musicians' music.' We said, 'No we're not! Do us a favour, Fela. We do all right as it is, actually. We sell a record here and there. We just want to use some of your guys.' But he got heavy about it, until in the end we thought, 'Blow you then, we'll do it all ourselves.'[32]

Despite the difficult encounter at the time, McCartney's experience in Lagos had a lasting effect on him. Speaking in 2021 during an interview with the legendary producer Rick Rubin, he fondly reminisced about visiting the Shrine.

'You were sitting right by him!' Rubin said,

'Front-row seats,' replied McCartney with his usual boyish enthusiasm. 'The energy was great. When he came on and his band kicked in, "Oooh". I still remember the riff.' He jumped up and started playing it on a nearby piano. 'The music was so incredible that I wept – just when it hit and the groove. That was one of the greatest music moments of my life.'[33]

McCartney wasn't the only global star to make a pilgrimage to the Shrine. In the early 1970s, former Cream and Blind Faith drummer Ginger Baker visited Fela in Lagos. Then, in 1977, the Afro-Brazilian singer Gilberto Gil, discussed earlier, travelled to perform at the FESTAC 77 Black Arts Festival at the venue.[34]

It was watching that McCartney interview a few years ago that convinced me I had to make my own pilgrimage to the Shrine. I arrived by taxi for the Thursday of Felabration, the annual festival that celebrates Fela's music, life and politics. The scene outside the Shrine was chaotic, pulsing with people drinking heavily already. The car vibrated to the booming bass from a roadside speaker system. As we crawled towards the venue, the car was surrounded by people peering through the window with cupped hands. Seeing me in the back, children banged on the door, only to be moved out the way by an older man who pressed a plastic petri dish of marijuana against the window. The car came to a stop and I stepped out into the madness. The show wasn't due to start that evening, but the party was well underway on the road outside.

I pushed my way to the entrance and was waved through to the backstage area. There, I was kindly given an access-all-areas pass with no real discussion about who I was or why I was there. I was christened Mr Joe English and handed a lanyard, while a plastic cup of booze was thrust into my other hand. I drank it in one gulp to calm myself and asked for another. White wine, red wine, vodka and an energy drink were mixed together and handed back to me with a warm smile. It tasted less horrifying than it sounds and a couple of cups was enough to create a near-instant buzz.

I was introduced to Tosin Akinbami from the festival's media committee and I asked if there was any chance of an interview with Femi Kuti, Fela's eldest son and a respected musician in his own right. He had played in his father's band Egypt 80 before starting his own outfit, Positive Force. 'No problem,' Tosin instantly replied. I had been trying to arrange an interview for some time with little success. While back in London I had managed to track someone down who said they could organise a meeting but just before I flew out, I was informed there would be an introduction fee.

There were no such complications with Tosin. She walked me into the building just behind the stage, up some stairs, knocked on a door, opened it without pausing and ushered me into the room. There, sat on a black leather office chair was Femi, trumpet in hand. On a double bed lay Yeni Kuti, Fela's daughter and the founder of Felabration. Completely unprepared, I explained I was writing a book and hoped to interview him. He looked exasperated, uninterested and inconvenienced, saying it was too loud to talk due to the ongoing soundchecks below. Nervously, I said I would return later, before fumbling for the door handle to escape the awkwardness.

I returned an hour later once the stage had fallen silent. Tosin knocked and ushered me in again without ceremony. Someone was applying cream to Femi's feet and he looked at me still unconvinced. 'Do you have a moment for that quick interview?' I tentatively asked. Just as I did so a band struck up on the stage below and he grumbled about me coming again while the music was playing. I apologised but persevered and he nodded for me to take a seat as he put on his boots. As I nervously sat and began to explain what I was hoping to discuss, he quickly interrupted. 'Just ask your questions. Time is going.'

Thankfully, as we began to chat, he softened a little, even smiling occasionally. He was clearly tired as the festival was in its fourth day and ran until the early hours each night. I started by discussing the Shrine and why it was that he had decided to rebuild it after Fela's passing. 'Many things are the same. The Shrine is in the same place. It's just five times bigger. The old Shrine, 500 people and it was completely full. So, it's much bigger.'

He wasn't wrong. The New Afrika Shrine is a cavernous building with a high corrugated iron roof from which hang a scattering of fans, the benefit of which isn't felt. A stage sits at one end and, along the walls, are stalls selling all manner of booze, cigarettes and nibbles. Technically, it's open to the elements at its sides, but little breeze passes through, making it a humid and dense atmosphere. Tin signs reading 'The Shrine Does Not Support Hard Drugs' are nailed to the wall but, as suggested, they prohibit only 'hard' narcotics; thick plumes of marijuana smoke dance through the beams of light, unincumbered on their way up into the night sky.

Femi began to thaw further when I asked why, so long after his father's death, people still revere him so much.

'I think it's because as a person he was very truthful with his compositions. He really meant what he was saying. The message still resonates today, twenty-six years after. Everybody, the economy, the situation is getting worse. All the things he said are still so truthful.'

'So would you class yourself as a political activist like your father?'

'I don't like the word "activist",' he interrupted.

'What word would you prefer?'

'I'm just someone who is concerned.'

'And what is it that you are concerned about?'

'We still don't have electricity. People are still poor. Same issues.'

I mentioned his 2010 record *Africa for Africa*, an angry collection of songs about African unity and the scourge of corruption set to pumping horns and infectious polyrhythms. Since arriving in Lagos, every person I asked bemoaned the crippling corruption that still blights the country.

'So does music still have a role in trying to change Nigerians' lives for the better?' I asked.

'Yes – any way you look at it, even if it just consoles you. You can't do anything without music. It consoles you when you are depressed or angry, especially when you speak truth with music like what Fela and I'm doing. People hear it and it gives them courage.'

I pushed further, wanting to know if music merely offers comfort or if it can have a profound impact, a means to create real change. 'What about your band Positive Force?' I asked. 'Wasn't that the objective – to bring about real change?'

He formed the band in the late 1980s after falling out with his father and leaving Fela's band Egypt 80, so I was worried I was on touchy ground.

'The name of the band was supposed to be the Universal Revolutionary Front, but my mother thought that was too political. So she suggested Positive Force. I left my father, but it wasn't for negative reasons. I wanted to be myself. So, it was her suggestion. I was a very angry person. I wanted to be very militant and my mother was like, "Hey, take it easy. You don't need to be bitter. You can still pass your message in a more subtle way.'

'Like all mothers,' I quipped nervously.

By now the fire in his eyes was beginning to flicker a little more, his famous anger and passion still there.

'I hope I influence people positively by inspiring people. I don't believe change can just happen like that. It's a very difficult question. Fela was singing for three decades and I've been performing for nearly four decades, and things have gotten worse. Ukraine, Israel, Palestine ... I was in America two years ago. I've never seen San Francisco and Philadelphia so poor. You go to England or France with the migrant crisis. Life can be so depressing so, for me, I use my music to keep my sanity as well. I hope it helps people. I practise and practise because when I don't practise, I have to think about all these other issues. It's very depressing, so I try to use that force, to energise myself, and I hope my compositions do that for other people.'

'So does that mean music *can* change the world?' I asked, pushing my luck with a final question.

'I think it can. If we use Fela as an example, people are very aware because of Fela's music. Fela's music changed me. Fela's music made me and it made many of us who we are. While we were going through the colonial and then post-colonial periods, Fela enlightened us. Fela gave us hope.

'So, I think music can change the world. Look at Bob Marley. Look at what jazz did. Look at what the blues did. Look at what funk did. Imagine if all of this music didn't exist. The world would be so bitter. It can be a love song or it can be political. Just imagine if there was no music. We would probably all be killing each other. Music gives that comfort. It makes you a deep thinker. So, yes, music can change the world.'

131

With that, I knew the interview was over. I can't pretend his intensity didn't scare me a little, but I was just glad to have met him. I couldn't tell if he didn't like me specifically, all journalists generally or if he was just tired. I shook his hand and, as I left, he nonchalantly picked up his trumpet and began to practise, the clarity of his tone sending a shiver through me as I closed the door. Later, as I decamped to a plastic table for some impossibly tough chicken, he walked behind me, patted me on the back and said, 'Enjoy the food.' As I looked round and realised it was him, he shot me a broad grin, so I guess the interview went OK.

The Shrine began to fill and, by 10pm, the place was pulsating with drunk people necking small pouches of neat gin. The festival organisers had packed the bill and the first few hours saw a procession of uninspiring rappers mumbling to a generally disinterested audience. That all changed at 11pm when Made Kuti, grandson of Fela and son of Femi, exploded onto the stage. His set started with a solitary drummer playing a djembe, a goblet-shaped drum played with the hands. Each strike produced a crisp popping sound that echoed around the room. The kit drummer joined in, perfectly replicating each beat to roars from the excited crowd. The rest of the band ran on, then three women and an impossibly muscular shirtless man gyrated across the stage. Finally, an effortlessly cool Made entered in a gold sleeveless shirt, playing his trumpet with one hand. It was magnetic. I was on the side of the stage dancing uncontrollably and sweating significantly more than was decent.

It was then that I noticed Femi Koleoso, bandleader and drummer of Ezra Collective, as well as drummer for Damon Albarn's virtual band, Gorillaz. I dripped over to him and asked about the possibility of an interview the following day, to which he enthusiastically agreed.

The next day, rehydrated, I made my way back to the Shrine for 2pm. Koleoso arrived on time looking excited but already tired: 'I went back to the studio with some local musicians last night, so didn't get much sleep.' It must have been a late one as we were dancing together on the side of the stage at 1am that morning. Clearly, he was determined not to waste a minute of the trip.

When Ezra Collective won the Mercury Prize for their album *Where I'm Meant to Be* in September 2023, it was long-overdue recognition that the UK jazz scene is bubbling and fizzing with talent. Off the back of the award, and soon after returning from Lagos, they were set to play a massive show at the Royal Albert Hall, making them the first jazz artists in the venue's history to go from playing its 150-capacity Elgar Room to selling out the main auditorium.

But if anyone thought that the Mercury Award was to be the highpoint for the band, they haven't been listening to Femi. 'What a special moment for me and all my friends. It was beautiful, but it's not the top of the mountain, so we just keep going.' Despite his lack of sleep, his infectious excitement still oozed out of him. 'This right now,' he said, pointing around a near-empty Shrine as the detritus of last night was still being cleared up around him, 'sat here is another version of something even greater than the Mercury Prize. I never sat down with a pen and paper and thought *I need to write something to win a Mercury Prize*, but I've definitely sat down and thought, *I need to get me and my brothers to the Shrine*. So, this is almost even more of a prize.' The band's tenor saxophonist James Mollison agreed, citing the band's first-ever show in Africa. 'It's a massive privilege and honour. It's kind of weird. I've been checking out Fela for so long that his music is in my heart. So, to actually be in Lagos to play is surreal.'

Despite the band's recent success, the show didn't come about like a normal booking. Femi wanted it so badly he made it happen himself. 'I came here in December last year and I spent ages in this building, asking how I could get my boys here. I don't care about money. I don't care about flights. Just tell me how to get on that stage. And I got it.'

As he spoke, he became visibly emotional. 'I wouldn't be surprised if I cry when I'm up there tonight because it's such a special, special feeling. This is actually who I am in a venue – in music form. It means so, so much. I can't eloquently put it into words.' To understand his emotion, you have to go back to when he first picked up drumsticks. 'I had two Nigerian parents, and they bought me a toy drum kit when I was about three or four years old. It was my favourite thing ever. But, also, my dad used to play Fela Kuti albums in the car. The drum kit was my favourite toy and Fela was why I fell in love with music. And the combination of the two ended up being why music is everything to me.'

You can hear that love of Fela's music in the very earliest Ezra Collective records. The band formed in 2012 at the Tomorrows Warriors organisation run by celebrated British jazz musician Gary Crosby. If you caught those very early shows, you'd have heard them play 'Zombie' or 'Colonial Mentality' by Fela, alongside tracks like 'Eye of the Hurricane' by Herbie Hancock and 'Strasbourg/St Denis' by Roy Hargrove. Femi went on to be taught by Fela's drummer Tony Allen. '"Zombie" is not "Zombie" without Uncle Tony,' he said with a fond smile. 'He taught me the way of leaning back, of letting beauty speak and letting the little you do be done with power.'

But the band's sound hasn't stood still. While always built upon those hours of practising the jazz standards and Fela Kuti records, they've now infused it with hip hop, salsa, dub and reggae to make a modern, powerful and uniquely British sound. 'I think London has such a melting pot of cultures and the jazz musicians are able to react to that eloquently. That's why it's amazing.'

James agrees, explaining how the band has absorbed the city's soundscape. 'We reflect our environment. If our environment has all these different sounds in it, then we're going to include all those sounds.' If Ezra Collective music reflects the musical diversity of London, it also shines a light on the troubles faced by the city. Politics was at the very heart of Fela Kuti's music. Indivisible from the sound was the message; the struggle against colonialism, police brutality, poverty and oppression.

For Femi Koleoso, Ezra Collective can make similar change, but in a different way. 'You will never hear me say "Vote for this", "I don't like that", "Campaign for this". That's not the language I'll use.' For him, the solution is for everyone to do whatever they can to help the people around them.

'I live in north London and I look poverty in the eye every single day. I'm working at a youth club attached to a food bank and I've got kids coming up to me talking about their schools crumbling before their eyes, literally and metaphorically. Youth violence is heartbreaking. I just don't feel the solutions are found in screaming "Vote for this" or "Campaign for that". I believe the solutions are in looking at what I can do to fix this. I will make my 1 per cent. What can you do?'

Femi also believes that the music he creates can have a positive impact on its own. 'A good bassline and a drumbeat puts everyone on the same page. And when you've got everyone on the same page, you can achieve change.' He looks around the Shrine. 'If you had the entire world stood in front of you and you pressed play on Fela Kuti's "Zombie", the whole world would start agreeing about things they didn't think they could.'

What time Ezra Collective would take to the stage was unclear; the festival had a flexible attitude to running orders and timings. 'I've been told both 8pm and 1am,' said Joe Armon-Jones, the band's wizard keyboard player while wrestling with the world's toughest pre-show chicken. Lateness would prove to do them a favour; the place was full as they arrived at the side of the stage just after 9.30pm.

A seated and sceptical crowd looked on, unsure what to expect from a British band at the Shrine. They needn't have worried. From the moment Femi thumped the opening beat of 'Welcome to My World' and the locked-in horns of trumpeter Ife Ogunjobi and tenor saxophonist James Mollison boomed across the venue, the audience knew they were in safe hands. By the time the cripplingly funky bassline of TJ Koleoso and the squelching keyboards of Armon-Jones joined in, plastic chairs were being abandoned as people rushed forward to the stage. The highlight came when Femi Kuti walked on unannounced during 'No Confusion' to roars of delight from both the audience and band. Bravely, they finished with a cover of Fela's 'Water No Get Enemy' that left the crowd in no doubt that Ezra Collective deserved their spot on that revered stage. They had delighted an audience of Afrobeat connoisseurs, with any scepticism long dissipated, along with the haze of hash smoke in the air. It was proof, as if any more were needed, that they are one of the most entertaining, powerful and exciting bands in the world right now.

'It's a beautiful thing that the kid who used to pick up a guitar because they wanted to be like Blur is now picking up a trumpet because they want to be like Ezra,' Femi smiled.

The band's conquering performance at the Shrine that night proved exactly why.

Mere moments after their set was over, I began to feel horrendously unwell. I hurried back to the hotel where I became uncontrollably sick, passing out on my bathroom floor. It may have been the ill-judged street food I'd eaten the night before or perhaps a waterborne bug, but the next week was a blur, punctuated by a tortuous flight back to the UK. The doctors feared it might be cholera, but I began to improve before there was any real concern. I emerged a few weeks later significantly thinner and able to look back on a magical, if difficult, trip. To stand in the Shrine had been an amazing experience. To visit the place where Afrobeat was born and hear it played by Fela Kuti's children and grandchildren was a remarkable thing. Seeing Lagos, it became clear why Fela still occupies such an important place in Nigerian culture.

The issues he sang about – the corruption and poverty – still blight the country. The anger he felt then is shared by many Nigerians today, which means the message in his music remains sadly relevant. The resistance he showed then still inspires people to resist now. One evening in Lagos, I had visited Freedom Park to watch a band play Fela Kuti covers. Before they came on, a compere referenced the Fela song 'Question Jam Answer'. 'What are the questions?' he asked. 'How, after decades, do we still not have working electricity? How do we still not have working roads? These are the questions!'

As with all musicians, the impact of Fela Kuti and his music is hard to measure. However, more than any of the other musicians or songs I explore in this book, his music was a means for education and his life was a source of inspiration. So many people I spoke with in Lagos explained how it was through his songs that they became politically conscious, how his lyrics had opened their minds and taught them about the crimes of colonialism and corruption that blighted their country. Through his music, Fela concentrated his anger on the military regime and the corrupt politicians that were bleeding Nigeria, which in turn radicalised people into resistance. Yet beyond his music, what inspired such lasting admiration was the way that Fela forged his radical and rebellious lyrics with his own life. He didn't just sing about resistance. He engaged in it too, often at huge personal cost.

FIVE

White Riot:
Rock Against Racism and
Two-Tone in Britain

Recommended Listening:
Billy Bragg – 'Waiting for the Great Leap Forwards'
X-Ray Spex – 'Oh Bondage, Up Yours'
Steel Pulse – 'Handsworth Revolution'
The Clash – 'White Riot'
Tom Robinson Band – 'Glad to be Gay'
Misty in Roots – 'Mankind'
Aswad – 'I A Rebel Soul'
The Beat – 'Stand Down Margaret'
The Selecter – 'On My Radio'
The Specials – 'Ghost Town'

–

THE O2 ACADEMY IN OXFORD is a pretty nondescript music venue: sticky floors, black walls and commercial lager. Located in an Edwardian building on Cowley Road, it was once home to the Oxford Co-operative Society. In the 1990s, Britpop conquered the British music charts and this Oxford venue, then called the Zodiac, played host to the city's contribution to the scene. Local bands such as Supergrass and Ride graced the stage and its highpoint came in 1992 when Radiohead filmed the video for their hit 'Creep' here.

It was a dank, rainy evening and I was in town in the spring of 2023 for a Billy Bragg charity gig in aid of the anti-fascist organisation HOPE not hate (HNH). Bragg, often dubbed the the 'Bard of Barking', is probably the first person British people think of when political music is mentioned. Since emerging as a singer-songwriter in the early '80s, Bragg's Essex drawl and spiky guitar has become instantly recognisable. The Irish novelist Ronán Hession once described his guitar sound as 'like someone dropping cutlery on tiles' and it's the perfect description.[1]

Bragg's first album, 1983's *Life's a Riot with Spy vs Spy*, still sounds urgent and angry, but also touching and soft. It's that combination that marks Bragg out. He may be best known as a political songwriter, with songs such as 'Between the Wars', 'There is Power in a Union' or 'Waiting for the Great Leap Forwards', but I've actually always preferred his love songs, whether it's the teenage longing of 'The Saturday Boy', the heartbreaking ode to his father 'Tank Park Salute' and, of course, his most famous creation, 'A New England'.

> I don't want to change the world
> I'm not looking for a new England
> I'm just looking for another girl.

I first met Billy Bragg when I was campaigning with HNH against the British National Party in 2010. We were in Dagenham, Bragg's home town and the BNP's national strong-hold. He came out to campaign with us, proving that, unlike many others, he didn't merely talk about politics, he got stuck in. Since then, I've been lucky enough to see him play live countless times. Doing so is a tonic, an injection of energy. Every time, I leave the venue feeling like I could walk through walls. Or, at the very least, like I can face going into work again on Monday.

We sat backstage in a grubby dressing room in Oxford, Bragg looking healthier than anyone who's been on the road that long deserves to, and me nervously fidgeting. I opened with a question I've asked musicians all over the world: Can music really change the world?

'My personal experience is that actually music has no agency.' It wasn't the answer I had been expecting. If anyone was going to outright claim that music can change the world, I presumed it would be Bragg, someone who has been singing political songs for forty years. I pushed him again. 'The role that music has to play is not to change the world, but to make you believe that the world can be changed,' he explained. 'The way that change happens is twofold. The first bit is that you realise that everything is fucked up. And the second bit is you realise that everyone else realises that everything is fucked up and music has a role to play in that process.' For Bragg, 'music is the thing that brings you together to see people express their anger about how fucked up everything is.' I understood what he meant. I'd been thinking about it too literally.

While Bragg's extensive back catalogue is worth every moment it takes to listen to it, it's at the live shows where his music really comes alive. There's something in the communal experience of his gigs that is elevating, euphoric even. 'There is a solidarity in song. It's not about politics, it's not about political songs. Solidarity isn't just about politics. There is emotional solidarity to be had there to. It's why they sing at the football. It's why they sing at church. It allows them to manifest something they believe in. To celebrate something. Or even when they're losing, they sing at football to express their sadness together. That power is in music. It is there to be picked on.'

It's for this reason Bragg plays so many benefit gigs, he sees it as part of his role, a key element of a tradition of which he is part. 'Woody Guthrie never did gigs like I do gigs. He never did a tour. Never sold T-shirts and all that shit. Basically, he did shows where they were raising money or focusing solidarity. So, if I'm going to be true to that spirit, I need to do these sorts of gigs where people are gathering together to try to change the world.'

With showtime fast approaching and time running out, I asked where it all began for Bragg, what lit the flame that has kept burning for decades. There's a simple answer. 'I went along to a Rock Against Racism march in 1978 and it affected me to the extent that I don't think I would be sitting here talking to you now as Billy Bragg without it.' The event saw a vast crowd gather in Victoria Park in East London to oppose the National Front, then on the rise in Britain. 'What it did was, it gave me the courage of my convictions. I realised that it was the Clash that transformed my perception. It was seeing 80,000 kids just like me, acknowledging that something was wrong. And I realised at that event that this issue, not just racism but discrimination of all kinds – homophobia, sexism, disablism, whatever – was going to be our Vietnam, the issue that was going to define my generation.'

It's remarkable how many similar stories there are of people being inspired by Rock Against Racism (RAR). As an anti-fascist, it has always been central to my understanding of the role that music can play in fighting discrimination. For a period in the 1970s, RAR fused pop and politics into a single and powerful force that changed the national debate. I knew that any book exploring the role of music as a form of resistance would be incomplete without it. Bragg checked his watch, jumped up from his seat, shook my hand and, barely a moment later, he was onstage, doing what Billy Bragg does best.

—

Contrary to popular belief, it was not the *Empire Windrush*, but rather the *Ormonde* that began the process of immigration that would shape modern Britain in the second half of the 20th century.[2] The *Ormonde*'s arrival in Liverpool in late 1947, with 108 migrant workers from the Caribbean onboard, was a watershed moment that fundamentally changed Britain and Britishness. This island's music, food, language, culture and identity were forever altered.

Despite its lasting impact, the arrival of immigrants in the post-war period was far from a historical aberration or irregular phenomenon. The historian Panikos Panayi has identified that Britain's history of immigration dates back to the age of invasions before the eleventh century; to the wave of continental tradesmen, craftsmen and Jews during the high and late Middle Ages; and to religious refugees, economic newcomers and slaves between 1500 and 1650, followed by a significant rise in the variety of groups that arrived from the mid-seventeenth century onwards.[3]

Between 1815 and 1945, the rate of migration increased greatly, with as many as a million Irish immigrants arriving in the UK between 1800 and 1900, along with tens of thousands of Germans, Russians and Jewish Poles. World War I saw 240,000 Belgian refugees arrive on these shores, while a further 200,000 other Europeans came to Britain during World War II. On top of all of this, Panayi estimates an additional 300,000 people moved to

Britain between 1815 and 1945 from a range of places including France, Spain, Greece, India and across Africa, bringing the total to between 1.5 and 2 million immigrants.[4]

On paper then, the arrival of the ships *Ormonde* in Liverpool and the *Windrush* at Tilbury dock should have been little more than the latest chapter in a history of immigration. However, their arrival has rightly been described by the historian Peter Hennessy as 'a turning-point in British history'[5] – or, in the words of Mike and Trevor Phillips, 'the Windrush sailed through a gateway in history, on the other side of which was the end of Empire and a wholesale reassessment of what it meant to be British'.[6]

The 1948 Nationality Act gave all imperial subjects the right of free entry into post-war Britain. However, due to the financial hurdle of paying for passage via boat, the immigration from the West Indies that started in 1947 remained modest for the first few years. This changed by the mid-1950s, with steadily increasing numbers making the voyage. In 1954, 24,000 people arrived, followed by 26,000 the following year; by 1958, some 115,000 people had left Kingston and Port of Spain and arrived in Britain to make a new life.[7] West Indians were not alone in making the journey to the imperial capital. Many thousands came from India and Pakistan, often as a result of the problems caused by partition. Sikhs, Hindus, Muslims and as many as 30,000 Anglo-Indians also made the journey to join their fellow colonial subjects,[8] bringing the total to nearly a quarter of a million Empire and Commonwealth migrants in the decade following the *Windrush*'s arrival.[9]

My own family, like so many others, plays an infinitesimally tiny role in this story of national change. My father's family emigrated from Ireland to England in the years following the Great Famine. My mother's family, however, is an altogether more recent story of arrival. In a move that still staggers me in its bravery, my maternal grandmother moved to the UK from Germany in either 1947 or 1948. What possessed an eighteen-year-old woman to leave her rural home near the small town of Dinklage in Lower Saxony and travel to England – just years after the end of World War II – to build a new life is hard to fathom. With swathes of London still largely rubble from Luftwaffe bombs, she took a job as a domestic worker. One can only imagine the welcome that a German would have received in Britain at that time, when countless families had only just buried their sons. It was perhaps with this in mind that her father refused to sign the forms required for her transit, forcing her to get her brother-in-law to forge the papers.

My maternal grandfather arrived in Britain later, disembarking at Tilbury Dock on the ship *Strathmore* on 20 May 1951, joining the many thousands of his fellow Indians who made the journey. My grandparents met each other at a tea dance in Hayes in west London and were married in 1954. The Catholic Church refused to conduct the ceremony, just one of the many indignities suffered by mixed-race couples at that time. A German woman just after the war, marrying an Indian man: it is hard to imagine a situation more perfectly designed to face discrimination in post-war Britain. Yet they prevailed and forged their lives together, making a very modern British love story.

My family is just one of countless similar stories of people making their way to Britain, falling in love and building new lives. Sadly, the response that many new arrivals faced goes some way to challenging the widespread myth of British toler-ance. Far more pervasive than overtly physical manifestations of racism was the more day-to-day prejudice and discrimination faced by new immigrants, with many struggling to find employ-ment, accommodation and social acceptance. The first necessity for many new immigrants was employment, but many industries and professions were essentially out of bounds to the new immigrants because of their colour. Writing in *Checkers Magazine* in 1946, R. Donaldson explained the experience of the average West Indian man in the UK at the time:

> Day after day he tries to get work. Day after day he hears the radio crying out for workers. He can't understand it, he begins to think: they want workers in the mills and in the mines, they want workers here and there, I see Poles and even Germans getting jobs, what's wrong with me? Ah! the light shines. My Colour.[10]

A study by Ruth Glass between 1958 and 1959 found that 55 per cent of West Indians underwent a job downgrade due to migration; those with professional and clerical experience had just a one-in-four chance of finding a similar job in Britain.[11] Most found work in unskilled or semi-skilled jobs despite their background as skilled workers or professionals. Employers often claimed to be rejecting Black applicants on the grounds of a lack of qualifications or a grasp of the language. However, research in the 1960s showed these excuses were inaccurate and that 'blatant racial discrimination in employment was taking place on a massive scale'.[12]

The other necessity was finding a place to live. When asked about the struggle to find accommodation in the early post-war period, Cecil Holness, a West Indian immigrant, painted the picture:

> It's either two or three of you in a room. In those days, as a Black man, it's very hard to get a room, you wouldn't get one. They always put on the board, 'Black-Niggers not wanted here', on the board you know, these boards

out there, 'No Niggers' or 'No Colour', things like that. So it's very hard to get a room.[13]

The difficulties faced by Holmes were by no means extraordinary but rather 'typical and characteristic'[14] of the problems new arrivals found when looking for accommodation. This is backed up by a private poll conducted in 1956 by John Darragh, a British journalist, which found only fifteen out of a thousand white people in Birmingham were willing to rent accommodation to 'coloured' people.[15] Glass carried out a similar study of adverts for rental accommodation in the *Kensington Post* in 1959 and found one in six adverts were 'anti-coloured'.

Perhaps the most poetic and articulate description of the hostile environment faced by many new arrivals comes via a fictional account of West Indian immigrants in 1950s London. Sam Selvon, a Trinidadian author and an immigrant to Britain himself, penned his classic novel *The Lonely Londoners* in 1956. It details the lives of West Indian immigrants in '50s London as they experience the failed promise of the 'mother country', the hostility of the locals and the struggles to build new lives, all supplemented by the heady excitement of being in a city they had read and dreamed about. While Moses, the main protagonist, mentions a modicum of tolerance – 'It have a kind of communal feeling with the working class and the spades, because when you poor, things does level out'[16] – the overwhelming reaction is portrayed as hostile and deeply racist.

The following passage from the novel, a discussion between Moses and Galahad, a new arrival, exposes the hypocrisy that lies just beneath the myth of English tolerance.

'Things as bad over here as in America?' Galahad ask.
'That is the point the boys always debating,' Moses say.
'Some say yes, some say no. The thing is in America they

don't like you, and they tell you so straight, so that you know how you stand. Over here is the old English diplomacy: 'thank you sir,' and 'how do you do' and that sort of thing. In America you see a sign telling you to keep off, but over here you don't see any, but when you go in a hotel or restaurant they will politely tell you to haul – or else give you the cold treatment.'[17]

The hostility – governmental, popular and far right – towards the arrival of immigrants of colour was overwhelmingly manifest in the form of prejudice and discrimination. However, in 1958, as a balmy summer drew to a close, intolerance turned into terror as some of the worst racial violence Britain has ever seen exploded on the streets of Nottingham and then Notting Hill in west London. This was not the first example of racial violence experienced by immigrants to Britain. There had been anti-Black rioting in Liverpool in 1948 and further riots in Deptford in south London in July 1949. The homes of Indian workers near Birmingham were also attacked that year.[18] Interracial violence broke out again in London in August 1954, with disturbances in Camden Town when a white mob attacked Black people with bottles, axes and a petrol bomb that burned out the home of a Black resident.[19] However, these racially motivated attacks were all overshadowed by the major riots of 1958.

What became one of the largest examples of racial violence in British history had humble origins. On the evening of 23 August, a shout of, 'Lay off that woman'[20] from a white man to a Jamaican immigrant in the Chase Tavern, a pub in the St Ann's area of Nottingham, led to eight people being hospitalised, two with stab wounds to the back. A scuffle between the two men engulfed the pub as others joined in, soon spilling out of the tavern and onto the streets. What began as a pub brawl evolved into a full-on race riot as a crowd of white people, that quickly swelled to 1,000-strong, set upon West Indians.

Simultaneously, a little more than a hundred miles to the south, a group of nine white men in Notting Hill – crammed into a car and armed with table legs, chains and pointed iron railings – were out 'nigger hunting'. The result of their racially motivated bloody rampage around west London that night was five seriously injured West Indians. Back in Nottingham, the following weekend saw a crowd of 4,000 white men and women disappointed by a prepared police force and a West Indian community that had largely gone to ground. With very few West Indians around to target, the crowd turned on itself and internecine fighting broke out.[21]

In London, however, despite a week of newspaper coverage predicting where racial tensions might next break out into displays of violence, the police of Notting Hill failed to put extra officers on the beat. As with the Nottingham riots a week previously, it is generally understood that what became known as the Notting Hill race riots were triggered by a single quarrel. The match that lit the tinderbox was struck on 29 August following an argument outside Latimer Road tube station between a 'mixed race' couple from Jamaica and Sweden. When the white woman sided with her Black partner, rather than the white crowd that had gathered, things turned violent.[22] Events escalated quickly and, by the following evening, mobs armed with improvised weapons were rampaging around the streets, leaving a path of destruction in their wake. What followed was a week or so of rioting and violence that shocked Britain.[23]

One of the more positive reactions to the horrifying events came in the music newspaper *Melody Maker*, which ran a front page declaring, 'At a time when reason has given way to violence in parts of Britain, we, the people of all races in the world of entertainment, appeal to the public to reject racial discrimination in any shape or form.'[24] That musicians and music fans were at the forefront of rejecting racism in Britain wasn't particularly new. Britain's Musicians Union, for example, had a proud history of anti-racism. As early as 1947, it passed a resolution at its annual conference making it clear that it would oppose the colour bar which refused people of colour service or made them drink in separate rooms, as well as launching an early boycott of South Africa following the creation of apartheid and working hard to oppose racism in music, dance halls and venues.[25]

In addition to *Melody Maker*'s principled stance after the riots was the creation of the Stars Campaign for Interracial Friendship, a collective that included a wide range of performers from Ronnie Scott to Laurence Olivier. The group opened the Harmony Bar in Notting Hill's Blenheim Crescent in January 1959, designed to challenge racial discrimination in arts venues.[26] Although the group didn't last long, the concept of using musicians and artists as a way to break down barriers between communities and to openly challenge racism had been set. The groundwork was laid for what would become Rock Against Racism in the 1970s.

—

On 20 April 1968, Enoch Powell, the Member of Parliament for Wolverhampton South West, took to the stage to deliver a speech that reverberated well beyond the walls of the Conservative Political Centre in Birmingham. His clipped moustache twitched as he delivered his poison:

Those whom the gods wish to destroy, they first make mad. We must be mad, literally mad, as a nation to be permitting the annual inflow of some 50,000 dependants, who are for the most part the material of the future growth of the immigrant-descended population. It is like watching a nation busily engaged in heaping up its own funeral pyre.[27]

His piercing gaze drilled into the audience as he concluded: 'As I look ahead, I am filled with foreboding; like the Roman, I seem to see "the river Tiber foaming with much blood".' Within a day of what became known as Powell's 'Rivers of Blood' speech, he was sacked from the Shadow Cabinet by the then Leader of the Opposition Edward Heath. Despite this principled stand, condemnation was far from universal. Powell reportedly received 110,000 letters, of which only 2,300 disagreed with him. This was echoed in a Gallup poll conducted at the end of April that year which found 74 per cent of respondents also agreed with his sentiments.[28] Famously, 2,000 London dock workers downed tools in protest at his firing, while the meat porters of London's Smithfield market submitted a lengthy petition in his support. Popular unease at the changing face of Britain was clashing with lofty post-war ideals of anti-racism.

In such a climate, it's no surprise that Britain's fringe fascist scene was working hard to exploit societal disquiet. Having formed in 1967, the National Front (NF) grew into Britain's leading fascist party in the 1970s. Under the leadership of John Tyndall and Martin Webster, the NF leapt upon growing concern about South Asian migration into Britain. When, in 1972, Prime Minister Edward Heath took the decision to grant asylum to many of the Ugandan Asians forced into exile by Idi Amin, the NF launched a ruthless but astute political campaign. Webster, deputy leader of the NF, instantly saw the possibilities for recruitment offered by the imminent arrival of thousands of immigrants of colour. The party seized upon the rapidly growing fear with remarkable speed, holding a demonstration outside Downing Street within twenty-four hours of the alarming news from Uganda beginning to percolate through Britain. They also held pickets outside Heathrow and Manchester Airport to ensure that the arriving Ugandans were made to feel as unwelcome as possible.

The result of the NF's swift opportunism was a rapid swelling of their rank-and-file membership and an understanding of the political capital that could be gained through anti-immigrant campaigns. The anti-fascist magazine *Searchlight* suggested that the NF's membership grew from just 4,000 in 1968 to a peak of 17,500 in 1972, dropping back down to 15,000 by the end of the decade.[29] While Enoch Powell continued his more eloquent but no less harmful anti-immigrant campaign, the National Front sought to advance their racist politics not only through the ballot box, but also with terrifying violence on the streets of Britain.

Sadly, the music world wasn't immune from the fascist creep of the 1970s. As the decade opened, Rod Stewart declared: 'I think Enoch Powell is the man. I'm all for him. This country is overcrowded. The immigrants should be sent home.'[30] As was the case with so many things, David Bowie took things even further. In May 1976, he became embroiled in controversy when images emerged of him greeting fans at Victoria Station in London with what looks like a fascist salute, although he later denied that it was. However, that September, he gave a shocking interview to *Playboy* in which he declared:

I'd love to enter politics. I will one day. I'd adore to be prime minister. And, yes, I believe very strongly in fascism. The only way we can speed up the sort of liberalism that's hanging foul in the air at the moment is to speed up the progress of a right-wing, totally dictatorial tyranny and get it over as fast as possible ... Rock stars are fascists, too. Adolf Hitler was one of the first rock stars.[31]

This was all during his Thin White Duke phase, when he blurred the lines between himself and a supposed character, while others have excused the behaviour by referencing his gargantuan drug intake at the time. That said, I've never come across any drug where a side effect is National Socialism. Whatever the cause, character or not, a global pop star was publicly toying with fascism.

However, the event that finally gave birth to Rock Against Racism came on 5 August 1976, when a drunk Eric Clapton took to the stage at the Birmingham Odeon. Each sentence is more shocking and revealing than the last:

I think Enoch's right, I think we should send them all back. Stop Britain from becoming a Black colony. Get the foreigners out. Get the w*gs out. Get the c**ns out. Keep Britain white.[32]

Each line drips with racist hatred. It was no mistake. Remarkably, the following week's *NME* barely referenced Clapton's rant. A few lines tucked away at the bottom of page forty-three read: 'Eric Clapton (no, we just don't believe it) enters the political arena – in support of Enoch Powell. Leastways, Eric is reported to have voiced support for the Wolverhampton Wildman onstage in Birmingham last week. He's a card, that Eric.'[33] He's a card, that Eric? What a revealing response. Where was the shock? The horror? The anger? A *card*?

A month later, Clapton sent a half-hearted handwritten apology to the music magazine *Sounds*: 'I openly apologise to all the foreigners in Brum ... It's just that (as usual) I'd had a few before I went out, and a foreigner had pinched my missus' bum. I proceeded to lost my bottle, well, you know the rest, anyway,

I'm off up the pub, and I don't live in America, and I think that Enoch is the only politician mad enough to run this country.'[34] It was hardly a full and frank apology. Thankfully, not everyone responded so nonchalantly. So, in 1976, a small group of artists, actors and hippies wrote a letter to a range of music and left-wing newspapers, calling out Clapton's horrifying comments:

> When I read about Eric Clapton's Birmingham concert when he urged support for Enoch Powell, I nearly puked. What's going on, Eric? You've got a touch of brain damage. So you're going to stand for MP and you think we're being colonised by Black people. Come on . . . you've been taking too much of that *Daily Express* stuff, you know you can't handle it. Own up. Half your music is Black. You're rock music's biggest colonist. You're a good musician but where would you be without the blues and R&B? You've got to fight the racist poison, otherwise you degenerate into the sewer with the rats and all the money men who ripped off rock culture with their chequebooks and plastic crap. Rock was and still can be a real progressive culture, not a package mail-order stick-on nightmare of mediocre garbage. Keep the faith, Black and white unite and fight. We want to organise a rank-and-file movement against the racist poison in rock music – we urge support – all those interested, please write to:

> ROCK AGAINST RACISM,
> Box M, 8 Cotton Gardens, London E2 8DN

> P. S. 'Who shot the Sheriff', Eric? It sure as hell wasn't you!

And with that, Rock Against Racism was born.

–

Finding Red Saunders, founder of Rock Against Racism, was easier than I had feared. He's still a working photographer, so has a website with an email address. I dropped him a begging message and he very promptly agreed to have a chat over Zoom with me. Despite his age, he exploded onto the screen – still a ball of infectious energy and righteous anger. He's retired to the countryside after a life lived in east London and it seems to be suiting him, the crisp light a delight for an artist.

I mentioned that I'd recently returned from Nigeria where I was researching the chapter on Fela Kuti. 'I was a colonialist's son,' he interjected. 'I was brought up in Nigeria in the 1950s. My dad was a colonialist.' He's a genuine storyteller, full of enthusiasm and charm and he drops into a yarn with only the briefest of prompts. It's a joy to listen to.

'My last visit to Nigeria was in the late '60s. It was a really weird scenario. But there was this guy who was an incredible music hustler. He had hustled his way into the middle of the Nigerian Civil War and tried to organise a concert, you know, a kind of UNICEF thing. And he knew the Beatles and he said he was going to bring the Beatles to Nigeria. It was a fantasy that never ever happened, but as part of the build-up to it all, I was there. The whole thing was a complete and utter shambles, from the day we arrived. I have a piece of paper somewhere from the military governor saying, "This is Mr David Saunders and he is bringing the Beatles group to Nigeria."'

Our conversation lasted a few hours and was full of fascinating asides like this. 'I learned in the past how easy it is to answer questions and forget to get to the root of the question. I've tried to make myself slow down. Because as my wife always says to me, "Oh God, Red, you're off and running . . ."'

Before RAR started, Red was in an agitprop theatre group putting on performances in prisons, occupied factories and the back rooms of pubs. Gathered around him was a group of left-wing artistic types: musicians, artists, actors and performers, all bustling around his studio in the heart of London's Soho. The group were already politically active, having been involved in campaigns for majority rule in then Rhodesia and anti-apartheid activism. One day, someone burst in waving a copy of *Melody Maker* newspaper with an article about Eric Clapton's racist rant. 'I'd never written a letter to anybody public in my life. But that evening after rehearsals I went, "This is just fucking outrageous."'

'And so I wrote a letter. We were outraged because we were anti-racist. We were a tiny, tiny group. We weren't representative of anybody. We were just a bunch of lefty hippies.' Three weeks after the letter was published, Red received a phone call saying his PO box address had received 500 responses. 'So it started with a letter. But it was born with the response. And then we started. We had to do something now.'

Remarkably, the average age of those who responded to Red's letter was between thirteen and seventeen years old. Looking back, it all sounds a little amateur and ad hoc. People wrote in, Red responded, making them head of RAR in their area, and told them to start organising concerts. It was that simple. It emerged organically and only later became a proper nationwide organisation with offices and staff.

The first proper RAR gig involved Carol Grimes performing at the Princess Alice pub in London's Forest Gate in November 1976. In Daniel Rachel's wonderful oral history of the period, *Walls Come Tumbling Down*, Roger Huddle of RAR's hastily assembled central committee remembered the evening: 'It was quite funny because one of Carol's band made an Irish joke and, when it was pointed out to her, she sacked him at the end of the gig.'[35] Saunders remembers the incident. 'We were doing the soundcheck and Carol's sax player comes on and goes, "One, two. Did you hear the one about the Englishman, the Irishman . . ." and does a soft, idiot joke. We were like, "What? Hold on, mate."[36]

Gigs across the country were hastily organised before Red launched the group's newspaper, *Temporary Hoarding*. It's a thing of beauty: all cut and paste, very Dada. The cover of the first issue had RAR's rousing manifesto: 'We want rebel music, street music. Music that breaks down people's fear of one another. Crisis music. No music. Music that knows who the real enemy is. Rock against racism. LOVE MUSIC, HATE RACISM.'[37]

The back page outlined the groups aims: 'RAR is a campaign. A political campaign. Its aims are: 1. To fight the influence of racism/fascism in popular culture, especially music. 2. To build an anti-racist/fascist movement WITHIN pop culture and use it to fight racism and fascism EVERYWHERE.'[38] The Winter 1977 edition had a summary of RAR's first year and gives a flavour of just how fast the operation grew. 'So we made it thru 1 year. What a year; from nowhere to 200 gigs; from pubs to the Roundhouse. Reggae soul rock and roll jazz funk and punk . . . especially reggae and punk this year that's something that RAR *can* claim credit for. NO punk and reggae ever jammed till we set up the environment and suggested it.'[39]

The anti-racism activist Rick Blackman explained that 'the rejection of prevailing attitudes and fashion, the anti-authoritarian stance and the DIY ethos of punk would dovetail perfectly with RAR's militant anti-racism and much of the imagery from punk and RAR overlapped and merged in the heat of the two temperature-breaking summers of 1976 and 1977'.[40] Blackman described the smaller gigs as 'an effervescent and omnipresent backdrop to the musical and political landscape in late 1970s

Britain'.[41] By 1978, there were fifty-two RAR clubs putting on shows in towns around the country.

However, those involved in RAR knew that music alone wasn't enough. One issue of *Temporary Hoarding* explained that 'racism is political. Fighting is extra political 'cause you can't stop NF thugs intimidating and petrol bombing people just by holding a dance. What we need if we are going to win is organisation. RAR is a small but vital part of the overall fight against fascism in this country.'[42]

When we spoke, Red explained how it was RAR's collaboration with the Anti-Nazi League and the wider labour movement that really ensured its success. 'You know, when that alliance came together, we could book coaches to go to demonstrations. It meant we could put on a really exciting series of gigs running up to a massive carnival that would spread the news, spread the excitement, spread the culture. When it came to organising hundreds of thousands of people, the alliance between the labour movement and this group of fucking nutty underground lefty loonies was what made it possible.' The scale of RAR made it part of one of the largest mass movements of the post-war period. The historian Dave Renton estimates that RAR and the Anti-Nazi League likely mobilised between half a million and 1 million people in just a few short years.[43]

Importantly, the ANL and the labour movement hugely expanded the reach of RAR. 'It brought in the whole of the United Kingdom,' said Red. 'Access to everywhere from Bangor to Norwich, to Aberystwyth to Carlisle to Plymouth. The whole fucking country, you know. And with trade union branches, suddenly you have access to teachers. Teachers in every county, every place in the entire United Kingdom.' He spoke fast and with energy, like he was still on the barricade.

With this vast reach, it became easier to attract big musical names. Remarkably, the first issue of *Temporary Hoarding* had interviews with both the Clash and Johnny Rotten of the Sex Pistols. Today they don't come across as particularly radical reads, but for their time, in the climate of widespread support for people like Enoch Powell and the rising National Front, it was so important for them to make a stand. 'All we think about the Blacks is we ain't gonna start blaming them for things they shouldn't blamed with,' said Joe Strummer of the Clash. 'I wouldn't wanna get rid of the Blacks because if they'd never have come to this country, we'd never have heard [Junior Murvin's] "Police and Thieves" and [Tappa Zukie's] "M.P.L.A." and [Big Youth's] "Ten Against One" . . . and all that gear.

'A lotta the new groups are raving on about Nazi parties. I mean, I think they're just a bunch of thickos. If they're gonna go on about that gear, they oughta fuckin think about it before they go on about it.'[44] His bandmate Mick Jones added: 'Well, basically we're dealing with oppression, which is like what we have in common.'[45] Meanwhile, when Rotten was asked about the National Front, he spat, 'I despise them. No one should have the right to tell anyone they can't live here because of the colour of their skin or their religion or whatever, the size of their nose. How could anyone vote for something so ridiculously inhumane.'[46]

In a later issue, Poly Styrene, lead singer of the mixed-race punk band X-Ray Spex, summed up the role of RAR in opposing the NF. 'I think the National Front are at their strongest when they've got youth following them. If they haven't got the youth, if you make the National Front unfashionable, then a lot of kids won't follow them. If they haven't got all the kids following them, they won't work.'[47] That was the whole point. RAR created a movement that made young people understand that racism and the National Front weren't cool.

The high point of RAR came in 1978 with a series of carnivals attracting vast numbers of music lovers and anti-racists. On 30 April, they organised a march from Trafalgar Square in central London, through the East End and into Victoria Park in Tower Hamlets. There were giant papier-mâché models of National Front leader John Tyndall and Adolf Hitler, which were built by Peter Fluck and Roger Law, who later made the hit ITV satirical puppet show *Spitting Image*. The march featured flatbed lorries, carrying bands such as the Southall-based reggae outfit Misty In Roots. By the time the music began in the park, 100,000 people had gathered to watch performances from the Clash, Steel Pulse and X-Ray Spex.

Also on the bill that day was the Tom Robinson Band, who had been central to RAR from the beginning. According to Red, Robinson was one of the people who replied to his letter to the music press. 'The first time I went to meet Tom, he was running a gay switchboard for teenage gay boys who were suicidal. And we did a gig with him raising money for that.' From there, Robinson stayed involved, even sporting the RAR logo on his guitar during a performance on *Top of the Pops*.

Best known for their hit '2-4-6-8 Motorway', Tom Robinson was a big star, but unusually for the time, he was also openly gay. Talking about his song '(Sing if You're) Glad to be Gay', during an interview with *Temporary Hoarding*, he said: 'I was talking to a straight man today, and he saw instantly the connection between being Black and being gay. I just said, "You get Black people saying, 'Hey you know we got nothing to do with no queens, we're respectable folks', and you go down to any gay club and all the queens will say 'No, we don't like niggers. Oh no'." I said this and the guy peeled with laughter 'cos where he's coming from, they're both just as bad – the queens and the niggers.'[48]

It's not the language we would use today, but the point about understanding that the enemy, in this case the National Front, hated all minority communities whether because of their sexuality or race was a fundamental part of RAR's ethos. When I spoke to Billy Bragg about the Victoria Park gig, he spoke at some length about the importance of Tom Robinson's performance:

When Tom Robinson sang '(Sing if You're) Glad to be Gay', loads of guys standing around me and my mates began kissing each other on the lips and cheering. Now I was nineteen, twenty. I'd never met an out gay man. And now these guys around me were kissing out the blue. We'd marched just in front of a big banner that read 'Gays Against Nazis', so when the march ended, we were just stood there. And my initial feeling was 'What are these gays doing? This is about racism, about Black people.' But it didn't take me long to grasp that the NF were against anyone who was in any way different, so they were part of this struggle. To know that those gay men were part of it, whatever the fuck *it* is, whatever the fuck they are and whatever the fuck I am, whether it's a punk rocker, or whatever the fuck, we're all in this together, me and them we're in it. The Clash were in it, all these kids were in it. This is a fight and we're in it.

In the autumn of 2023, I attended an anti-fascist demonstration outside a pub in south London against a group of far-right transphobes. Someone set up speakers and played '(Sing if You're) Glad to be Gay' and the crowd joined in: '*Sing if you're glad to be gay / Sing if you're happy that way . . .*'

There were only a few dozen people singing, but the song hasn't lost any of its bravery and power, and gave me a small flavour of what it must have been like to hear it at Victoria Park back in 1978.

Later, in the summer of 1981, RAR organised the Northern Carnival Against Racism in Leeds, this time staging the Au Pairs, Misty in Roots, Joolz the Poet and, importantly, a band called the Specials.

—

In the late '70s, in England's industrial Midlands, a musical revolution began – quiet at first, but soon to change the musical map of Britain. A group of mates from Coventry started the Specials. By 1979, the band's keyboardist and visionary, Jerry Dammers, had formed 2 Tone Records as a way to release their own music, in effect creating a whole new genre and movement that united Black and white musicians.

That same year, Margaret Thatcher won the general election and began her own revolution, one that stratified Britain into winners and losers. It was no great surprise that people had voted for radical change. The 1970s had been a depressing decade, plagued by shortages and strikes, and typified by the three-day week (when working hours were reduced to conserve coal stocks), the chronic water crisis resulting from drought in 1976, and the now-infamous 'winter of discontent' when the country was gripped by widespread strike action.

The Conservatives' new economic path was laid out by Sir Geoffrey Howe's 1979 budget and led to a schism of opinion within Britain, due to its profound effect on both the economy and society. Top priority was given to reducing inflation rather than maintaining employment, the result being a dramatic rise in joblessness. In 1978, unemployment stood at 1.25 million but, by October 1980, it had reached more than 2 million. By January 1982, a staggering 2.67 million were lining up in the dole queue.[49] By 1984, unemployment had reached 11.9%.

In her first term of office, Thatcher sought to free the Local Education Authorities from the duty of providing meals, transport and milk, to make less people eligible for supplementary benefits, to reduce local authority housing and generally to abdicate responsibility for the worsening situation by delegating to other organisations. While parts of the economy would later boom, whole industries were decimated and communities destroyed. For many millions of working-class people, it became a hopeless decade.

As these clouds gathered, the Specials released their first record in 1979, the Prince Buster-inspired *Gangster*. The record was championed by Radio 1's John Peel and interest in both the band and the label began to increase, with avid music fans being captivated by the energy and brilliance of their live performances. With the record's success, 2 Tone became a real record label and, in the coming months, Dammers signed bands such as Madness, the Selecter and the Beat. Critical and commercial success was swift in arriving and this collection of like-minded musicians became a nationwide phenomenon among the youth of Britain, soon transcending its origins and blossoming into its own genre. Pauline Black of the Selecter noted that 'Two-Tone became in a similar way to Motown, that it was described as a type of music, not just a record label . . . It was rapidly becoming clear that Two-Tone was becoming far more than just a record label.'[50]

This new sound was an energetic mixture of punk, ska and reggae which, while angry and loud, was backed by an undeniably danceable rhythm on the upbeat. They fused the music of the Caribbean with that of the British working-class to make an identifiably new sound that reflected the country's post-war multicultural identity. 'Musically, it meant our punky tunes could still be played fast,' explained Horace Panter of the Specials, 'but with a swing that made them eminently more danceable.'[51] The performance poet Phill Jupitus described it perfectly: 'Here was the skank and groove of reggae, but delivered in a kind of psychotic double-time.'[52]

Like all real musical movements, Two-Tone had more than just a sound. It had a style and a message. Much like the mods and skinheads before them, and influenced by both, Two-Tone artists wore close-fitting, Italian-style suits, slip-on shoes and high-collar, button-down shirts. Importantly, it was all black and white, a not-so-subtle nod to their politics. Much of the identity of the movement was eventually cemented by Walt Jabsco, the fictional character who adorned the early record sleeves and subsequently spread the multicultural, mod-influenced image to a generation of youths.

One fan from the time explained how central this was to the whole scene. 'I think the clothing and everything else was just as important as the music. From the minute I saw my first gig, that was it. I was in school within two or three days with a Harrington jacket, Fred Perry, sta press trousers and loafers.'[53] However, though the music and fashion were central, it was all underpinned by a powerful political message. The NME journalist Adrian Thrills agreed. 'It worked on three or four different levels,' he explained during a BBC radio documentary. '[There was] the initial excitement of going to see the bands live. There was the dress, the kind of rudeboy look that went with it and there was the lyrics and the underlying sentiment, promoting racial unity, giving a voice to a lot of disaffected teenagers.'[54]

If one was to simplify the broad political message of Two-Tone, it would be anti-Thatcher and pro-racial unity. Another Two-Tone band, the Beat, also brought together white and Black musicians to make this new British ska music. 'It wasn't fair as far I was concerned,' said the Beat's Ranking Roger. '[Thatcher] went on like she cared about the unemployed and didn't care about the unemployed. We just saw that go higher and higher . . . We saw thousands and thousands and thousands of people losing their homes.'[55] The Beat made clear their opposition on their song 'Stand Down Margaret', with the catchy refrain of 'I see no joy, I see only sorrow, I see no chance of your bright new tomorrow, so stand down Margaret.'

However, it was anti-racism that was the overriding message of the whole Two-Tone scene. With most of the band's line-ups being made up of both Black and white musicians, they were living proof of the success of multiculturalism. They mixed their fashion, culture and music to form something new, something genuinely British. 'One of the most important messages promoted by the Two-Tone acts was one of racial harmony,' said Pauline Black.[56] Speaking years later on a TV documentary, she observed that 'there was no blueprint for these things. People who are looking at the Selecter see a Black man and a Black woman up the front of a band, telling them how they think things are, starting that conversation. That's quite rare.'[57] Horace Panter shares a similar outlook. 'Racism was a big thing. I mean, the Specials were a multiracial band and we mixed Black and white music . . . It was a role model for how Black people and white people can work together musically and, consequently, why not off the stage as well.'[58] It was this politics that led to the Specials' involvement in RAR and later other forms of anti-racist activism.

The highpoint for the 2 Tone label came in 1981 with the Specials' single 'Ghost Town' reaching number one in the charts before going on to define the decade. The band sang of youths fighting among themselves, of the paucity of jobs, of the desperate social and economic situation. *'Can't go on more / The people getting angry . . .'*

Its angry and profound lyrics were set to a haunting carnival-esque but doom-laden reggae tune, one which conjured up images of derelict streets and boarded-up housing. Dammer's wrote the song after seeing the state of the country while on tour. 'In Liverpool, all the shops were shuttered up, everything was closing down. Margaret Thatcher had apparently gone mad. She was closing down all the industries, throwing millions of people on the dole. You could see that frustration and anger in the audience. It was clear that something was very, very wrong.'[59]

The day that 'Ghost Town' reached number one in the charts, Britain exploded, with riots engulfing whole areas of London, Handsworth in Birmingham, Leeds and Leicester among many others. Few records have captured a moment more powerfully or accurately. Britain was on fire and 'Ghost Town' was the soundtrack.

Just as Britain was pulling itself apart, so were the Specials, with the band splitting up backstage at *Top of the Pops*.[60] The Selecter would only last a year and the 2 Tone label continued until 1985, but it was all over by the middle of the decade. In 1984, Dammers released the protest song 'Nelson Mandela' under the name of the Special AKA and threw himself into Artists Against Apartheid, but more on that in a later chapter.

The scene may not have lasted long, but its impact was enormous. For Red Saunders, Two-Tone was the realisation of everything he had been fighting for with RAR. 'When you saw

Two-Tone, you went "Job done. That's it! This is what we dreamed of in 1976." Two-Tone music and their spirit and their story and everything Jerry Dammers went on to do for Nelson Mandela trumped the whole fucking lot of us.'[61]

Similarly, music historian Daniel Rachel has described Two-Tone as 'the practical realisation of the anti-discriminatory ambitions of Rock Against Racism: Black and white musicians not just sharing a stage, but playing in the same bands'.[62] It became one of the most exciting musical movements to ever emerge in Britain and at its core was a radical politics that made manifest the dreams of Rock Against Racism. Importantly, Two-Tone didn't just challenge the racism and austerity of the period. It offered a living blueprint of what a modern multi-cultural Britain could look like.

SIX

Back in the USSR:
Rocking the Eastern Bloc

Recommended Listening:
Dmitri Shostakovich – 'Adagio (Lady Macbeth of the
Mtsensk District)'
The Beatles – 'Back in the USSR'
Stas Namin & Gruppa Tsvety – 'Мы желаем счастья вам'
Mashina Vremeni – 'Povorot'
Illés – 'Keresem a szót'
Dezerter – 'Tchórze'
David Hasselhoff – 'Looking for Freedom'
Scorpions – 'Wind of Change'

–

I ENTERED THE LIFT on the third floor of the grand neo-
renaissance building at 60 Andrássy Road in Budapest. The
doors closed, blocking all outside light and cloaking me in an
uneasy darkness. A sharp staccato violin strike shocked through
the speakers as a previously unnoticed TV screen flickered on.
As the lift descended at a punishingly slow speed, a black-and-
white video of a suited man started to play.

I read the subtitles with increasing shock as he described in
considerable detail the means by which executions took place.

The victim was woken early, no last meal, final letters ripped up, and a noose placed around their neck – not too tight, he explained – before the stool was kicked away from below their feet. Each line was punctuated by another screech of the violin. 'Comrade Doctor' would then place a stethoscope to their chest and confirm the death. The screen returned to black as the doors opened and I walked into the cellar. Despite the claggy summer heat above, it remained noticeably, eerily even, cool down there.

I quietly walked from cell to cell. Black and green mould-stained plastered walls looked like the undulating sea in J. M. W. Turner's *The Shipwreck*. The detention cell, its dimensions just sixty by fifty centimetres, with two splitting lightbulbs puncturing the prisoners' eyelids at all times. The wet-cell, so named as this was where presumed traitors were forced to sit in water. The so-called 'fox-hole', with ceilings too low to stand up. Then, with grim inevitability, the condemned cell, where those who had survived the torture and finally confessed to real, or likely imagined, crimes were held before being taken for execution.

This final room showed the gallows, shocking in their power and simplicity. The laminated guide explained that this set was originally employed at the nearby Vác penitentiary before being moving to Kozma street prison, where it was in use until 1985. An addendum nonchalantly stated that no formal executions happened at 60 Andrássy Road, only 'fatal bashings and suicides.'

I stepped from the chill of the cellars back into the sticky oppression of the evening sun. Turning right, I ambled along the grand boulevard that runs to the river, passing luxury shops. The streets vibrated with the competing chants of Roma and Seville football fans, in town for the Europa League final. The sulphurous smell of red flares choked the evening air, with the crack of bangers and the moan of police sirens diverting my thoughts from the imagined screams of 60 Andrássy Road. As I reached the river, the sun was calling time, the horizontal beams catching each gentle ripple, making them sparkle. The Danube is a silken length of turquoise cloth that gently divides Buda on one bank and Pest on the other, held elegantly together by the famous Chain Bridge.

With the river to my left, I followed the dusty bankside path towards the Parliament building. The dramatic hillside on the western side of the river demands attention, each building more magnetic than the previous. Looking down knowingly is Fisherman's Bastion, a turreted jumble of neo-Gothic and neo-Romanesque towers, seven in total representing the Magyar tribes.

Looking back down to the path, I noticed a small pair of iron shoes fixed to the stone embankment. Then another pair. And another. Boots, brogues, slip-ons, some with thick square heels, others flat, all cast in iron and now rusted. Sixty in total, the most powerful was a small pair of children's boots. It was the remarkably moving memorial, 'The Shoes on the Danube Promenade', created by the film director Can Togya with the sculptor Gyula Pauer. The work commemorates those people, many of whom were Jewish, who were walked to the edge of the river, forced to remove their shoes, and then shot by members of the fascist Arrow Cross Party. The memorial's power is engulfing, the empty shoes conjuring the ghosts of their owners. Moments of horror, cast into permanence.

Together, 60 Andrássy Road and this memorial create a painful reminder that much of Eastern Europe experienced decades of traumatic oppression, first at the hands of fascism, then communism. Its swapped one set of secret police for another; different ideologies, different uniforms, but the same terror. By the time the cannons fell silent across Europe in 1945, the leading architects of fascism were dead. Mussolini was hung upside down from a metal girder in the Piazzale Loreto in Milan, while Hitler was hurriedly cremated after swallowing a cyanide capsule and shooting himself in the head.

With much of Europe reduced to rubble, few families were left untouched and the newsreel footage of Jewish bodies being pushed into mass graves was seared into societal consciousness. Yet, for many in the East, the respite was short-lived. In the words of Winston Churchill during his famous 'Sinews of Peace' speech in Fulton, Missouri in March 1946, 'a shadow has fallen upon the scenes so lately lighted by the Allied victory'. He continued:

From Stettin in the Baltic to Trieste in the Adriatic, an iron curtain has descended across the continent. Behind that line lie all the capitals of the ancient states of central and eastern Europe: Warsaw, Berlin, Prague, Vienna, Budapest, Belgrade, Bucharest and Sofia, all these famous cities and the populations around them lie in what I must call the Soviet sphere, and all are subject in one form or another, not only to Soviet influence, but to a very high and, in some cases, increasing measure of control from Moscow.[1]

The dividing lines of the post-war world had begun to solidify and the first frosts of the Cold War could already be felt. The communist takeover of Eastern Europe was not instant-aneous, varying in its timing and nature from country to country. The historian Hugh Seton-Watson argues that it generally happened in three stages: a coalition of left-wing and anti-fascist forces; a fake coalition where communists neutralised those not willing to accept communist dominance; and, finally, complete communist domination.[2]

The Union of Soviet Socialist Republics (USSR) eventually grew to fifteen republics and, in addition, was the 'Eastern bloc', a term often used to describe USSR-aligned countries, including East Germany, Poland, Czechoslovakia, Hungary, Romania, Bulgaria and Albania. While ostensibly independent countries, they were under the heavy influence of the USSR, which was run from Moscow.

Looking back from a post-Cold War world, it's important to avoid the binary simplifications of 'West = Good, East = Bad'. Indeed, other chapters in this book explore the ongoing oppression suffered by many in the capitalist West, but this takes nothing away from the spirit-crushing authoritarianism and terror experienced by so many in the USSR during the second half of the twentieth century.

—

As with most dictatorial and authoritarian regimes, censorship of music was the norm within the communist bloc. From the 1917 Russian Revolution onwards, the state took an interest in what was being played on people's gramophones and what was being performed on stages. From 1932, socialist realism was the official doctrine of the state. Writing in 1960, J. B. Borev explained that:

> Socialist realism is a method, type or form of figurative emotional thinking which corresponds to the objective esthetic [sic] wealth of reality, to the practice of revolutionary struggle of the proletariat, and to the building of socialism. Socialist realism is a means of truthful reflection of reality from the position of socialist esthetic ideals.[3]

Doesn't sound easy to dance to does it? In reality, this meant that artists were expected to 'represent reality truthfully' and that music 'had to be simple and easy to remember so that it could become a source of collective unity when sung or hummed together'.[4] Though some found ways to create remarkable art and music within these constraints, it severely limited people's scope for expression. Great works such as Shostakovich's opera *Lady Macbeth of the Mtsensk District* fell foul of the communist censors and were banned.

When it comes to understanding musical censorship across the bloc, it is impossible to grapple with all the nuances and changes over location and time in a book like this. What was permissible in one country was banned in another – and vice versa. 'Styles, rhythms, songs, artists, dances, even instruments, came in and out of official sanction,' writes Stephen Coates, a music producer and world expert on banned music in the communist east. 'Exceptions were made and then rescinded. Records of popular stars once sold in every music store were taken out of circulation when those stars became forbidden; singers might suddenly be allowed only to perform a fraction of their repertoire, or to perform but not record.'[5]

If musicians in the East faced strict controls over what they could create, there were also rules on what music recorded elsewhere in the world could be listened to, with quotas being issued for the amount of foreign music allowed to be played on the radio and even at social events. What made this even harder for eager music fans was that what was and wasn't permissible was ever-changing – although, generally, Western popular music faced tight restrictions and often outright bans. Comically, however, one route around the censors was via parodies. More amusingly, it was sometimes permissible if being performed by the bad guys in films.[6]

Following the death of Vladimir Lenin in 1924, Joseph Stalin rose to power and cupped the ears of the communist bloc ever tighter. Alexander Zhdanov was made director of cultural policy and, by 1932, all culture was subject to approval by the censors. All manner of exciting and cutting-edge music from early electronic to experimental classical was declared decadent and banned, often with horrifying consequences for the creators. With time, the noose tightened until what was left was only what Stalin and his fawning apparatchiks personally liked – which was a mixture of classical music, mawkish movie scores, Georgian folk songs and, of course, stirring Soviet hymns.[7]

Jazz was especially targeted, with improvisation prohibited, valved trumpets and mutes supressed, and the saxophone was completely outlawed following the comically sinister claim that 'it is just one step from the saxophone to a dagger'.[8] In 1928, the socialist realist Maxim Gorky published his influential article 'On the Music of the Gross', which included a remarkable description of jazz that is worth quoting at length:

There are rumblings, wails and howls like the smarting of a metal pig, the shriek of a donkey, or the amorous croaking of a monstrous frog. Bestial cries are heard, neighing horses, wild screaming, hissing, rattling, wailing, moaning, cackling. The insulting chaos of insanity pulses to a throbbing rhythm. Listening to this screaming music for a few minutes, one involuntarily imagines an orchestra of sexual maniacs led by a man-stallion beating time with an enormous phallus. The monstrous bass belches our English words; a wild horn wails piercingly, calling to mind the cries of a raving camel; a drum pounds monotonously; a nasty little pipe tears at one's ears; a saxophone emits its quacking nasal sound. Fleshy hips sway, and thousands

175

of heavy feet tread and shuffle. The music of the degenerate ends finally with a deafening thud, as though a case of pottery had been flung down from the skies.[9]

I don't think I've ever heard a description of a live gig that I would like to have been at more. Everything Gorky hated about jazz is what makes it so electrifying and appealing to me.

This censorship continued into the post-war period. Between roughly 1946 and 1964, first under Stalin and then Nikita Khrushchev, the record industry in the Soviet Union was heavily controlled by the state. What was permissible to play, record and dance to was decided by faceless men. Yet, finding ways around these official censors became something of dark art in communist countries. Creativity is like water: it seeps into cracks and finds ways to drip through seemingly impenetrable walls. The best example of this is the remarkable phenomenon of Roentgenizdat, aka Ribs, or jazz on bones or, simply, bone music.

I attended the launch of Stephen Coates's wonderful book *Bone Music* at the rather odd Horse Hospital in London's Bloomsbury. It's an underground venue just behind Russell Square tube station and, on that night, its walls were covered in remarkable and disturbing photographs that made up an exhibition titled *Augenblick Press: Rain Time*: 'a collection of photographs documenting the self-portraiture of one person's penchant for deep-sea submersion via the burgeoning world of rubber fetishism'.

More interesting than the black-and-white pictures of aroused divers were Coates's stories about staggeringly brave music obsessives who ingeniously found ways to distribute banned music. While all culture faced censorship, it was jazz and rock 'n' roll that were most stridently banned, seen as subversive articulations of Western culture.[10] But, as Coates explains, 'bans did not reduce their desirability, only their availability'.[11] This was especially the case amongst the stilyagi, or 'style hunters', of the 1950s – trendy young people with a flair for loud clothing and loud music.[12] Much like the mods in the UK, who saw clothes as a way to escape the drudgery of post-war British society – clean living under difficult circum- stances – the stilyagi donned coloured zoot suits, bright shirts and jackets as a way to subvert the rigidity of their monochrome existence.[13] Just as they were enamoured with Western clothing, the stilyagi wanted Western music. This was easier said than done in Stalin's Soviet Union.

One way to hear international music was via the children of diplomats who smuggled back vinyl records from stints beyond the Iron Curtain, renting out records to young music lovers.[14] Others, such as Ruslan Bogoslovosky, devised a technique to soften and flatten the grooves of shop-bought records, thereby cutting banned music from the West right onto recordings of Stalin or Lenin's speeches.[15] But these sort of techniques were never going to be enough to meet the demand, so people created bone records.

With vinyl in short supply, innovative bootleggers began to use discarded x-rays, cutting the songs onto images of shattered bones, ribs, sternums and chest cavities with a lathe. They are remarkable items, at once beautiful but also haunting and unsettling. If music is really what makes us human, then there is no better example than these records – music etched into images of the inside of us. All manner of banned songs were bootlegged; some Western jazz and rock 'n' roll, but also banned music made by people from the East. Around 1946, a group of music lovers in Leningrad began cutting their own records; they were described by Coates as 'anti-establishment, music-loving chancers whose defiance was as much technological and entrepreneurial as it was cultural'.[16] The practice spread to Moscow and then across the Eastern bloc in both the Soviet Union and its satellites, such as the People's Republic of Hungary.

Listening to recordings of interviews of those who made or bought the bone records has striking similarities to stories told by drug dealers, tales of back-street deals, avoiding police and scuffles with other gangs selling the same merchandise. It was thrilling, but also dangerous. The best-known group of bootleggers were the Golden Dog Gang, who started out in Leningrad and were central to developing and spreading x-ray records. But, on 5 November 1950, the Soviet financial police – the OBKhSS – rounded them up, arresting sixty of their number and confiscating the group's equipment.

Following a trial, Ruslan Bogoslovsky, Boris Taigin and Konstantin Sankova were found guilty of, 'producing and distribution of gramophone records on x-ray film with recordings of émigré Russian repertoire'. Bogoslovsky was sentenced to three years in prison, while Taigan and Sankova received five following the additional charge of 'composition, performance and recording onto disc of songs of the criminal genre'.[17] They were by no means the only ones to face persecution and imprisonment for the creation and distribution of bootleg records.

When the stakes were so high, one wonders what motivated these remarkable young people to take these risks. It seems that there is no single answer. For a young bootlegger called Mikhail Farafanov, it was a range of reasons. 'To be honest, my first motivation was money and I did well. It brought me a good income; I made a lot sometimes. When you make things well, you'll always have an income. And the thing is, you see,

I was eighteen years old – I was very energetic. Secondly, it was a desire to introduce people to jazz, which I loved so much.' Another bootlegger, Rudy Fuchs, explained his reasons: 'We weren't doing it only for money, but for adventure. Good romantic adventures! We were young. It was our energy.'[18]

After interviewing so many of these young people, Coates summed up their motivation. 'These people were not trying to bring the system down. They were sometimes accused of that by the authorities, that they were trying to pervert young people, that it was some anti-communist conspiracy. It wasn't really like that. But they were anti-establishment in the sense that they wanted to listen to what they wanted to, when they wanted to.'[19]

The era of the bone records was short-lived. With Stalin's death and Khrushchev's softening of state terror, there was a cultural thaw. Yet it was the arrival of reel-to-reel tape machines that eventually made records cut on x-rays redundant by the 1960s. Though the medium passed into history, the objects still retain their power and beauty. Despite most of the recordings being poor quality, riddled with pops, jumps and fuzz, it was what they stood for that made them so important. They are proof that no matter what the state tries to do, no matter how repressive they are, how censorious and dictatorial, people's ability to innovate and our desire to listen to what we want – not what we are told to – can overcome it.

After Coates's talk at the Horse Hospital, I bought a bone record from him. Not an original one, but a reissue they had made to distribute with the book. But even though I knew it wasn't real, it was oddly exciting. I didn't know what was on it or how it would sound or whether it would even work on my record player. In a world where we can open our phones and listen to almost anything we want to in seconds, it was a thrill. I ran home desperate to play it. Even though I faced no danger at all for owning it, it gave me a tiny glimpse into what it must have been like for a young person in Leningrad in the 1950s, rushing to the sanctity of their home to put their bone record on their gramophone.

—

I used to live just off Penny Lane in the Mossley Hill suburb of Liverpool. It wasn't a coincidence. I may have technically moved to the city to attend university, but the real reason involved my twin loves of Everton football club and the Beatles. It's impossible to say anything new about the most famous band on the planet, but thankfully that hasn't stopped people trying. As a student, I veraciously tore through endless articles and books which forensically detailed every moment of the Fab Four's lives, hungrily looking for new, irrelevant but pleasing facts about their upbringing and love lives, from the tuning on their guitars to the stool that Ringo sat on (usually a Premier drum chair, but sometimes a Ludwig Timpani throne, if you're interested).

I sat with friends debating their albums long into the night, heated arguments between those of us who were correct and argued *Rubber Soul* to be their best and those who were wrong and made other choices. If you had asked me then whether the Beatles meant as much to anyone else as they did to me, I would have said it was an impossibility, but it turns out I was completely wrong. Locked behind the Iron Curtain, there had been an army of Beatles fanatics who had a relationship with their music I couldn't comprehend. For them, the Beatles were the chink of light that illuminated their prison cell, a fundamental source of life and hope.

On Wednesday, 22 August 1962, a young British film director called Leslie Woodhead recorded a lunchtime concert at the Cavern Club in Liverpool. It was the first time the Beatles had been filmed.[20] Woodhead later explained the moment he first heard the band: 'Tangled up with a woozy cocktail of disinfectant and sweat, it felt physical, dangerous, like an assault.'[21] The film that he shot that day was one early step towards the Beatles conquering of the world. This dominance would prove easier in some places than others; the Soviet Union was determined to resist the invasion at all costs. Woodhead developed a fascination with those fellow fans behind the Iron Curtain, the result being *How the Beatles Rocked the Kremlin*, a 2009 documentary and an accompanying book, packed with interviews with Beatles fans who risked it all to listen to their favourite band, despite state bans and suffocating censorship. The undeniable star is Kolya Vasin, a Beatles obsessive who dressed like a pirate and who created the John Lennon Temple of Peace and Love in Leningrad. Surrounded by walls dripping with all manner of memorabilia, his pure passion oozes from the screen:

> It was the salvation of my soul. It's not a buzz, not a high, not a pastime, not a hobby . . . I was really afraid. During the Soviet era, my whole life was lived in fear because the pressure from the propaganda was enormous. They were so angry and aggressive about our favourite band that it frightened me. If I said anything good about the Beatles I could have been arrested.[22]

Vasin was, in fact, arrested on numerous occasions for amassing Beatles bootlegs and memorabilia, but it didn't stop him. For him, music was a way to escape, to build his own Beatles 'republic'. 'I decided to emigrate to a "free territory" of Russia.

In 1964, I said to myself, "I will live without the Soviets, in my room with the Beatles".'[23] Sadly, he died in 2018, leaving a suicide note that reportedly read: 'It's impossible to live in a country where nobody supports a Temple of John Lennon.'[24]

Vasin was not alone in seeing the Beatles as a way to engage with the wider world and subvert the restrictions of life in the Soviet Union. Some even argue that they played a role in bringing it down. The Russian music commentator Artemy Troitsky is one, believing their impact to be seismic. 'In the big bad West, they had whole huge institutions which spent tens of millions of dollars for undermining the Soviet system and I'm sure that the impact of all those stupid Cold War institutions has been much much smaller than the impact of the Beatles.'[25] The way this happened, Troitsky argues, was that 'the Beatles more or less melted the hearts and brains of millions of Russian youngsters, and prepared them for the end of the Soviet Union'.[26]

Similarly, the Russian journalist Vladimir Pozner has claimed that 'if you look at all the factors that led to the ultimate loss of belief in The System, which was its downfall – it was held together by fear and by belief – and the Beatles played a role in first of all overcoming the fear and that showing the belief was actually stupid'.[27] This argument has been succinctly summarised by the historian William Jay Risch: 'The new music turned young people away from Vladimir Lenin to John Lennon.'[28]

The Beatles are perhaps the best example of how ostensibly non-political music can have an enormous political impact. While later songs, such as 1968's 'Revolution', were more overt, it would be hard to find any notable political message in their early work. Even if there were, many of the Russian youths listening to it wouldn't have spoken English anyway. Yet the energy, vibe, style and sound stirred something within them. For this alone, the regimes of the Eastern bloc instinctually knew it was dangerous.

Just as in the West, the Beatles also inspired countless people to pick up instruments, spawning – numerous bands in the East. 'The party leaders were stodgy, middle-aged men,' explains the historian of Eastern-bloc rock, Timothy W. Ryback. 'Marx and Engels were dusty relics of the nineteenth century. The Beatles, in contrast, were impulsive, iconclastic, and exuberant.' For this reason, they 'provided inspiration for hundreds of upstart Soviet-bloc rock musicians . . . The Beatles provided a tangible model for the modern rock ensemble.'

By the early 1970s, there was a thriving underground music scene in Russia, with countless amateur rock 'n' roll bands like Rubinovia (Ruby Attack), Arax and Vysokosnoe (Leap Year Summer) playing covers of Western hits. Remarkably, one estimate from the middle of the decade put the number of unofficial bands at 100,000.[29] One of the most influential in Russia was Tsvety (The Flowers), formed in 1968 by Stas Namin and sometimes called the 'Soviet Beatles'. 'They [the Beatles] changed everything,' explained Namin. 'Our music, our way of dressing, our way of living. Officially, the Beatles were called things like "Long-haired bastards". Very rude and unpleasant. But at that time everything that came from the West was forbidden.'[30]

However, Tsvety were different to many of their Beatle-obsessed counterparts. While their peers were content with playing underground gigs at venues like Moscow's Institute for Architects or the Institute for Civil Engineering, Tsvety recorded for the state-owned record label Melodiya and under-took national tours. Namin even became the first rock musician to be inducted into the Soviet composers' union.[31] The state's leniency wasn't to last, though, and in 1975 the band was dissolved, with its name banned by a decree of the Ministry of Culture.

Another significant Soviet band to have been influenced by the Beatles was Mashina Vremeni (Time Machine), formed by Andrei Makarevich in 1968. Their records from the 1970s undoubtably echo those of Lennon and McCartney – touching and melodic acoustic records with lush instrumentation, while others thump like Led Zeppelin or Deep Purple with heavier and funkier electric guitars. While their sound is undoubtably derivative Ryback has explained how their lyrics were distinctly Soviet. 'While vocal instrumental ensembles cheerily recounted the exploits of cosmonauts and the accomplishments of five year plans,' Ryback explained, 'Makarevich chronicled young people's sense of indifference and passivity, their despair over the conformity and hypocrisy of daily life.'[32] Avoiding overt attacks on communism or the regime, he produced coded lyrics that signposted discontent; lines like, 'There's no point in believing the promises any more', in reference to state propaganda.[33] By the end of the decade, Mashina Vremeni cassettes were being circulated in their millions, with some commanding the same price as Western music bootlegs.[34]

This use of rock music to subtly articulate discontent wasn't just happening in the USSR, but also emerged right across the Eastern bloc in this period. One of the best was the Hungarian band Illés. I must admit I had never heard of them until one afternoon when I was digging through crates of old vinyl in Kalóz Records in Budapest. I was looking for bone records and the painfully cool young man working behind the desk was staring at me blankly. At first, he thought it was the name of the band, but when I explained I was actually searching for old x-rays with music carved on them, he looked at me with pity, as if I were a lost grandparent walking the cold streets in my pyjamas.

'If you are looking for banned music, you might find some in there,' he said, pointing me in the direction of some boxes of old vinyl from the '60s and '70s. The first one that caught my eye was *Illések és pofonok* by Illés. Released in 1969, the sleeve was an explosion of colour, unmistakably '60s with its red, orange, purple and blue squares: some with circles, others with flowers, and five with headshots of the band that could have been members of the Rolling Stones, the Beach Boys or, of course, the Beatles. When I opened the gatefold sleeve there was a pop-up rainbow and a piece of card with a band picture covered in psychedelic paint.

I hurried over to the turntable, took off whatever repetitive electronic thumping was being played and placed the vinyl down. If I thought the sleeve was an homage to *Sgt. Pepper's* . . . the first song was not far off a cover. A recording of a passing train was interrupted by a blast of horns and a marching snare before a jolly and melodic pop song emerged. The album was full of sound effects and one song even featured a Beatles-like sitar. Other than the lyrics being in Hungarian, you'd be forgiven for thinking it was a collection of rejected Beatles songs that didn't quite make the grade. But there was something endearing about it. Magical, even. The idea was intoxicating; that a group of musicians had managed to get hold of copies of Beatles records behind the Iron Curtain and loved them so much they were inspired to try and recreate what made them so special.

Illés had formed as a jazz ensemble in 1957, but switched to beat music, and then later produced Beatles-influenced records, from the middle of the '60s onwards.[35] They weren't alone in loving rock music during this period. A 1969 book titled *Beat* claimed there were approximately 4,000 rock bands in Hungary at the time and that 92 per cent of Budapest's young people had attended rock concerts.[36]

Under the communist leader János Kádár, Hungary had more liberal rules than much of the Eastern bloc when it came to rock music, but this didn't stop Illés eventually crossing a line. In early 1970, the band travelled to West Germany and England where they gave interviews that criticised the Hungarian government's 'rigid' policy towards popular music. They were castigated upon their return and the government imposed 'measures limiting their appearances', which included a ban on them playing live in Budapest, a proscription of radio and television appearances, and the shelving of their third album.[37]

The restrictions were subsequently lightened, but the band continued to butt heads with the regime over the coming years. As I was paying for their album, the guy at the record store suggested I also get a copy of the bands' 1971 *White Album*, which I happily did. It wasn't until I got it back to London and opened the sleeve that I realised the words 'human rights' were printed in small letters on the vinyl label. Then a small postcard fell out. It was a picture of the American civil rights activist Angela Davis. Perhaps I was wrong, but I read it not just as a statement about human rights in the United States at the time, but perhaps also a more universal call for them, including in Hungary.

While rock music had an impact all over the Eastern bloc, I knew that if I wanted to properly understand its possible role in the eventual collapse of the communist system, I had to travel to where it first imploded. And that meant heading to Poland.

—

A banger exploded right at my feet with a thunderous boom that forced my right leg from under me. The sound hammered on my eardrums and left them ringing, before my right ankle began to sting like it had been singed. I looked down, dazed, but there was no mark. To the amusement of a passing neo-Nazi, another exploded down the road and the 'BOOM!' made me flinch.

I was at the 2023 Polish National Day demonstration in Warsaw, an annual event that attracts tens of thousands of marchers, a sizeable number of whom are explicit neo-Nazis. I first attended the demonstration back in 2018, but even when knowing what to expect, the sights are still shocking. It's a horrifying mixture of families waving Polish flags while walking alongside some of the most extreme fascists in Europe. There are also massive banners with homophobic declarations, graphic images of abortions, biker gangs and Catholics carrying crosses or images of Pope John Paul II.

Not everyone on the march is a fascist, but no one seems to mind marching alongside those who are. Before it started, in the shadow of the Palace of Culture and Science, the vast brick edifice that towers over central Warsaw, activists from All-Polish Youth – a virulently homophobic far-right youth organisation – and the National Radical Camp (Obóz Narodowo Radykalny, or ONR) – named after an antisemitic organisation from the 1930s – set up their stalls. Small gazebos, selling badges, stickers and flags, were doing a healthy trade. Another sold books, including one title with a caricature of a Jew hanging from a lamppost and another emblazoned with Hitler's face on it. They even sold Ted Kazinkis Unibomber manifesto. In front of the stalls, Gay Pride and European Union flags had been laid on the ground. Protestors gleefully took pictures of themselves wiping their feet and spitting on them with hateful cackles. A speaker blasted out bad Nazi metal, a reminder that music can be used for bad as well as good.

As the time approached for the march to start, a group of roughly 200 neo-Nazis began to muster. Clad in balaclavas, combat trousers, bomber jackets and black Dr Martens boots, they waved the flags of the various fascist groups they represented. They had travelled from all over, including the US, France, Germany, Denmark, Hungary, Italy and the UK. Some wore scarves emblazoned with the white supremacist version of the Celtic cross, while others had tattoos or badges of the Odal Rune or the Nazi SS Black Sun. Their faces were obscured by skull facemasks, leaving only their hateful eyes visible. They marched down the road before passing under a bridge. I stood at the exit as they lit dozens of red flares that made it hard to see or breath. As they emerged from the tunnel's exit, it looked like the gates of hell had opened, a battalion of skulls emerging out of a cloud of thick red flare smoke. Nazis escaping the underworld, climbing out of the sewers once more. It reminded me of Chumbawamba's song 'On the Day the Nazis Died':

We're told that after the war
The Nazis vanished without a trace
But battalions of fascists
Still dream of a master race.

That's when the banger exploded next to me, nearly making me drop my camera. The Nazis finally gathered in a park, laying their banners on either side of a stage, before lighting more flares and chanting, the sound echoing across the city. As the final flares spluttered out and they disappeared into the night's darkness, I made a quick exit back to my hotel. The last thing I saw as I reached the train station was a man carrying a Solidarnosc (Solidarity) flag, the famous trade union that helped bring down communism in Poland. I was surprised to see this symbol of hope and change at a demonstration filled with so much hate. The following morning, I woke early and boarded a train to Gdansk, the birthplace of Solidarity. As I stepped out the station, the first thing I saw was a bronze statue of five children among a clutter of luggage. The plaque read: 'Dedicated to the Jewish children of the Kindertransports from the Free City of Gdańsk 1939 who were rescued from German Nazi persecution by leaving for Britain without their parents so their lives could be saved.' The Kindertransport programme has always left me with mixed feelings, at once both proud Britain saved the lives of some children, but also ashamed we didn't do more. After the horrifying scenes I had witnessed the previous day, the statue took on additional poignancy. How could we let such horrors return to the continent of Europe?

The historian Dan Stone convincingly argues that 'the further from the war we get, the more its impact is being felt and the more its meaning are being fought over', meaning that 'the years since 1989 should be understood as the real post-war years'.[38] What Stone is arguing is that opportunity for real debate and a serious reckoning with the events of World War II has only become possible since the end of the Cold War and the reunification of Europe. Prior to that, the continent was divided, with each side of the Berlin Wall experiencing its own distinct 'post-war consensus' – the West in the form of welfare-capitalist states; in the East, communist dictatorships.

While not downplaying the fundamental importance of this ideological divide, Stone offers an alternative framework through which we can understand the post-war period that helps, in part, to understand the return of far-right politics since the fall of the Berlin Wall. He argues that the post-war consensus was entwined with a particular memory of World War II and that competing notions of anti-fascist (an instrumentalised tool in eastern Europe and the intellectual basis of political and social stability in the West) was, in essence, a fire blanket supressing the flames of far-right politics. As such, the end of the Cold War and the 'collapse of the political project of social democracy in the West and communism in the east went hand in hand with the death of antifascism, hence the reappearance of ideas and values which had long been assumed to be dead, or at best marginal and lunatic'.[39] The beast was injured, but not dead. And since the end of the Cold War, it has begun to reawaken. But I was in Gdansk to explore altogether happier historical events: the fall of a communist dictatorship.

I must admit that my expectations for Gdansk were low, picturing an industrial city with little to see beyond its famous shipyards hugging the Baltic. I couldn't have been more wrong. As the sun began to set and a bitter chill tightened my face, I walked from the train station towards the city centre. I entered the old town through a large stone gate to find a warren of beautiful cobbled streets that reflect its history as a powerful trading city. The centre is cluttered with magisterial buildings that date from the sixteenth and seventeenth centuries, and tall, thin houses fronted in painted plaster. It's a mixture of Gothic, Renaissance, Flemish and Dutch architecture that, in places, looks remarkably similar to Amsterdam, especially along the banks of its canals. It was a Sunday evening, but the bars and restaurants were busy with people hugging heaters and drinking mulled wine.

I woke the following morning, still heavy from too many Polish dumplings, and made my way towards those famous shipyards, the cradle of Polish freedom. The wind picked up as I got closer to the coast, like fine sandpaper brushing my face. I walked past a fragment of the Berlin Wall displayed by the side of the road. The sign read: 'A symbol of Europe divided into a free and an enslaved realm.' I kept walking, using the towering green cranes on the horizon as my guide, until I reached a vast monument to the fallen shipyard workers who died in 1970. On 12 December, the government again displayed their remoteness from the people by drastically increasing fuel and food prices just days before Christmas. With workers' salaries remaining frozen, the ensuing outrage was swift, with indignant workers spilling onto the streets, enraged by communist leader Władysław Gomulka's decisions and timing.

The anti-Gomulka sentiment of the industrial action was clear from the off, with some 3,000 workers marching on the police headquarters. The response was dramatic and swift, resulting in 10,000 workers attacking the party building and setting it on fire.[40] Unsurprisingly, Gomulka responded by labelling the workers as counter-revolutionists. The following morning, workers arriving at the Gdynia railway station were fired upon, with some estimates labelling the death toll as high as seventy-five, despite the official line initially claiming 'just' thirteen fatalities, before eventually declaring that twenty-six lives had been lost. It was at this stage that Gomulka unsuccessfully attempted to bring in the might of the Red Army, his request rejected by the Kremlin. Gomulka was replaced by Edward Gierek, following a forced resignation. The events of December 1970 marked the first time in Europe since World War II that workers had successfully unseated a ruler.[41]

The memorial manages to be both vast in its scale but also touching. Three enormous crosses, with ships anchors crucified in place of Jesus, brush the clouds. At its base, a plaque reads: 'A token of everlasting remembrance of the slaughter victims. A warning to rulers that no social conflict in our country can be resolved by force. A sign of hope for fellow citizens that evil need not prevail.'

In the remarkably modern Solidarity Museum, which now sits on the site, one of the most poignant artefacts is a leather jacket sprayed with bullet holes. It belonged to Ludwik Piernicki. Just twenty years old, he was shot down on 17 December 1970 in Gdynia. When his lifeless body was searched and his pockets emptied, they found a medallion of the Virgin Mary and a blood donor card, reading: 'Giving blood is the greatest of humanitarian acts. Proof of great social solidarity.' The bloody events of that winter marked a turning point in the history of Poland and for the future leader of Solidarity, Lech Walesa.[42] He recognised the mistakes made, but also acknowledged their importance for his development as an activist. 'I had plenty of time later to think things through,' he observed, 'and realise just where we had gone wrong. It was an apprenticeship, a necessary stage.'[43]

Throughout the 1970s, Walesa maintained his activism and, as such, spent much of his time under surveillance, being incarcerated regularly. In 1976, he was dismissed from the Gdansk shipyard where he was employed as an electrician, but this did not mark the end of his affiliation with the site; by 1978, he had begun to agitate for free trade unions along the Baltic coast. However, it was the events of 1980 that were to be a watershed, the moment that the wheels of change began to turn in earnest. More price increases, this time on meat, were introduced in July, which immediately led to a rash of strike activity across Poland. Despite the government's wage concessions and their attempt to rush meat into the shops, the workers were unwilling to concede. By the end of the first week in August, more than 150 stoppages had taken place and the focus was soon shifting to the site of the 1970 unrest, the Gdansk shipyards.

The Baltic region of Poland was already simmering following the dismissal of trade union activist Anne Walentynowicz from her job at the Lenin Shipyards in Gdansk in August 1980. Workers claimed that she was 'dismissed from work a few days earlier and subsequently persecuted'. They were demanding 'pay increases and the introduction of a money bonus to offset the hike in prices.'[44]

The widespread discontent developed into a movement led by Lech Walesa. Within days, the board of directors conceded to the workers' demands in an attempt to avert major industrial action in a period of such economic uncertainty. As such, the planned strike action was temporarily suspended on 16 August. However, surrounding firms called for the support of the Lenin Shipyard and many labourers refrained from returning to work. Sensing he had misjudged the mood of the workers he represented, Walesa changed tack and, despite the generous concessions offered by management, he called for a solidarity strike and an occupation of the factory.[45]

The Gdansk Inter-factory Strike Committee (MKS) was created and proceeded to produce a list of twenty-one motions with a wide array of demands, including pay increases, work-free Saturdays and a limitation on censorship. Most important of all the points, though, was the demand for free trade unions, independent from the influence and constraints of the party and the state. Such demands swiftly galvanised support for the cause and, just two days later, 156 factories had been recruited. By the end of the month, 700,000 people were on strike in 700 factories across the whole country.[46] The workers pulled together in defence against the state's traditional tactic of attempting to divide one factory from another, through separate concessions. The results astonished a watching world.

Unlike during the unrest in 1970 and 1976, the intellectuals pledged their support from the start, which greatly bolstered both the workers' morale and their chances of success. Discussions with the then deputy prime minister Jagielski were imminent and the workers needed assistance articulating their demands. Tadeusz Mazowiecki arrived in Gdansk with a six-strong team of intellectuals at the behest of Walesa and work began in earnest. 'It was a difficult task, and a round-the-clock marathon, with Walesa . . . a relentless taskmaster.'[47]

The consequential talks resulted in the signing of a historic agreement that permitted the existence of an independent mass social movement for the first time since the 1940s in communist eastern Europe. Walesa and Solidarity had seemingly succeeded, despite the acceptance of several unavoidable concessions to the party. The sanctity of both the party and the Warsaw Pact – a collective defence treaty established by the Soviet Union and its satellite states – were officially accepted by Solidarity regardless of more radical members' protests.

However, despite the brief period of euphoria, it soon became clear that the government 'had no intention of relinquishing in fact the authority it had signed away in theory'.[48] Firstly, the party attempted to apply the agreement just to Gdansk, leading to three weeks of strikes in an attempt to gain nationwide application. The movement also struggled to gain the legal recognition it believed it had been promised in the Gdansk charter. The power of Solidarity became clear when recognition was provided following a threatened strike; however, the moderate nature of the organisation's reactions to events infuriated much of the radical rank and file.

Walesa, who had been so integral to the early successes of the movement, was being marginalised and, as such, Solidarity was to move beyond being a trade union to embracing a wider political agenda. The positions held by the party and Solidarity fast became irreconcilable to the detriment of the movement. Walesa remembered the mistakes of 1970 and 'warned against any action which might cause bloodshed, and insisted that Solidarity do nothing which suggested that it was seeking political power for itself or questioning Poland's membership of the Warsaw Pact'.[49]

Walesa's warnings were ignored by the newly elected, radical congress and, as a result, de facto leader of Poland, Wojciech Jaruzelski, made the dramatic decision to suppress the movement. Martial law was declared, Solidarity leaders were arrested (including Walesa) and the Military Council of Salvation was created. Despite Solidarity's attempts at resistance, the organisation was officially abolished by the autumn of 1982, forcing those determined to continue their activism to operate underground. The underground solidarity movement slowly grew throughout the 1980s, feeding off the back of the economic turmoil in Poland.

Unintentionally, the imposition of martial law in 1981 'jolted the Polish rock scene from a half decade of lethargy'.[50] For many young people, hope of a better future had been dashed and, just as in Britain years before, it was punk music that gave voice to their frustration and anger. Between 1982 and 1985, a raft of punk bands released musical attacks on the Jaruzelski regime. One famous song from the band Dezerter articulated this sense of anger and hopelessness: 'No goal, no future, no hope, no joy!'

I managed to track down the band's drummer Krzysztof Grabowski to ask him what it was like to make Polish punk music during that period. 'Imagine if every song you wanted to sing had to be approved by a government official,' he told me. 'It was not possible to enter the studio without the consent of the censor. Album release? Forget it. The authorities wanted to control everything. But there were ways to bypass the system, and that's what we did. We played songs at concerts that could have landed you in jail. But we were young. We weren't afraid.'

The band faced constant censorship and even had to change their name. Like many other subversive bands working within the Eastern bloc, they weren't necessarily overtly political. 'We have always avoided calling ourselves a political band, rather we are an anti-political band. This was because we did not want to be associated with any side of the political conflict in Poland. Of course, everyone secretly supported Solidarity. But we were anti-regime and anti-totalitarian.'

Dezerter were not alone in using music as a statement about their circumstances at the time. In a corner of the Solidarity Museum was a small exhibition about music. There was a short but powerful video with interviews of rock musicians from the time. 'Rock 'n' roll is a force the communists didn't foresee,' said Marek Piekarczyk of the Polish band TSA. 'It blew the world, the whole situation, to pieces, because how can a Russian soldier shoot an American soldier if they both listen to Hendrix or the Beatles?'[51] Muniek Staszczyk, from the band T.Love, noted that 'it would be an overstatement to say that, together with my friends, I dismantled communism. The honour goes to the people who really risked their lives. We, just like the other bands, made our contribution by making a small hole in the wall. Polish rock 'n' roll of those times simply gave hope of independent thought.'[52]

All the musician interviewees mentioned the importance of the Jarocin Festival, which was first held in June 1980 and dubbed 'the first All-Polish Review of Music of the Younger Generation'.[53] The historian Tom Junes argues that it 'represented the most important arena in which bands that could not get access to the official distribution channels managed to present themselves to the public'.[54] Most importantly, said Junes, the festival 'represented an oasis of freedom for those who attended it'.[55] One of the festival's co-organisers Marcin Jacobson described it as 'something unheard of in those times: it was an enclave of freedom marked by geopolitical division',[56] noting that 'there was no festival in this part of Europe that would so openly represent so called independent thought and underground culture'.[57] What I really wanted to know was whether these festivals, and music in general, had a real impact on the collapse of communism in Poland. I asked Krzysztof Grabowski for his take on it.

'We certainly inspired a group of rebels. They can be found today in various institutions, in important positions on all sides of the political puzzle. Personally, I receive a lot of signals that we were, and are, very important to people, because we give hope or encouragement. But let's be realistic. Music is just music. For some, it gives energy. For others, it gives food for thought. It is important, but it will not change the world.'

It struck me that this was something I had heard from musicians all over the world: the idea that music alone isn't enough to create change. But what it does do is produce hope. It makes people feel that change is possible, and I guess that is enough.

Martial law was suspended in December 1982; Walesa had been released from incarceration the previous month. However, the peace was fragile and discontent grew rapidly as the decade progressed. Despite heavy surveillance, Walesa remained active within the illegal Solidarity movement and, by the middle of the decade, a resurgence looked likely. Anger among the populace further spread following the murder of the anti-communist party clergymen Jerzy Popieluszko in 1985. Tension was rising fast and, by 1988, industrial action was once again widespread, as was support for the once-broken Solidarity movement. It mobilised on a mass scale and pushed for industrial action to combat price increases and, 'by the spring of that year, the illegal union had unleashed industrial guerrilla warfare with a rash of strikes across the country'.[58]

The situation became untenable for the grossly unpopular party, which was left with little other option than to negotiate with Solidarity. Following a series of unsuccessful talks between the party and opposition representatives towards the latter part of the decade, Walesa formed a civic committee within Solidarity. He worked to purge the movement of its more radical elements in an attempt to engage in more successful dialogue with the party.

The historic negotiations began in February of 1989 and were to last just short of two months. That the state would seek accommodation with society through bargaining was a huge step and a departure from the norm throughout the communist period.[59] Remarkably, Solidarity managed to secure the re-legalisation of the movement, wide-ranging economic reforms and, most breathtaking of all, the assurance that the next election would allow 35 per cent of seats to be genuinely contested. 'Unwittingly, the Polish communist government had taken the first step to the dismantling of its power and in doing so had begun the revolution of 1989.'[60]

The subsequent election results were an overwhelming success for Walesa and a crushing blow for Jaruzelski. The party's hope of 'socialist pluralism' was rejected comprehens-ively, with Solidarity gaining approximately 65 per cent of all votes cast, translating to 40 per cent of the total elect-orate.[61] Following protracted debates, the only feasible option seemed to be that Solidarity should form a government and, on 24 August 1989, Jaruzelski stood down and Tadeusz Mazowiecki formed the first non-communist Polish govern-ment in decades. The following April, Walesa was re-elected chairman of a divided Solidarity party and was sworn in as president of Poland on 22 December. His long struggle against oppression had begun in 1970 and, twenty years later, he found himself president in a period of dramatic change and reform.

The victory of Solidarity didn't mark the end of communism across the whole region, but it was the beginning of the end. In the months that followed, regimes fell with a surprising peacefulness, like an elderly person slipping away, long ready for death. On 9 November 1989, the Berlin Wall crumbled followed by the Soviet Union itself in 1991. The Cold War was over and, with it, what British historian Eric Hobsbawm called the short 20th century.

I've always wondered what all those remarkable musicians and brave music fans, who had risked so much to listen to what they wanted, when they wanted, made of David Hasselhoff, wearing a piano-keyboard scarf and leather jacket, while singing 'Looking for Freedom' at the Berlin Wall. As elsewhere, when dictatorial and oppressive regimes fall, it would be wrong to say that it was music that brought down the Polish regime or the Soviet Union. But music was what gave millions of people hope that it would fall. Getting hold of smuggled Western records, or making their own rebellious music, gave young people a window into what was beyond, what they were missing out on. Music also kept the spirit of individualism and rebellion alive when states were working to crush it out of them. It was people who smashed the Iron Curtain, but music gave some of them the strength to swing the hammer.

SEVEN

Free Nelson Mandela: Anti-Apartheid Music and South Africa

Recommended Listening:
Miriam Makeba – 'Beware, Verwoerd! (Ndodemnyama)'
Miriam Makeba – 'Soweto Blues'
Enoch Sontonga – 'Nkosi Sikelel' iAfrika'
The Jazz Epistles – 'Blues for Hughie'
Hugh Masekela – 'Grazing in the Grass'
Hugh Masekela – 'Bring Him Back Home (Nelson Mandela)'
Abdullah Ibrahim – 'Mannenberg'
Irene Schweizer and Louis Moholo – 'Free Mandela!'
National Wake – 'International News'
Kalahari Surfers – 'Prayer for Civilisation'
Johannes Kerkorrel – 'Sit Dit Af'
Gil Scott-Heron – 'Johannesburg'
Peter Gabriel – 'Biko'
The Special AKA – 'Nelson Mandela'
Artists United Against Apartheid – 'Sun City'

–

IT WAS A SCORCHING thirty degrees when I landed in Cape Town on New Year's Day, 2024. The receptionist at my hotel had raised an eyebrow when I explained I wanted to walk down to the city's waterfront, a mere fifteen minutes away. I'd taken less than five steps beyond the front door before a hotel employee joined me and insisted that they too happened to be walking in the same direction.

It was of course a lie. They were worried about my safety, which was sweet of them, but made me feel instantly guilty as the young man had clearly been tasked to chaperone me through the punishing heat. South Africa is one of those countries that is sometimes greeted with a grimace and an 'Oh, do be safe' when you tell friends and family you're planning a trip. This can range from a gentle 'Be sensible' to an alarmist 'Don't leave your hotel room without an armed escort and air cover'. But plenty of sensible and informed people had encouraged caution before the trip, so I was happy to be accompanied.

I reached the city's waterfront sweatier than I'd have liked, to find an undeniably beautiful orgy of modern consumerism. Top-end shops competing to sell eye-wateringly priced handbags and watches while yachts and pleasure boats bobbed around the harbour's translucent tributaries, dropping off day trippers and picking up well-dressed locals for their sunset cruises. Restaurants overflowed, with flustered waiting staff frantically rushing between tables, weighed down by armfuls of seafood linguine and trays of white wine. For those on a different budget, there was also a healthy smattering of fast-food outlets spitting out burgers at a ferocious pace. The whole scene was watched over silently by Table Mountain, which felt close enough to reach out and touch. As much as I tried to hate everything about the waterfront, I found it joyous, undeniably beautiful, and I couldn't stop smiling.

At the waterfront's centre was a small amphitheatre, its rows of wooden benches thronging with delighted revellers.

A mediocre cover band churned out contemporary pop songs to a genuinely delighted audience who danced with infectious abandon. The audience was one of the most diverse I'd ever seen in any country. Large groups of Black people singing along to every word, women in headscarves thrusting their iced coffees into the air instead of clapping, a group of elderly Indian men concentrating intently on each lick of their artisan gelato, a cluster of white teenagers with backwards caps unselfconsciously dancing, and a ring of unconvinced denim-clad fathers, arms resting on stomachs somehow both wobbly but also taut like a drum.

Looking around, I wondered if this was the Rainbow Nation that Nelson Mandela had talked about, the unrivalled melting pot, the multi-racial ideal. It certainly looked like it. But, after an hour, I realised that all of these groups were next to each other but not actually together. I moved to a restaurant to continue my unscientific survey, watching groups pass as I tucked into prawns. Again, I didn't see a single mixed group. That's not to say they don't exist; of course they do. It's just I didn't see any. It was a reminder that the end of apartheid wasn't that long ago and that while people of all races can now visit the same restaurants, dance next to each other while listening to poor cover bands and empty their wallets at the same expensive shops, it may be some time before deeper integration becomes the norm.

The following morning, I rose to find the roads around my hotel in the city's central business district were all closed. Metal barriers lined each street and a tented village stretched either side for miles. Families were hurriedly erecting gazebos, putting out plastic chairs, ice-coolers, shisha pipes and picnic equipment. 'What's all this?' I asked a passing woman as she hurriedly shuffled passed, eager to secure herself a good spot.

'The Kaapse Klopse!' she bellowed back over her shoulder. Once known by the horrifying name of the 'Coon Carnival', it is now officially called the Cape Town Minstrel Festival and is an annual celebration within the Cape coloured community. I have always winced at the use of the term 'coloured', but it is an accepted ethnic group in South Africa and is used to describe people of mixed African, Asian and European heritage. The festival dates back to the colonial period when slaves were given the second day of January off, and used it 'for revelry and self-expression through vibrant song and dance in the streets'.[1]

By the time I returned to my hotel that evening, the festival had transformed the area with an explosion of sound and colour. The parade is comprised of troops of competing dancers and musicians, all with painted faces and wearing astonishingly loud silken suits. Each troop had its own marching band with a huge brass section and a drum corps that mixed booming bass drums and clapping snares with a range of bassy African drums. It was similar to the marching bands you get at American football games, but far more ramshackle, which was no bad thing. It was messy, sloppy, overlapping, chest-rupturing and ear-to-ear grin-inducing. They played with infectious enthusiasm and combined well-known pop songs with intricate and innovative drum patterns that seemed to electrocute the hips of everyone watching. The rest of the troop danced with impressively consistent enthusiasm for hours, blowing whistles, twirling batons and shaking tambourines. There were people dressed as devils or monsters who ran towards the crowds, scaring the children and causing hoots of delight from their parents.

I walked the night streets for hours listening to the sound of horns echoing off the buildings. It was joyous. I mean,

genuinely fucking joyous. I must admit to finding it less enjoy-
able four hours later as I lay awake in bed, my room still
shaking as ever more bands passed, but that was my fault for
going to bed too early. I had only just arrived in South Africa
and to find Cape Town vibrating to the sound of music boded
well for my trip.

South Africa is a country of stunning natural beauty, remarkable wildlife and fascinating cultural diversity. Yet for many
people, myself included, it is impossible to separate the modern
country that it is now from its history of apartheid. For those
on the left, especially anyone involved in anti-racist politics,
apartheid is a spectre that haunts the post-war period; it's the
go-to example of racism and state brutality.

While South Africa was a state built on the notion of white
supremacy, it was the 1948 election victory of the Afrikaner
National Party, in alliance with the smaller Afrikaner Party (AP),
that formalised and instituted a comprehensively apartheid
system. However, the formal introduction of apartheid was more
of a continuation than a break. The South African system was
already built on the model of racial segregation, meaning that
1948 merely marked the formal and legal entrenchment of a
system that sought to concentrate and secure white dominance
over all aspects of South African life.[2] Its roots can be traced
much further back, perhaps as far as the first arrival of European
explorers in 1488, or the establishment of the first European
settlements by the Dutch East India Company in Cape Town
in 1652, or the eventual defeat of the Zulu kingdom in 1879,
the most powerful indigenous state in the region.

However, the fallout from the Anglo-Boer War, fought
between the British Empire and the two Boer Republics between
1899 and 1902, played a central role. The bloody conflict
resulted in a comprehensive victory for the British and the

defeat of the Transvaal and the Orange Free State. The war's brutality was staggering, with an estimated 28,000 Boers dying in the British-run concentration camps.[3] The Boers were understandably deeply bitter about their defeat and their treatment during the war which unsurprisingly sparked 'unprecedented Afrikaner unity'.[4] Once folded into the British Empire, the Transvaal and Orange River Colony were granted self-governance in 1906 and 1907 respectively. The unification of South Africa followed in 1909, codified by the Act of Union in 1910, bringing together the British colonies of the Cape Colony, Natal, Transvaal and Orange River.

During the act's drafting, it soon became clear that London intended to ensure power resided with the white minority, failing to safeguard either rights or influence for the Black majority and entrenching the colour bar within the constitution.[5] The subsequent Native Land Bill ensured the white population was guaranteed 90 per cent ownership of the land, while just 7.3 per cent was available to the African population.[6] The racist intentions were never hidden, with the statesman Jan Smuts explaining, when addressing a crowd at London's Savoy Hotel in 1917, that 'it has been our ideal to make it [South Africa] a white man's country'.[7] Support for this position was widespread within the white community, with Smuts going as far as to pronounce: 'There are certain things about which all South Africans are agreed, all parties and all sections, except those who are quite mad. The first is that it is a fixed policy to maintain white supremacy in South Africa.'[8] For this reason, as the historian David Welsh explains, 'until the 1920s, there was a tacit agreement among the parties that colour policy ought to be kept out of party politics'.[9] One of the earliest legislative manifestations of this racial consensus was the Native Land Act of 1913, which prohibited the purchase of land by Africans outside of designated reserves.

However, despite South Africa already being segregated along racial lines, the passing of the formal apartheid legislation in 1948 entrenched the status quo still further.[10] Historians roughly divide the history of apartheid which followed 1948 into three defined periods. Guy Arnold suggests the first ran between its formal imposition, through the establishment of what is referred to as 'grand apartheid' and ending in 1960 with the Sharpeville massacre and the withdrawal from the Commonwealth in 1961.

The second phase ran until 1976, which was a period of increasing international isolation, while the final stage, sparked by the Soweto uprising of 1976, ran until the system's collapse in 1990 and the election of Nelson Mandela as president in 1994.[11] Similarly, David Welsh argues that the first phase between 1948 and 1959 was typified by the entrenchment of the National Party power and the extension of discrimination; the second, between 1959 and 1966, saw a supposedly more 'positive' version, called 'separate development', typified by the preparation of Bantustans, a euphemistic name for separate racial homelands, for self-government; and the third ran from 1966, when the apartheid system began to erode ever quicker and Afrikaner solidarity began to splinter until the system's eventual disintegration.[12]

Over these periods, apartheid was buttressed by rafts of legislation that entrenched and formalised the society's racial hierarchy and sought to quell organised opposition, such as the 1950 Suppression of Communism Act and the Group Area Act, the 1953 Criminal Law Amendment Act, and the 1967 Terrorism Act. Perhaps most important was the 1959 Promotion of Bantu Self-Government Act.[13] The 1963 Bantu Laws

Amendment Act further downgraded the status of Africans working within the 87 per cent of South Africa designated for whites. Previously referred to as 'guest labourers', their role and status was now reduced to that of chattels.[14]

The removal of African landowners from designated white areas was enforced on a vast scale, with an estimated 3,548,900 people being removed between 1960 and 1983.[15] One area which suffered from this policy of forced removal was the Sixth Municipal District in Cape Town. Once a thriving community of newly freed slaves, labourers, traders and artists, some 30,000 inhabitants were 'cleared' to make way for white settlers. 'The government declared District Six was a crime-ridden slum full of dens of vice, only fit for clearance. Many believed this was a convenient cover story and that, in fact, their desire to demolish District Six was because it was a prime piece of land, nestled between the city centre, Table Mountain and Cape Town's harbour.'[16]

Today, the story of forced removal and the decimation of communities is kept alive by the District 6 Museum. Stepping inside its walls, the pounding heat and noisy street bustle falls away instantly. It is cool and calm, like entering a library. An old Methodist church, the building has high, vaulted wooden ceilings and a balcony running around its edges, all held up by ornate pillars rising from the floor. What's most powerful about this small museum is not just the way it highlights the injustice and brutality of apartheid policies, but also its emphasis on what was lost. Its poignant displays and touching artifacts offer glimpses of a destroyed community, a lost world of craftsmen, artists and musicians.

One small corner is dedicated to the importance of music and dance to the area's former community. Before the clearances, there was a vibrant scene centred around 'langarm', the term given to a quickstep style of dance. 'It's just ballroom dancing,' explained Joe Schaffers, the senior education officer at the Museum. 'The extended arm that you're dancing with is where our term langarm came in.'[17] Sadly, when the forced removals began following the Group Areas Act, successful bands were forced to split up after the musicians were scattered to other areas of the country. It is an important reminder of the impact of apartheid policies on the cultural life of the coloured and Black population.

As I ambled past the informative display boards, I looked down from the balcony to see a bench with the words 'Europeans Only' painted across its back. Artifacts like these never lose their emotive power. Even shorn from their historical time period and context, they maintain their ability to shock and appal. Just those two words – 'Europeans Only' – somehow encapsulate an entire worldview. As I gazed down, a group of South Asian women in headscarves shuffled over to the bench and took turns having their picture taken while sitting on it. They seemed to find it amusing, each laughing and smiling, perhaps a slight subversive thrill. It made me smile. More than that, it made me feel hopeful. There were Black people in the museum that morning who will have remembered seeing horrendous signs like that plastered all over this city, constant reminders of their subjugation, dehuman- isation and oppression. Yet, now, women in headscarves laughed at the absurdity of it, mocked it even. Problems remain of course, but it was a reminder of the progress and change that has happened in South Africa.

—

On 21 March 1960, the world saw the willingness of the South African regime to use murderous violence against those who opposed their unjust laws. Crowds gathered across the country to protest the pass laws, a system of internal passports designed to restrict the movement of the Black population. Longstanding anger and opposition towards the system culminated in horrifying scenes at a protest in Sharpeville, a township in the Transvaal Province.

Six Sabre jets and eight Harvard planes, as well as a fleet of armoured cars, were used to intimidate those who had gathered, numbering between 3,000 and 25,000, according to differing estimates.[18] When a drunk petty criminal fired two shots into the air while stones were being thrown from the crowd, a massacre erupted, carried out by an already nervy, scared and undertrained police force.[19] The police emptied their weapons on the crowd for an estimated twenty seconds, killing sixty-nine and wounding a further 182.[20] Allegedly, fifty-two of those killed were found to have been shot in the back.[21]

Justifying the massacre, the local police commander, Colonel Pienaar, declared that 'it all started when hordes of natives surrounded the police station. My car was struck by a stone. If they do these things, they must learn their lesson the hard way.'[22] Far from condemning the bloody actions of the police, Prime Minister H. F. Verwoerd 'commended the police for the courageous, efficient way they handled the situation'.[23] However, as Nelson Mandela explained in his autobiography, the Sharpeville shootings plunged the government into turmoil. 'Outraged protests came in from across the globe ... The Johannesburg stock exchange plunged, and capital started to flow out of the country. South African whites began making plans to emigrate.'[24] The state's response was swift, authoritarian and had important ramifications for the nature and radicalism of the anti-apartheid struggle.

The African National Congress (ANC) had been founded back in 1912, following a conference of African leaders in Bloemfontein who met in response to the formation of the Union of South Africa. 'Chiefs of royal blood and gentlemen of our race,' cried the lawyer Pixley ka Isaka Seme when addressing attendees, 'the white people of this country have formed what is known as the Union of South Africa – a union in which we have no voice in the making of the laws and no part in the administration. We have called you, therefore, to this conference so that we can together devise ways and means of forming our national union for the purpose of creating national unity and defending our rights and privileges.'[25]

The gathering bore fruit, with the founding of the South African Native National Congress, later renamed the African National Congress. In the decades that followed, the ANC's influence, size and radicalism fluctuated. In 1959, a group of ANC activists broke away to create the Pan-Africanist Congress (PAC) and the two organisations campaigned against apartheid as uneasy collaborators. In the days that followed the Sharpeville massacre, the ANC and the PAC, which had both been running separate anti-pass campaigns, held a day of mourning, resulting in the biggest strike in the country's history.[26] The state responded swiftly, announcing a state of emergency on 30 March that gave the authorities sweeping power to detain people and ban meetings, the result being the detention of 11,503 people by the end of August.[27] There was also a rapid enlargement of the security branch of the police, with officers beginning to be trained in the use of Sten and Browning machine guns.[28] The government also banned both the ANC and the PAC, engendering their shift towards more clandestine and overtly confrontational and violent means.

At 1:30, on the morning that the state of emergency was passed, Mandela was arrested. 'I was awakened by sharp knocks at my door. "The time has come," I said to myself as I opened the door to find armed security police,' he later wrote.[29] 'By morning, we totalled forty in all. We were placed in a tiny cell with a single drainage hole in the floor, which could be flushed only from the outside. We were given no blankets, no food, no mats and no toilet paper. The hole regularly became blocked and the stench in the room was insufferable.'[30]

Mandela and his comrades had been rounded up to attend the so-called Treason Trial, a laborious ordeal that had been dragging on since 1956 when 156 people had been arrested on spurious charges of treason. 'I did not know whether to laugh or despair,' remembered Mandela, 'but in the midst of this thirty-six hours of mistreatment and the declaration of a state of emergency, the government still saw fit to take us back to Pretoria to continue their desperate case against us.'[31] In time, all defendants were found not guilty, but famously, however, the South African authorities had not given up on the idea of imprisoning Mandela.

In the wake of the Sharpeville Massacre, the ANC jettisoned its fifty-year commitment to non-violence with the launch of its armed wing, Umkhonto we Sizwe (The Spear of the Nation) – or MK for short. 'I, who had never been a soldier, who had never fought in a battle, had been given the task of starting an army,' explained Mandela.[32] He quickly recruited the white communist Joe Slovo and former ANC secretary general Walter Sisulu to form the group's high command. They began a campaign targeting government buildings, and while taking care to avoid civilian deaths, they were behind more than 200 explosions.[33] In 1963, they transitioned towards a form of guerrilla warfare with activists receiving military training abroad.

However, on 11 July that year, the police descended on the group, arresting seventeen members. Slovo avoided the raid as he was abroad while Mandela was already imprisoned for a previous conviction for incitement. The subsequent trial, famously known as the Rivonia Trial, began in October 1963, lasted eighty-six days, and resulted in eight of the accused being handed life sentences: Nelson Mandela, Walter Sisulu, Govan Mbeki, Ahmed Kathrada, Denis Goldberg, Raymond Mhlaba, Elias Motsoaledi and Andrew Mlangeni. On 20 April 1964, Mandela addressed the court for four and a half hours, concluding with a statement of such reasoned beauty and bravery that it caught the attention of the world:

During my lifetime I have dedicated myself to this struggle of the African people. I have fought against white domination, and I have fought against Black domination. I have cherished the ideal of a democratic and free society in which all persons live together in harmony and with equal opportunities. It is an ideal which I hope to live for and to achieve. But if needs be it is an ideal for which I am prepared to die.

Mandela and his fellow accused avoided the death penalty, but the sentence handed down was intended to ensure they spent the rest of their lives behind bars. Following the sentencing, they were transported from Pretoria to the infamous prison at Robben Island, where Mandela would live for the next eighteen years of his life.

Today, the prison is a UNESCO World Heritage site, attracting tourists from all across the globe. The boat that bobs and bumps towards the island is a time machine. It picks you up in the very heart of modern cosmopolitan Cape Town and transports you back to the darkest days of apartheid. Upon arrival at the dock, I passed under a sign reading 'ROBBENEILAND: We Serve With Pride'. The first thing I noticed was a World War II concrete pillbox to my left, the sort that are scattered all over southern England, giving the place an oddly familiar feeling. The island was militarised during the war by the British but saw no action.

I was ushered onto a coach and my tour guide introduced himself. 'My name is Modise Phekonyane. I served five years on Robben Island between 1977 and 1982.' There was an audible intake of breath throughout the bus. He had been arrested for taking part in anti-apartheid student protests and detained without trial for six months under Section 29, before being unceremoniously tried and sentenced to his fate on the Island. It was clear from the off that he was finding it hard to relive in front of an audience the trauma of those years. 'To be brought here, you must have done something against the apartheid regime,' he explained. He spoke with a terrifying passion that stunned the bus into silence. 'Every aspect of life was about race,' he said, bellowing into the microphone until it distorted and popped. It may have been more than forty years since he had been released, but the pain and anger seemed not to have faded.

Eventually he cracked, overcome by emotion, tears escaping from his eyes. 'One night, I decided I will hang myself,' he said, his voice wobbling. He became briefly incoherent, offering words out of order and without context. 'Drowning syndrome. Electric shocks.'[34] He fell silent, dropped his head and tried to gather himself. The coach driver took this as his sign to start up the bus and get us moving. 'Sorry, I've only been doing this for five days. Yesterday was the hardest and today is the second hardest.' I wanted to run to the front and hug him. I could tell every other passenger felt the same.

We circled the five square miles, stopping at the various sites dotted across the island. Sat at the entrance of Table Bay, this tiny island has been used as a prison in various forms for centuries. We disembarked at the southernmost point, which had staggering views back towards Cape Town and Table Mountain. I can't imagine what torture that beautiful vista must have been for the prisoners on the rare occasions they glimpsed it, a tiny stretch of gently undulating, azure water separating them from the rest of the world.

I approached Modise to shake his hand and he almost looked a little embarrassed. I wasn't sure what to say and my pathetic Englishness subdued the urge to throw my arms around him – not, I'm sure, that he would have wanted me to. We chatted a little about his time on the island and I asked if there was any music allowed. 'Of course,' he replied. 'The Red Cross would sometimes get us instruments we could play. But we are a very vocal people, so we would just sing.' With that, we were ushered back onto the bus and driven to the island's quarry. 'This was my university,' he explained. It was among the dust and rubble kicked up by prisoners doing hard labour that Modise received his political education, learning from the elders.

As the coach approached the actual prison, he closed his eyes, raised a clenched fist and began to sing. It was haunting, inspiring, emotional.

'What is that song?' I asked.

'I can't remember its name, but it's about how we Africans are crying out for our land, the land taken from us by white people.'

Inside the actual prison walls are rows of cells, barely six feet square, adorned with nothing but a bedroll on the floor and a tiny wooden table. I felt claustrophobic just poking my head inside. The idea of living there for eighteen years was beyond my comprehension.

As I headed back towards the ferry that would return me to Cape Town and modern South Africa, I ambled along the dock front and spotted Modise walking towards me. A few yards away, he raised his fist in what I thought was another salute. In a moment that has haunted me since, I followed suit and raised mine. It was only as we passed each other I realised that he was going in for a fist bump. I flushed instantly red as I realised that me, a boy from Woking in England, had incomprehensively thrown a Black power salute to a former inmate at Robben Island. He pulled an understandably confused face and it took every ounce of self-control to not instantly turn left and walk directly off the dock to avoid the crushing embarrassment. Luckily, he chuckled. We nodded at each other and I sheepishly got on the boat.

–

Having seen where Mandela and his comrades were incarcerated, I took the short flight up to Johannesburg – or Jozi as the locals call it. Considering its vast scale and its status as the economic powerhouse of South Africa, I found remarkably little to recommend the place. I drove its streets for hours and took numerous tours, but beyond its remarkable apartheid history, the city seems devoid of notable landmarks, impressive buildings or pleasant vistas. The city's open-topped bus tour was reduced to pointing out notable coffee shops and lingering too long on unremarkable bridges that cross trainlines.

Founded in 1886, following the discovery of vast gold deposits along the Witwatersrand plateau, the city suffers from its location. There is no water. It lacks the rivers, lakes, canals or seafronts that are fundamental to a great city. Johannesburg is dusty; the vast mine dumps created unstable and toxic hills around the city's edge and wind blows fine grains into your eyes. Then there's the pollution – you can taste it, especially in the poorer districts of the city, of which there are many. The once-imposing centre has been gutted, with multinational companies moving their headquarters out to shiny suburbs like Rosebank that have the clinical feel of identikit American cities.

What has been left is a crumbling centre now occupied by migrants and asylum seekers from across the continent, many living in upsettingly depressing squats and shared housing. Every tour guide and hotel employee told me to avoid the centre, especially after dark. Ironically, however, it was the only part of the city that felt alive, real, bustling and busy. By contrast, social life for the wealthy seems to centre around shopping centres and hotels, with their clusters of restaurants that make you feel you could be in any country in the world.

It's this striking inequality between rich and poor that is perhaps the most noticeable feature of the city. Johannesburg is home to more dollar millionaires than any other place on the continent, with the Africa Wealth Report describing it as the 'most affluent city in Africa'.[35] That's believable. Whole sections of the city are occupied by enormous mansions hiding behind towering security walls that are draped in electrical wire. Yet, drive just eleven miles south-west of the city centre and you enter the township of Soweto.

With a population of roughly 2 million inhabitants, almost all Black, Soweto is not merely a suburb of Johannesburg but its own city with all the diversity that suggests. Parts of it are remarkably middle class with beautiful detached houses, pristine streets, manicured and lush green gardens, and driveways cluttered with expensive German cars. Other areas, such as

Motsoaledi, are gripped by an unconscionable and heart-breaking poverty. The area is an informal settlement, or 'squatter camp', where dense clusters of iron shacks are linked together by narrow dirt roads. Though painted brightly, the tiny houses are boiling in the summer and freezing in the winter. In the midday heat of mid-summer, I could hear the metal tingle. The homes lack running water, so locals use communal pumps dotted around the area, transporting heavy buckets back home for washing and cooking. Not officially linked to the electricity grid, the supply is pilfered from nearby buildings, with high-voltage black wires running down each road, precariously held up by makeshift pylons. That people live in such conditions just moments away from the tree-lined avenues and gated mansions of Johannesburg is a crime – and a painful reminder that the end of apartheid might have created political parity but not economic equality.

Among the warren of winding roads that makes up Soweto is Vilakazi Street, one of those rare places where history is piled on top of history. It was formerly home to two Nobel Peace Prize winners, Desmond Tutu and Nelson Mandela, along with a memorial to Hector Pieterson, who was killed by police in the 1976 student uprising. Mandela's house still stands and is now visited by endless streams of eager tourists crushing into its cramped rooms. The tiny red-brick building was inhabited by Mandela and his first wife Evelyn Ntoko in 1946 and remained his home when his second wife, Winnie Madikizela Mandela, moved in in 1957. It is also where he briefly returned upon his release from prison later.

'That night I returned with Winnie to No. 8115 in Orlando West. It was only then that I knew in my heart I had left prison. For me, No. 8115 was the centre point of my world, the place marked with an X in my mental geography.'[36] Today, its walls are plastered with the countless honouree doctorates and certificates bestowing the freedom of numerous cities on the great man, even if the bullet holes and fire-blackened bricks of its turbulent history are still visible.

Just a few steps from its front door is the dilapidated memorial to Hector Pieterson and, a little beyond that, is a museum telling the story of the 1976 Soweto uprising. By the mid-1970s, apartheid seemed immovably entrenched, with many of its leading opponents either in prison or exiled. Despite this, with much of the rest of Africa now independent from their former colonial rulers, the unstable foundations of the South African regime were continually rocked by external and internal pressure.[37] In 1976, the township of Soweto erupted in protests that would spread across the country and shake the regime to its foundations.

The catalyst for the outbreak of opposition was the government's plans to introduce Afrikaans, seen as the tongue of their oppressor, as a language of instruction within schools for young Black students.[38] On 17 May 1976, the students at Orlando West Junior Secondary School began a strike, voicing their opposition at being taught in Afrikaans. Things escalated and, on 16 June, violence erupted, starting what has been described as 'a seminal event in the decline of apartheid'.[39] An estimated 15,000 students marched towards the school, only to be met by a phalanx of soldiers who, as at the Sharpeville massacre, opened fire on the defenceless protestors, many of them children. Police estimated that twenty-five people were killed and a further 200 injured in the massacre.

Their murderous actions compounded longstanding fury and resulted in widespread rioting. The police response was horrifyingly brutal, with reports of child protestors being beaten and tortured. In eight days of rioting, an estimated 176 people were shot dead and thousands more left bloodied and broken.[40] Unrest spread, with Cape Town's coloured community organising solidarity demonstrations which were also brutally put down by the state. By the end of the unrest, the *Rand Daily Mail* had identified a staggering 499 deaths, though some estimates suggest a figure to be well in excess of 1,000.[41] However, while the uprising was relatively short-lived, the events of 1976 'turned out to be the beginning of a process rather than a one-off explosion of violence; from this time onwards permanent, smouldering antagonism was likely to erupt at any time'.[42]

At the Hector Pieterson Museum, which tells the story of the uprising, there is a small board which quotes a protestor explaining how they had been singing as they marched that bloody day. 'As we led the Big March, our spirits lifted and the songs began to be more spontaneous and full of vitality. "Sizobadubula ngembhay'mbhayi", a song by Miriam Makeba, was among the most popular freedom songs on that morning, but we also made up songs as we marched, converting religious hymns and choruses to freedom songs.'[43] Two years before the Soweto Uprising, the state had passed the Publications Act of 1974, which created the Directorate of Publications, charging it with the power to ban material deemed unacceptable to the regime. Censorship existed beyond formalised bans, with the government-run South African Broadcasting Corporation refraining from playing songs deemed undesirable.[44] However, as is so often the case, oppressed people found ways to subvert the bans and continued to create and use music as a form of resistance.

This tradition of oppositional protest music dated back decades. In the 1950s, the ANC choir had been launched and protest songs became increasingly popular with musicians joining the increasingly organised and overt political opposition.[45] In August 1956, women from across South Africa descended on the streets of Pretoria to protest against proposed amendments to the already unjust Pass Laws.[46] As they marched they sang, 'Wathint'a bafazi, way ithint'imbodoko uzaKufa', which translates to 'Now that you have touched the women, you have struck a rock, you have dislodged a boulder, and you will be crushed.'[47] Another popular song from the period was composed by the political activist Vuyisile Mini and included the line 'Naants'indod'emnyama, Verwoerd bhasobha, naants'in-dod'emnyama' which translates to 'Behold the advancing Blacks, Verwoerd. Beware of the advancing Blacks.'[48] A warning to the then prime minister H. F. Verwoerd. The song was later recorded by perhaps the best-known anti-apartheid singer, Miriam Makeba.

Known as the 'Empress of African Song'– or simply as 'Mama Africa' – Makeba combined a remarkable musical career with an undying commitment to opposing apartheid, as she explained in her inspiring autobiography. 'I look at a stream and I see myself: a native South African, flowing irres-istibly over hard obstacles until they become smooth and, one day, disappear – flowing from an origin that has been forgotten toward an end that will never be.'[49]

Her life and career read like an epic tragedy, with global musical success combined with personal misfortune, five husbands, cancer and heart-breaking exile from her South African home. Yet she was a survivor, once declaring that 'there are three things I was born with in this world, and there are three things I will have until the day I die: hope, determination, and song.'[50] Makeba's first break came in 1954 when she joined the well-known Manhattan Brothers, but her international fame exploded with the help of the American singer and civil rights activist Harry Belafonte. However, after moving to New York and recording her first solo album in 1960, she fell victim to the South African regime's clampdown following the Sharpeville massacre. When attempting to return upon news of her mother's death, her passport was revoked and thus began thirty years of painful exile. 'He takes a rubber stamp and slams it down on my passport. Then he walks away. I pick up my passport. It is stamped "INVALID" . . . And now, with the single impression of a rubber stamp, I am in exile.'[51]

The decade that followed saw Makeba release a string of influential records, the most famous being 'Pata Pata' in 1967, which became a hit in the US. In 1977, she released 'Soweto Blues', written by her former husband and the 'father of South African jazz', Hugh Masekela (of whom more later). Makeba's gentle but haunting vocals tell the story of the previous year's uprising: 'The children were flying, bullets, dying / All the mothers were screaming and crying'.

Upon Makeba's death in 2008, Mandela remembered how 'her haunting melodies gave voice to the pain of exile and dislocation which she felt for thirty-one long years. At the same time, her music inspired a powerful sense of hope in all of us.'[52] Decades before, Mandela had sung the Vuyisile Mini-penned and Makeba-recorded song 'Ndodemnyama we Verwoerd' while imprisoned at the infamous Johannesburg jail known as 'The Fort'. 'Every day, Vuyisile Mini, who years later was hanged by the government for political crimes, led the group in singing freedom songs . . . We sang at the top of our lungs and it kept our spirits high,' remembered Mandela.[53] Keen to see the prison where Mandela himself had sung protest songs, I left Soweto and headed back into Johannesburg.

As I entered the courtyard of the former prison, ominous clouds gathered above me. Johannesburg experiences cataclysmic thunderstorms in the summer with heart-stoppingly loud flashes of lightning and torrential downpours that turn the streets to rivers. A storm was coming in and a cloud of darkness fell over the city. The wind whistled past the open cell doors. The Old Fort Prison complex, now a museum and including the infamous area known as Number Four, is a haunting space. Since its last inmates in the 1980s, it has been left to age naturally. It feels frozen in aspic, the paint and plaster peeling from its brick walls, the communal toilets left untouched, the barbed wire rusting slowly, the rows of isolation cells unlocked and left open as though someone had just walked free. Information boards have been put up and films are projected on the walls of the large communal cells, but it feels more like walking around a derelict prison than a museum. The eerie sensation was exacerbated by its emptiness; I was completely alone for most of my visit.

Number 4 is the section of the prison that housed 'native prisoners', meaning Black men. It was a brutal, degrading, disease-ridden and violent place where rapists, murderers and thieves were mixed with political prisoners incarcerated for fighting apartheid. Its roster of inmates was staggering. At various times in its history, locked behind its walls were Mahatma Gandhi (for intentionally breaking laws that discriminated against Indians), the founder of the Pan Africanist Congress, Robert Sobukwe, and former ANC president Albert Luthuli. Nelson Mandela was imprisoned in the fort twice, while the women's section held important anti-apartheid activists including Barbara Hogan, Fatima Meer, Albertina Sisulu and Winnie Madikizela-Mandela.

In one of the large communal cells, a short film was showing, with interviews of former inmates talking about the importance of singing for their sanity and survival. 'Some are singing and clapping because there is no radio,' explained one former prisoner. 'There's lots of clapping and you can take a dish and spoons, and use them as drums. Take a dish and turn it upside down and you beat them with the spoons. We start dancing.'

'When I first went to the Fort Prison,' recalled a second former inmate, 'I went there as a detainee. The music was wonderful because it hid the fact that we were talking among ourselves.' A third explained the importance of singing the national anthem, presumably a reference to the pan-African liberation song 'Nkosi Sikelel' iAfrika', a hymn popular with the anti-apartheid movement and later adopted as the dual national anthem in 1994. 'One moment that we always looked forward to was when we sang the national anthem. At eight every evening, we were given a signal before we had to switch off the lights and we had five minutes before they come back again and switch off. We took that period to sing our national anthem. That was a happy moment in my life, in our lives. We enjoyed it. And as we sang, the whole of Number Four shook as they sang with us.'

Finally, another former prisoner encapsulated the importance of the communal singing. 'When we sang, we would forget about everything. You'd think about being a hero. Whether I felt dead or alive, it was the same when you sing.' It was a powerful reminder that music can be overtly political, but it can also merely be a tool to remind someone that they are human when they are being treated like animals. That in itself is a form of resistance.

—

By the 1980s, those opposing apartheid set out to make South Africa ungovernable and, to a large extent, they succeeded. Black resistance during the decade had learnt from previous battles, even though it intensified beyond what had gone before, surpassing even the explosions of revolt after Sharpeville or during the Soweto Uprising.[54] The conflict had been in dead-lock for some years but, as the decade progressed, there was a 'consolidation of Black resistance and the growing recognition among white elites that the old racial order had to change.'[55]

While the struggle was overwhelmingly one of Black resistance, there was also pressure placed on the government by white liberals and left-wing activists, including musicians. An interesting part of this resistance was the anti-apartheid record label Shifty Records, launched in 1983 by Lloyd Ross. 'The political slogans of the time were "Forward to People's Power" and so on,' explained Ross on his label's website, 'but in my subculture, the music subculture, there was also a spirit of "Fuck apartheid, let's dance". Young people were ignoring boundaries, listening to each other's music, and playing together. Some even believed it was possible to rock apartheid into oblivion. But nobody was recording the music.'[56]

That's when Ross and his collaborators kitted out a caravan with recording equipment to create a portable studio. Their first project was a session with the exiled band Sankomota across the border in the independent enclave of Lesotho. One of Ross's early collaborators at Shifty was Warrick Swinney, who I sat down with to discuss the music scene of the period. Warrick changed his name from Swinney to Sony and released a string of studio projects under the name Kalahari Surfers, a fictional collective designed to protect him from oppression by the state. He released various collections of songs from 1982 onwards, along with a string of albums throughout the decade, the first being 1984's *Own Affair*.

I bought a vinyl copy of his compilation *Tropical Barbie Hawaiian Surf Set* from Roastin Records in Cape Town and it didn't leave my turntable for a month. His music is hard to describe, drawing from punk, German 'Krautrock', audio collages utilising apartheid propaganda, tape-splice edits, and a bass style that draws on reggae and dub, but also Zulu music, where the looping basslines copy the melody. It's a bit like a mix between Frank Zappa and Talking Heads. The songs are often fiercely and confrontationally political with records like 'Dance of the Young Fascists', 'Prayer for Civilization' and 'Potential Aggressor'. With EMI refusing to cut the vinyl records in South Africa, they were forced to send them to the UK to be pressed by Recommended Records and then sent back.

Unsurprisingly, Warrick and his fellow white anti-apartheid musicians soon caught the eye of the authorities. 'When we had concerts, the police would roll tear gas in,' he told me. 'It was strange. The police found it so hilarious that they'd laugh. They'd see these long-haired music fans or punks or the rock 'n' roll kids having fun and they'd fuck up the evening and they'd laugh about it. They'd roll gas into the concert hall and then laugh as you ran out. I think the cops enjoyed that.' They also faced surveillance. Talking about the multi-racial punk band National Wake, Warrick explained how founder Ivan Kadey 'had a house, right in the heart of Johannesburg, that he lived in with his Black band. And the cops used to climb trees and spy on them.'

Terrifyingly, things went well beyond breaking up concerts and surveillance, however. 'Shifty had our studio on the outskirts of Johannesburg near Soweto and the person that had the lease was Jackie Quinn,' explained Warrick. 'It turns out her husband, who was a coloured guy, was an ANC member. She was assassinated with her husband – one of nine people who were taken out by security forces.' Most shocking was when he told me about one particular state assassination. 'There was a guy who got a cassette player as a present and put the earplugs in, pushed play and it blew his head up.' These attacks weren't directed at Shifty Records, or even musicians, but are a horrifying reminder of the climate in which they were operating – and of the possible ramifications of attacking the regime of the time.

Warrick humbly played down his own influence. 'I'm not a Billy Bragg. I've never had a successful music career. I've never had a record that sold anything. So the cultural outreach is what I'm more interested in. I'm sixty-nine now and I think I've communicated through my music something that I've wanted to. In other words, the message I intended has reached people.'

He may be downplaying his influence and how important it was for white musicians like him to make a stand, to take risks and to fight against a system that ostensibly was supposed to benefit them. Of course, he wasn't alone in this. In the late 1980s there was even an anti-apartheid music scene comprised of white Afrikaans speakers known as Voëlvry (which translates as 'free as a bird'). The scene included bands like Die Gereformeerde Blues Band (The Reformed Blues Band), which parodied the name of the Dutch Reformed Church, and artists including Johannes Kerkorrel and Bernoldus Niemand.[57] As with others who produced anti-apartheid music, they faced persecution, surveillance and the banning of their performances. The scene's output is typified by songs like 'Sit Dit Af' (Switch it Off), a honky-tonk piano number that implored listeners to turn off their televisions whenever conservative state leader P. W. Botha appeared on screen.[58]

However, while Shifty Records, Warrick Sony and the Voëlvry scene played their part in convincing young, often white music fans to oppose apartheid, it was exiled Black musicians who were at the forefront of raising awareness and building pressure internationally. Along with Miriam Makeba, there were influential jazz players like Abdullah Ibrahim (formerly Dollar Brand), Zim Ngqawana and the fiercely confrontational avant-garde jazz drummer Louis Moholo.[59] In 1988, the *NME* published a profile on South African jazz, focusing on Ibrahim and his sometime bandmate Basil Coetzee. 'Racism, repression, exploitation, exile, drink and destruction echo through the music's last sixty years,' explained the article, 'leaving a legacy of abuse and crudely romanticised anecdotes which only hint at the lost brilliance of township players.'[60]

Ibrahim, then based in New York, is credited as holding together 'the broken strands of this South African music with a remarkable sound soaked through with echoes of *marabi* and Monk, of South African revolution and Islamic spirituality'.[61] He 'created a sound which provides an unbroken affirmation of political struggle'.[62] A good place to start with his music is his 1976 song 'Mannenberg'. Described as 'a sublimely singular South African anthem', the song is a laid-back amble through Xhosa ragtime with traditional African melodies and a heavy American jazz influence that was said to have 'reverberated through the 1976 Soweto school children's uprising'.[63]

Earlier in his career, Abdullah Ibrahim had been part of the influential though short-lived bebop band the Jazz Epistles, alongside Hugh Masekela. Aside from his former wife Miriam Makeba, Masekela is the South African musician most associated with the anti-apartheid struggle. Having topped the US charts back in 1968 with his interpretation of 'Grazing in the Grass', Masekela became a regular at international solidarity concerts and, in 1987, released the joyously catchy protest song 'Bring Him Back Home (Nelson Mandela)'.

Bring back Nelson Mandela
Bring him back home to Soweto
I want to see him walking down the streets of South Africa
Tomorrow.

In the 1980s, Masekela became entwined in the international furore that surrounded Paul Simon's global hit album *Graceland* after he joined the album's tour. Simon's undoubtably brilliant record was a breach of the UN-approved cultural boycott of South Africa that had been passed in December 1980. The ANC had been calling for a boycott as far back as the All African People Conference in 1958 and a UN resolution supporting sanctions had been adopted in 1968.[64] That year, Gram Parsons famously resigned from the Byrds rather than join their tour to South Africa playing to segregated audiences.[65] However, the 1980 UN declarations made a powerful appeal 'to writers, artists, musicians and other personalities to boycott South Africa'.[66] The appeal, supported by the ANC, was by no means universally adhered to, with major stars like the Beach Boys, Cher, Dolly Parton, Rod Stewart, Elton John and Status Quo, among others, all ignoring it and travelling to South Africa to play.[67] Perhaps most notably, Queen's tour of the country in October 1984 sparked a considerable and well-deserved backlash, prompting the Specials' Jerry Dammers to describe them as 'the prototype Nuremberg band.'[68]

However, Paul Simon's situation was deemed to be more complex; not because he'd performed there, but rather that he'd collaborated with Black South African musicians. Reflecting on the controversy many years later, he explained: 'Let me point out the difference. Going to South Africa to perform in front of a segregated audience is to support the apartheid regime . . . Going to record is not the same thing. And it was never specifically declared to be something that shouldn't be done.'[69] However, upon release of the album, he soon found out that many thought otherwise. 'Personally, I feel I'm with the musicians,' Simon said when challenged by journalists at London's Mayfair Theatre in August 1986. 'I'm with the artists. I didn't ask the permission of the ANC. I didn't ask permission of [Zulu leader Mangosuthu] Buthelezi, or Desmond Tutu, or the Pretoria government.'[70]

Unsurprisingly, for those Black activists engaged in a struggle for their very lives, Simon's position was met with anger. Speaking in the documentary *Under African Skies*, Dali Tambo, a founder of Artists Against Apartheid and son of former ANC president Oliver Tambo, explained how the boycott was designed to be universal, describing it as 'all or nothing. We couldn't allow Simon, any more than a tank coming in.'[71] The argument that he was helping introduce South African music and musicians to the world – undoubtably true in the case of *Graceland* contributors like Ladysmith Black Mambazo – also made some bristle. 'So, it has taken another white man to discover my people?' said Jonas Gwangwa, the influential trombonist and former member of the Jazz Epistles. Gwangwa was also leader of Amandla, the cultural ensemble of the ANC that toured the world raising awareness.

Despite the controversy and criticism, Masekela, Makeba and Ladysmith Black Mambazo all joined the 'Graceland' tour. Being associated with such prominent anti-apartheid musicians placated some but not all. Between 7 and 13 April 1987, Simon performed six sold-out shows at London's Royal Albert Hall. Concert-goers were met by protestors outside the venue, who included Jerry Dammers, Paul Weller from the Style Council and Billy Bragg. With debates about South Africa and the cultural boycott raging in the press, it was almost impossible for musicians to avoid taking a position. Even pop stars like George Michael, then in Wham!, were rigorously questioned about it by music journalists.[72] The 1980s were a time when pop and politics seemed indivisible and whole rafts of musicians enthusiastically got involved in anti-apartheid activism.

There had been examples of major international stars penning protest songs about apartheid before – the best being Gil Scott-Heron's typically funky 1976 record 'Johannesburg' – but it was during the 1980s that the musical fraternity really became engaged with the struggle. The decade opened with former Genesis frontman Peter Gabriel releasing his haunting eulogy to the murdered anti-apartheid activist Steve Biko. Biko, who had created the all-Black South African Students Organisation and was a central architect of the Black Consciousness Movement, died in police custody on 12 September 1977.

> When I try and sleep at night
> I can only dream in red
> The outside world is black and white
> With only one colour dead.

Unsurprisingly, the record was banned by the Directorate of Publications, limiting its impact and reach within South Africa, but it became a mainstay at anti-apartheid concerts around the rest of the world. Other stars also released specifically anti-apartheid records such as Stevie Wonder's 'It's Wrong (Apartheid)' and Eddy Grant's 'Gimme Hope Jo'Anna'. However, in 1985, Steven Van Zandt, the guitarist in Bruce Springsteen's E Street Band, brought together a vast collection of famous musicians in the same vein as Bob Geldof's Band Aid project the previous year, to record 'Sun City'. The pro-boycott record took aim at the Sun City Casino Resort in South Africa – technically a bantustan rather than *in* South Africa – which had played host to a roster of boycott-busting musical megastars from around the world. 'Sun City' included a staggering variety of famous names, including Bob Dylan, Lou Reed, Ringo Starr, Peter Gabriel, Run DMC, Bono, Ronnie Wood, Pete Townsend, Herbie Hancock and many more. Together, they were billed as Artists United Against Apartheid.

The song is perhaps the most '80s-sounding record ever made, with drums that sound like they were recorded in an aircraft hangar, pop synths and stadium guitars. Coming in at more than seven minutes long, it's a punishing listen, save for Miles Davis's interesting contribution. A good half of it is the ensemble singing 'Nah, nah, nah, nah, nah, nah / I ain't gonna play Sun City.'

While it hasn't aged well, the song itself isn't really the point. Van Zandt was a passionate spokesperson against apartheid and assembled a remarkable array of influential voices who drew a line in the music industry between those who would support the cultural boycott and those who wouldn't.

However, when it comes to anti-apartheid songs, 'Nelson Mandela', written by Jerry Dammers and recorded by the Special AKA, with lead vocals by Stan Campbell, is by some distance the best. And I don't just mean the best anti-apartheid song. I mean the best protest song about anything, full stop. Released in 1984, it is more upbeat than most and includes an instantly catchy and simple chorus – 'Free Nelson Mandela!' – that would go on to be sung by vast crowds of protesters in London, South Africa and then around the world. Its success is down to it not just having a powerful and simple message, but it being a genuinely great song in its own right. Its magic is that it manages to be extremely catchy while never becoming annoying; the perfect recipe for a song with a message that needs to hook people instantly but not drive them mad on repeat playing.

Dammers spearheaded Britain's musical contribution to the international anti-apartheid struggle. In the UK, activists focused on advancing the cultural boycott and targeting Margaret Thatcher's government for its vocal opposition to financial and commercial sanctions against South Africa. This was nothing new, with Britain having consistently shielded South Africa, even using their veto power to block UN attempts to impose sanctions upon the apartheid regime.[73] This extended to the 1963 United Nations arms embargo, which was circumvented by Britain through the indirect licensing of South African firms.[74] However, by the 1980s, Thatcher's obstinate refusal was widely condemned at home and prompted exasperation and angered criticism from the Commonwealth.[75]

By the middle of the decade, British artists and musicians had caught up with their American counterparts. Dali Tambo contacted Jerry Dammers after hearing 'Nelson Mandela' and encouraged him to launch Artists Against Apartheid in the UK.[76] A flurry of gigs were organised across the country, culminating in a huge festival on Clapham Common in south London in the summer of 1986. An estimated 250,000 turned out to see Big Audio Dynamite (the new band from the Clash's Mick Jones), Hugh Masekela, Boy George, Billy Bragg, Princess, Sting, Sade, the Communards, Gil Scott-Heron, Paul Weller and Peter Gabriel among others. ANC representative Thabo Mbeki read a message from Desmond Tutu to the gathered crowds: 'Our children are dying, our land is burning and bleeding. I call on you, the people of Britain, in God's name to appeal to your government to apply sanctions against the evil system of apartheid.'[77]

Building on the momentum of Clapham, the entrepreneur Tony Hollingsworth proceeded to organise a concert to mark Mandela's seventieth birthday at Wembley Stadium in June 1988. The event not only filled Wembley, but was broadcast in at least sixty-seven countries to an estimated audience of 600 million people.[78] The line-up on the day is too long to list, but included superstars like Dire Straits, Eurythmics, George Michael, Joe Cocker, Whitney Houston and Miriam Makeba.

The television broadcast of the concert proved controversial, with the BBC being accused by a group of Conservative MPs of 'giving publicity to a movement encouraging the ANC in terrorist activities',[79] while in the United States, Fox News censored explicit references to apartheid and Mandela, billing it instead as 'Freedom Fest – A Concert for the Freedom for the World'.[80] Despite this, it proved a huge success and further raised global consciousness about the plight of Mandela and the evils of apartheid. When asked if Mandela knew about the concert, his lawyer, Ismail Ayob, said: "I've been told he knows and is enthusiastic about it. I'm certain that the noise you hear tomorrow he will hear too.'[81]

The tangible impact of concerts such as these is always hard to measure. How many of those who packed into Wembley Stadium or watched around the world on TV had their minds changed? Beyond the money raised, did it actually put pressure on the South African regime? In the case of the Wembley concert, it seems that the answer is, in fact, 'yes'. The ANC website noted how:

The worldwide campaign for the release of Nelson Mandela and political prisoners made a decisive contribution ... One event in particular symbolised that campaign – the 'Nelson Mandela 70th Birthday Tribute' ... The ANC owes an enormous debt of gratitude to the artists and performers and all those who made that event possible.[82]

Mandela himself, when speaking at a second Wembley concert in 1990, just fifty-four days after his release, said:

> I would like to take advantage of this occasion to extend our special thanks to the artists of the world who have, for many years, lent their talents to the common effort to end the apartheid system. We thank you especially for what you did to mark our seventieth birthday. What you did then made it possible for us all to do what we are doing here today.[83]

Of course, while concerts and protest songs undoubtably played an important role in raising international awareness and put pressure on the regime, it was the struggle of Black people in South Africa that actually brought down apartheid. In 1983, more than 400 organisations came together to form the United Democratic Front, which organised rent boycotts and strikes. Then, in 1985, the ANC shifted strategy towards a 'people's war' that linked guerrilla activity to mass mobilisation.[84] The result showed whites that any existing sense of security was fragile. Some, including even young army conscripts, decided to join the struggle against apartheid.[85]

The ferocity of Black resistance in the 1980s might not have been sufficient to topple the regime, but it forced an impasse and made the country ungovernable. With time, it became unavoidably clear that that negotiations with Mandela and the ANC were an inevitability. As early as 1984, there were attempts by national intelligence figures inside the government to make contact with the ANC and, in November 1985, minister of justice Kobie Coetsee first met with Mandela. Negotiations continued via sporadic meetings for the next four years, resulting in his release on 11 February 1990. However, while the world rejoiced at the newsreel images of Mandela walking to freedom, the work to build a new South Africa had only just begun. Negotiations to end apartheid formally began that year and culminated in democratic election in April 1994, following which Mandela became president.

Music might not have brought down apartheid, but there are few examples in history of it being more important to a political struggle. At a time when Black and coloured people were treated like animals, music was a way to reaffirm their humanity. In the prison cells of Robben Island or Number 4, they sang to escape the conditions imposed upon them. As they marched and protested, they sang to steel themselves and then sang again to mourn those cut down by bullets and batons. Musicians in exile played to dull the pain and recapture a fleeting moment of home, but also raised awareness of the plight of their brothers and sisters. Then, finally, musicians around the world came together to lend their voice to the struggle, pressuring their own governments and isolating South Africa's. Music didn't bring down apartheid, but I'm not sure its demise could have happened without it.

EIGHT

Kyiv Calling:
Musical Resistance in Ukraine's War Against Invasion

Recommended Listening:
Valentin Bibik – 'Crying and Prayer'
Mykhailo Starytsky and Mykola Lysenko – 'Nich yaka misyachna' (What a Moonlit Night)
Pavlo Zibrov – 'Я так хочу додому' (I Want to Go Home So Much)
Clasps – 'Peacedove'
Lostlojic – 'Space Bus (DMX Krew Remix)'
Poly Chain – 'Leopard 2A4'
Beton – 'Kyiv Calling'

–

As I NEARED THE Ukrainian border, the motorway emptied. The bustle of traffic that had weaved around us on the road leaving Krakow slowly fell away as cars turned off into the monotonous expanse of the dank Polish countryside. By the time the crossing appeared on the horizon, the bus had the road to itself. As we pulled into the austere, corrugated-iron checkpoint, I saw a group of American GIs, stars-and-stripes patches Velcroed to the sleeve of their combat fatigues. They were directing a slow procession of Ukrainian soldiers towards waiting buses, presumably off to be trained in Poland.

My bus driver rested his head on the wheel, a clear sign that he was expecting a long wait and that I should too. He flicked on the radio, and a mournful ballad crackled through the speakers. I hurriedly pulled out my phone and opened Shazam, the song recognition app, and a jumble of Cyrillic letters popped up. I copied them into my translation app to discover it was by the Ukrainian baritone pop singer Pavlo Zibrov. The song, translated as 'I Want to Go Home So Much'[1], dripped with longing and pain, none of which was lost in translation:

Scattered around the world, separated families,
The heart is used to ache, drinks the news drop by drop,
what can be heard from the son over the roar of the shells,
Did the houses survive the hailstorms?[2]

It was undoubtably cheesy music, the type I'd not ordinarily entertain, but reading the lyrics from my phone while sat at the Ukrainian border, it was hard not to be moved. It was just days away from the one-year anniversary of the start of the full-scale Russian invasion and it was easy to imagine that the Ukrainian soldiers boarding the buses, loaded heavy with two rucksacks, a sleeping bag, a floor mat and a helmet, and with boots slung around their neck, understood the sentiment of Zibrov's song better than I ever could.

The crossing took two hours, a stamp on each side of the border, and was uneventful – save for a young man being ordered off the bus and firmly ushered into an office, not to return before our coach departed. Just a few hours later, we pulled into a wet and windswept Lviv as the sun was setting.

The first thing I noticed was how dark the city was. Street lamps, along with the usual punishing floodlights that ordinarily illuminate a city's grand monuments, statues and streets, were turned off, likely part of the country's efforts to significantly reduce energy consumption. Despite being hundreds of miles from the front line, Lviv was littered with tiny reminders of the war. Ornate church windows hidden behind metal covers and emergency generators outside bars and restaurants served as a reminder that, even this far west, Russian bombs had landed with fatal effect.

The Old Town's status as a UNESCO World Heritage site is well deserved with its mixture of eastern and western European architecture looming over quaint, cobbled streets. I popped into a small bar where a squat man with an ill-considered combover first played an accordion, then the piano, both with consummate skill. I sang along as he thundered through a raucous version of 'Bella Ciao'. Originally an Italian folk song lamenting the harsh working conditions in the paddy fields of northern Italy, it became an anti-fascist anthem after being adopted and modified by Partisan fighters during World War II. It felt an apt choice, no doubt a nod to Ukraine's current resistance fighters. As he thumped out the last few stirring notes with gusto, I drained my glass and made for the station to board the overnight train to Kyiv, nervous about what I would find when I arrived.

I must admit to knowing almost nothing about Ukrainian music before the trip. I had heard of Kalush Orchestra and their song 'Stefania' following their victory at the 2022 Eurovision Song Contest, but that was about it. Interestingly, their mix of contemporary music with elements of traditional Ukrainian folk was a tradition I would encounter a great deal on my trip. It didn't make me enjoy the song any more, but it did help me to understand it as part of a musical trend that was a result of the war.

The idea for my Ukraine trip came after attending a lecture-concert titled 'Yiddish Glory: The Lost Songs of World War II' at Birkbeck, University of London, a few weeks before. The event featured a lecture from Anna Shternshis from the University of Toronto and songs performed in Yiddish by Grammy-nominated singer Psoy Korolenko. The occasion breathed life back into a series of songs written by Jews during the Holocaust and recently discovered in the Vernadsky Ukrainian National Library. It was a touching evening which explained how music was used by Ukrainian Jews as a way to document their experiences, raise their spirits and continue to live.

An almost throwaway comment by Shternshis revealed that she had given an online lecture to students at the University of Mariupol during the ongoing siege of the city and that they empathised with the messages of resistance in the songs she talked about. It was at that moment that I realised it was impossible to write a book about the role of music in resistance movements and not travel to Ukraine to explore what musicians were doing right now during Russia's war of aggression. I found myself on the night train to Kyiv just a few weeks later.

The train vibrated into life with a clunk, then a thud – du dum, du dum – and crept out of Lviv station at 22:44 on the dot. Even during a war, their trains beat those back home when it came to cleanliness and punctuality. We trundled through dimly lit suburbs, flashes of damp streets illuminated by sporadic yellow lights. In just fifteen minutes, darkness had engulfed the train, total blackness punctured only by occasional flickers on the horizon. Unsure what to expect when light returned, I was gently rocked to sleep by the wobble of the carriage. I woke early, still heading east, and the rising sun revealed a dour, flat and seemingly endless landscape. The countryside looked like a faded watercolour, a wintery scene painted with a limited palate of grey, brown and yellow. Churches, with glistening, golden domed roofs, provided the only splashes of colour.

I stepped off the stuffy night train, made hot by human breath and bubbling water urns, and into the dramatic chill of the Kyiv morning. The escalators leading down from the platforms into the grand baroque entrance hall thronged with men in camouflage on their way to board trains to the front. The departure screens flashed with names of once-unfamiliar cities made familiar by evening news updates of bloody fighting: Kherson, Donetsk, Mykolaiv . . . Large black netting was hung in front of the main station window to stop lethal shards raining down on passengers in the event of a missile strike. The need for this precaution was made plain upon exiting the station and seeing the battered remains of the nearby Samsung skyscraper, its once-glistening blue glass stripped away and its innards exposed. A few months earlier, in October 2022, a Russian missile landed some 150 metres from the building, but the blast ripped open its right side. Since I had crossed the border, Ukraine had felt relatively normal, but upon leaving Kyiv-Pasazhyrskyi station, it was clear this was a country at war.

—

Ukraine is a country that straddles the East-West divide, often pulled in both directions simultaneously. It is the bridge between Eurasia and Europe, a thoroughfare through which people, ideas and trade have passed for 'generations'.[3] It is also a land sadly accustomed to occupation and the crimes that can accompany it. For centuries, it has been claimed by central European and Eurasian empires, being ruled from St Petersburg, Vienna, Warsaw, Istanbul and Moscow. 'Each of the empires claimed land and booty, leaving its imprint on the landscape and the character of the population and helping to form its unique frontier identity and ethos,' argues the historian Serhii Plokhy.[4] The twentieth century gave little respite to its citizens, with bloody periods of Nazi and Soviet rule, starvation, genocide and oppression. Yet, through all this, Ukrainians survived unbowed, steeled by a determination to rule themselves, to make their own mistakes, to shape their own nation.

Soviet rule lasted until December 1991, when Ukrainians went to the polls and voted for their independence, contributing to the Soviet Union itself dissolving just one week later. It was a chance to build a new nation and live up to the lines of the first stanza of their long-banned national anthem:

Ukraine's freedom has not yet perished, nor has her glory,
Upon us, fellow Ukrainians, fate shall smile once more.
Our enemies will vanish like dew in the sun,
And we too shall rule, brothers, in a free land of our own.

If only building a nation was as easy as singing an anthem. The following decades were turbulent, with democracy evolving only the shallowest of roots. In the general election of October 2004, Ukrainians thought they had a choice between twenty-four presidential candidates, the front runners being pro-reform candidate Viktor Yushchenko and pro-Russian candidate Viktor Yanukovych. Independent exit polls suggested a clear lead for Yushchenko, so Ukrainians were shocked when the official results announced Yanukovych as the surprise winner with 49.5 per cent of the vote. It had been rigged: people knew it and then leaked telephone intercepts of Yanukovych's team proved it. Outraged Ukrainians flooded onto the streets, some 200,000 gathering in Maidan, Kyiv's Independence Square, for what became known as the Orange Revolution. Ukrainians had to fight for democracy again and the number of protestors swelled to half a million.[5] The Constitutional Court annulled the result and Ukrainians returned to the polls, this time electing Yushchenko, whose 'road to the transformation of Ukraine led through the European Union'.[6]

The administration which followed disappointed many after the hope that had been inspired by its troubled birth. While Yushchenko's government ended the tradition of persecuting political opponents and ushered in new freedoms for the media, disquiet remained, in part due to his failure to combat widespread corruption and a sense of continuing unfairness in Ukrainian society.[7] The hoped-for union with Europe also stalled, due to both a cautious approach by the European Commission and important players such as Germany having economic and political concerns regarding the ongoing expansion of the EU.

By the time Yushchenko left office in 2010, many Ukrainians felt disillusioned and bitterly disappointment that the promises of the Orange Revolution had not been realised. Citizens remained sceptical about the robustness of Ukraine's young democracy, with 40 per cent expecting vote-rigging at the 2010 elections.[8] However, despite these disappointments, many continue to credit Yushchenko with helping to manifest a distinct and robust Ukrainian identity through a greater understanding of the country's history. '[He] relentlessly tried to educate his people and the world about Russia's efforts to destroy the Ukrainian nation,' wrote the journalist David Kirichenko.[9]

In February 2010, Yanukovych won the general election and set Ukraine on a path that ultimately led to war. Upon victory, he began to centralise power in the office of the president of which he was head. Most significantly, though, he once again turned Ukraine's gaze towards Moscow rather than Brussels, a decision that ultimately turned political disquiet into revolutionary protest.

Yushchenko had begun negotiations with the EU to create a free economic zone and visa liberalisations, a move, the historian Tony Judt describes as an attempt to assert its Europeanness as a 'defence against history and geography alike. Summarily released from Muscovite empire, these post-imperial orphan states looked now to another "imperial" capital: Brussels'.[10] For many Ukrainians, 'identification with "Europe" was not about a common past, now well and truly destroyed. It was about asserting a claim, however flimsy and forlorn, upon a common future.'[11] When Yanukovych came to power, all that remained was the signing ceremony at an EU summit in Vilnius in November 2013. To the horror of many Ukrainians, he refused to sign, dashing their dreams of closer union with Europe.

Outrage led to action. Thousands of protestors, mainly young, descended on Maidan on the evening of 21 November, for what would grow into the so-called Revolution of Dignity. It was a cold and damp night; their sodden Ukrainian and EU flags hung heavy and limp. 'I came here because several days ago our government crossed out the future of Ukraine, and the aspirations of Ukrainian youth,' explained one protestor. 'I came here to defend my future, the future of my children, compatriots and country.'[12]

The crowds blew horns and chanted 'Ukraine is part of Europe!' After days of peaceful protest, the Berkut, Ukraine's special riot police, moved on the square. Flailing batons illuminated by camera flashes landed with dull thuds on the bodies of terrified protestors, with chants of 'Re-vo-lu-tion' snuffed out by police in military-style fatigues swinging batons indiscriminately. 'They didn't act like human beings,' said one protestor as blood dripped from his face and stained the floor of Maidan Square.[13]

These images of state thugs attacking young protestors shocked the nation and inspired new impetus. On 30 November, thousands more gathered to protest the violent scenes. The Ukrainian singer Ruslana Lyzhychko addressed the crowd: 'No bruise will be forgotten! No beating must be forgotten!' she declared. The crowd responded with chants of 'All together, we are strong!'[14] Numbers continued to swell and, on the eleventh day of protest, they held the March of the Million, at which another singer, Svyatoslav Vakarchuk, announced: 'I'd like all of us to remember that there are two European values – freedom and human dignity – and no one can deprive us of them. These are fundamental rights that we must fight for.'[15]

The proportion of Ukrainians with a positive view of Russia would drop from 80 per cent in January 2014 to less than 50 per cent by the September of that year, while support for joining the European Union had jumped from 39 per cent in November 2013 to 64 per cent. Perhaps most worryingly for Russia, support for joining NATO rose from one third of the population in April 2014 to more than half. The people of Ukraine were turning westward fast.[16]

The day after the March of the Million, barricades were erected in Maidan, creating a sense of permanence. Soon people occupied the Kyiv City State Administration building. A woman in a red coat played the piano and filled the grand hall with music as protestors began to dance. By mid-January 2014, however, a new level of violence rained down on those fighting for their right to look west. A draconian law designed to stifle protest and empower the police was passed, causing protestors to march on parliament. Clashes with the police took place to a pulsing drumbeat hammered on riot shields and burnt-out vehicles. The peak of the violence came in the middle of the following month. On 18 February, protestors marching towards parliament were stopped at Mariinsky Park. The police's rubber bullets had been swapped for real ones and the massacre began. The icy streets of Kyiv caught fire, with burning tyres throwing a black canopy over the city.

The footage of those days is staggering, showing nothing short of a warzone, with protestors in hard hats and carrying wooden shields facing off against police snipers. Over three days, at least seventy-seven people were dead: nine police and sixty-eight protestors.[17] By the end of the revolution, 125 people had been killed, sixty-five were missing and 1,890 had been treated for injuries.[18] The images shocked the world and the pressure for change became overwhelming. On the night of 21 February 2014, CCTV footage captured President Yanukovych fleeing Kyiv via helicopter. A subsequent vote in parliament removed him from office and he claimed asylum in Moscow.

The protests had worked. The people of Ukraine had defended the fragile rights they acquired after independence and had resisted returning to Russian domination. Anyone who watched footage of the courage of the Ukrainian people in Maidan over that bloody winter wouldn't be surprised by the nation's remarkable resistance to Russia's invasion years later. Sadly, however, jubilation was short lived. The people of Ukraine may have been looking towards Europe, but Putin had other ideas and, on 26 February, a band of armed men took control of the Crimean parliament. With the embers still smoking in Maidan, the Kremlin engulfed the whole peninsula.

By the spring, paramilitary units trained and funded by Moscow expanded into the Donbas region. Years of bloody fighting ensued and, by the spring of 2016, 9,000 lives had already been claimed. By the winter of 2022, vast Russian forces had amassed along the Ukrainian border, ready to escalate the conflict beyond most people's comprehension.

—

On 24 February 2022, Vladimir Putin launched his euphemistically titled 'special military operation'. Soldiers and tanks crossed into Ukraine from the north, east and south, and hurried towards Kyiv. A widely covered US intelligence report, released just days before the full-scale invasion, estimated that the Russian military could reach the capital within two days.[19] At that moment, the world, including myself, wildly underestimated the resolve and skill of the Ukrainian people. Death came not just from the armoured vehicles that rattled and grunted towards Kyiv, but also from above as missiles drenched Ukraine in molten hail. In towns and cities across the whole country, people burrowed underground, finding shelter from the missiles in basements, car parks and metro stations. In the first months of the war, these barren concrete cocoons were transformed into new homes, underground havens where life could go on.

In Kyiv, one small group of locals chose to take shelter within the thick brick walls of the city's most iconic nightclubs. 'Pack the most necessary things, charge your phones and power banks. Use this map of bomb shelters or come to the club. Together we are strong!' read the first message on the club's work chat on the morning of 24 February 2022.[20] Colloquially known as K41, the venue actually uses the ∄ symbol instead of a name, part of the long tradition of the coolest clubs and bars being awkward. Often described as Ukraine's answer to Berlin's techno mecca Berghain, K41 occupies a former brewery, a vast brick building in the north of the city. What it looks like inside remains more of a mystery; cell phone cameras are taped up on entry and photography is banned. It's part of the venue's commitment to creating a genuinely safe space for the queer community. 'There are many gay people there,' explained Volodymyr Baranovskyi, the Kyiv-based DJ and founder of the electronic music label Mystictrax. 'Everyone is naked or in some leather, or chains.'

I had contacted Volodymyr online after I came across a sixty-five-track compilation he compiled to raise money for defence initiatives. He enthusiastically agreed to meet me for a chat while I was in Kyiv and gave me the address of a bar that, as far as I could tell, also had no name. I walked up and down the same dark street for ten minutes trying to find the place. It's not easy to ask for directions to a place with no name; maybe that's the point. I tried several wrong bars, a random block of flats and a shop before I spotted a man with a stark bowl-cut rolling a cigarette in a dank alleyway with no lights on. It was Volodymyr.

Behind an unmarked door was a small underground bar. It was empty, save for the barman and a painfully cool man sipping a shot and playing with an old film camera. We took a seat, ordered a drink and attempted to talk over the unnecessarily loud music until Volodymyr's friend and collaborator DJ Taras Clasps joined us. He bowled in with a disarming and friendly energy, and began talking about the first day of the full-scale invasion with barely a prompt. 'Everyone was like "What to do? What to do? Let's meet in the club and figure out what to do next."'

With tanks fast approaching the outskirts of the city, people had a choice to make: grab what you could carry and flee or hunker down in Kyiv and hope the city's defences held. Some of the K41 team took the completely understandable decision to leave and boarded the packed trains heading west. Thirty of the club's 130 employees landed in Berlin, where they had networks in the music scene, relationships that had been forged on the dancefloor.[21] Some of those who remained in Kyiv, including Taras, decided to turn the nightclub into a bomb shelter. It soon grew into a mini community with more than 100 people sleeping and eating where they once partied.

The new community of the club staff, DJs, musicians, family, friends and even pets stayed huddled together until April 2022 when the Kyiv region was finally liberated. The first two months of the war saw ground fighting come perilously close to the capital with a strategic airbase being captured by Russian special forces just fifteen kilometres away from Kyiv's historic city centre. Daily life was soundtracked by exploding rockets, with fires on the horizon illuminating the dark winter nights.

Unsurprisingly, for both Taras and Volodymyr, those early days of the war were about survival, not music. 'I was so affected by war that, for me, doing music was something inappropriate at that moment,' explained Taras. 'I was more into volunteering, collecting money, helping soldiers and stuff like that. Every time I thought I should maybe work on something, it didn't feel right. I had this inner dilemma because electronic music is associated with partying, like having a good time, so I stayed away.'

But as the Ukrainian forces pushed back the Russian invaders and the rockets abated for long enough for people to tentatively emerge from their subterranean homes, Ukraine's cultural scene also came up for air. 'It was like total chaos for a few months,' said Taras, 'but then we started to crawl out. It was safer than it was, so I started to work on things.'

While some musicians, such as Taras, understandably found it impossible to create during the traumatic early months of the war, others felt compelled to continue playing. While feverishly consuming press reports about Ukraine before my trip, I came across Vera Lytovchenko, a violinist for the Harkiv State Academic Opera and Ballet Theatre and a teacher at the I.P. Kotlyarevsky Kharkiv National University of Arts. Vera realised that live music could bring comfort to people huddled underground. The city of Kharkiv, her home, had been under near-constant bombardment since the start of the Russian invasion. Images of the punished city echoed those of Dresden after World War II, with whole neighbourhoods surviving only in memories. I had hoped to visit Vera but with fierce fighting still raging in the east, travel there would have been unwise. At Lviv's main train station, I had seen dilapidated departure boards reading 'Kharkiv' in faded yellow paint and watched as a procession of soldiers boarded the train after a period of rest in the west. I felt lucky that I had the luxury of choosing to go no further than Kyiv.

Inspired by Vera's story but unable to visit in person, I contacted her via WhatsApp to find out more about her story. 'In the first weeks of the war,' she wrote, 'we weren't sure we would survive. We hid in basements, bomb shelters and underground stations. I was sure that I would never be able to play the violin again. I regretted that my profession was so useless.' That all changed when she saw a video of one of her students playing for her neighbours. 'They listened and became less scared and lonely. I realised that it was also a way to fight and help people.'

Vera was inspired to pick up her violin again, first in shelters, then in centres for displaced people and in hospitals for civilians and soldiers. Videos of her playing went viral and she was flooded with messages from around the world, which led to her beginning to raise funds for those affected by the war. 'It's a form of resistance to our enemies. Together with other people who continue their normal life, we show them and the whole world that we aren't scared. We are determined to fight for our lives and our culture, still remaining humans.' I asked if it was safe for me to write about her and her location. 'I've been in Kharkiv since the beginning of the war,' she answered defiantly, 'and I'm not going to leave.' While Vera created music in a totally different genre from that of Taras and Volodymyr, there were striking parallels between the way they all saw music not just as a comfort but as a weapon.

Many of the musicians who emerged from the bomb shelters after months underground were not the same as when they had entered them. 'For a few weeks, music stopped, maybe months,' explained Volodymyr. 'Then people who didn't go to be military guys started producing something to resist the enemy, some kind of resistance music.' As the fighting on the frontline raged, a cultural front was launched by musicians and artists all across the country. Their weapons of choice were not tanks, missiles or guns, but paint brushes, guitars, drums and, for the electronic musicians, beats.

Yet just as with the musicians who made it, the music that began to emerge was shaped by the conflict. 'There was a whole wave started of tracks that have this message of like "Fuck off Russia", like "Get out of this territory",' explained Taras with fire in his eyes. 'People even made tracks using the words of Zelensky.' 'It was very inspiring for people,' nodded Volodymyr before Taras interjected again: 'It's like "Russian military are shit, fuck off".' This time there was anger in his voice.

The war inescapably permeated the musical landscape, changing musicians' purpose and subsequently their sound. 'A lot of my friends produced music for dance floors,' explained Taras of their pre-war creativity. 'It had no certain message, except "Have a good time, listen to the beat." That was it. But now it's like, everyone is naming their tracks after the situation, or are connected to the situation.'

Empty glasses now cluttered the table in front me. I offered another round. 'Maybe some shots, just to get warm,' joked Taras, pointing beyond the walls to the punishingly cold night closing around us. We made a toast – 'To the victory!' – before draining a sweet red liquor in one and resuming our conversation without a pause.

'Every day, I'm feeling like I must do something for the culture,' said Volodymyr, 'to keep the fire burning. I chose the cultural war. I started to understand that everything is political and culture is political too.' His first volley was the creation of a vast compilation of electronic music alongside Sasha Zakrevska, who creates music as Poly Chain.

'She texted me: "What you doing?"

'"Nothing, just sitting in a basement under a missile attack."

'"Let's create a compilation and collect donations for volunteers."'

The result was the sixty-five-track *РАЗОМ ЗА УКРАЇНУ / Together for Ukraine,* which included tracks by a range of Ukrainian and international electronic musicians, including the legendary French producer Laurent Garnier. Released as a collaboration between Volodymyr's label Mystictrax and another of the city's underground labels, Standard Deviation, the compilation raised more than €20,000 for non-military causes related to the war; the compilers were frustratingly aware that many Europeans wouldn't fund combat supplies. 'German people have money and they want to help us,' explained Volodymyr, 'but they don't want to buy guns. They still believe that if you bring more guns, you prolong the war.' 'But if you don't give them guns, they're going to lose,' added Taras with a touch of exasperation in his voice.

Volodymyr, using his DJ name Lostlojic, contributed his own hypnotic and pulsating acid house-inflected techno track, 'Sich 11', with its infectious squelchy synth line. Taras, aka Clasps, offered 'Scale Violence', an ominous, brooding and percussion-driven electronic track. It has the vibe of a dystopian movie or computer game soundtrack, which comes as no surprise when he explained the circumstances under which it was created. 'I actually made the track while staying in a shelter. I couldn't sleep properly and I had my laptop with me . . .' Since the start of the war, he had released this and another track, the Prodigy-like 'Peacedove', a satirical assault on those musicians calling for appeasement not victory. Its title sounds like the Ukrainian word for 'cunt'. 'I was super stressed,' he explained. 'I didn't sleep well. It was total madness. I can't even recollect how I did it.'

As Kyiv stabilised and the gaps between air raids became long enough for snippets of normal life to re-emerge, so too did opportunities for this new, more political music to be played to crowds. The same curfew that loomed over my evening with Volodymyr and Taras has forced club nights to be reimagined as day raves. Often happening underground, essentially in bomb shelters, all parties now raise money for the war effort. Both were adamant that no one would dare hold an event that didn't involve a collection, be it to fund a car or a drone, or to benefit victims of the war. 'During the party, you can spread some messages and thoughts,' said Taras. I asked whether they were scared at the thought of so many people gathered in one place when air raids were still so regular. 'Hopefully Russia don't target the parties,' smiled

Volodymyr. 'If a rocket lands, it won't be the first time Ukrainian culture would have to restart from the beginning.' He chuckled, half joking, half serious.

—

The morning after my evening with Volodymyr and Taras, I woke up, showered and headed out into the city's crisp morning sun. Life plays out in Ukraine to the daily wailing drone of the air raid sirens echoing and bouncing off buildings. Whenever they sounded, I frantically hurried to the nearest shelter, running past nonchalant locals made complacent by their regularity. Worst, for the locals, is the constant fear for loved ones fighting further east on the frontline. People dread the ping of their phone with more bad news.

The fact that I was there to mark an anniversary that almost no one predicted would happen made it all the more surreal. Ukraine had resisted beyond the expectations of most international commentators. Many Ukrainians, however, thought differently. Just days before the full-scale invasion, Illia Ponomarenko, writing for the *Kyiv Independent,* defiantly delcared: 'To many in the world, Ukraine seems to be doomed. But I refuse to accept that the situation is that simple ... Ukraine's fall is not predestined – at least, as long as the nation does not accept it without a fight. We in Ukraine might be standing on the gate of hell, but Russia is facing a nightmare as well.'[22] He proved to be correct.

In the first month of the war, Ukrainian troops only just held back Russia's dart for the capital. Armoured vehicles flanked by infantry rolled into Kyiv's suburbs, setting up checkpoints and cutting off access to utilities, internet and food. As of 9 March, the United Nations Office for Human Rights had recorded 1,424 civilian casualties since the start of the invasion, but conceded numbers were likely to be 'considerably higher'.[23] News began to emerge of atrocities and mass graves from the town of Bucha, just thirty kilometres northwest of Kyiv. 'Nearly every corner in Bucha is now a crime scene,' said Richard Weir of Human Rights Watch, 'and it felt like death was everywhere.'[24]

By the end of March 2022, however, the Battle of Kyiv had remarkably been won, with Russian soldiers forced to withdraw. Throughout April, Ukraine forced Russia back further. By June, Zelensky announced that Russian forces held just 20 per cent of Ukrainian territory, but that the losses on both sides had been terrible. The horrifying scenes from the siege of Mariupol shocked viewers of the evening news.

By the autumn, Ukrainian forces began to rout Russia from parts of the south and east of the country. In September, the Kharkiv counter-offensive saw steady gains until the city was fully liberated on 3 October. More hope followed when, in November, after eight months of brutal Russian occupation, the southern city of Kherson was also liberated. By the time I arrived in Kyiv for the one-year anniversary, estimates suggested that 200,000 Russian troops had been killed or wounded, while Ukraine had seen some 100,000 killed or wounded in action, and 30,000 civilian deaths.[25] The frontlines had solidified into a bloody crescent along the easternmost territory of the country.

I had no intention of heading east to the frontline. I'd been stupid enough to bungle my way towards danger in Iraq in 2014 for a previous project and had vowed never to be so foolhardy again. But I had heard stories that even there, in the trenches around Bakhmut and Solidar, people were using music as part of their resistance. Before travelling to Ukraine, I had read about a punk band who were still making records, despite one of their members being a military surgeon on the frontline. The band, Beton, had made international headlines after releasing 'Kyiv Calling', a thumping cover version of the Clash's 1979 classic single 'London Calling' with altered lyrics, including lines like 'Phony Putinmania has bitten the dust'.

I dropped the band a message online and received an almost immediate response. There was no way to meet in person, so I arranged a phone call with the band's guitarist Andriy Zholob one evening while I was in Kyiv.

With time to kill until the call, I spent the day hanging around St Michael's Golden-Domed Monastery in central Kyiv, trying to catch a glimpse of the far-right Italian prime minister Giorgia Meloni on her fleeting visit to the city. After hours of waiting, she whistled past me and a gaggle of waiting press, and was ushered quickly into the grand Intercontinental Hotel by a phalanx of security guards. Her presence in the city, designed to show solidarity with Zelensky and Ukraine, illuminated the complexities of the political situation. I had been appalled when Meloni, leader of the fascist Brothers of Italy party, had won the 2022 Italian election. It was another landmark in the uneven but terrifying rise of the European far right. Yet here she was, in Kyiv, reiterating Italian support for Ukraine in front of the world's media. It's hard to judge Zelensky when he's locked in a war for the very existence of Ukraine and Italian supplied arms are required, but it made me feel uneasy nonetheless. A luxury on my part, perhaps.

With Meloni safely in her room away from the prying media, I grabbed a much-needed cup of tea in the bar of the hotel before perusing the small gift shop just off the lobby. The first thing I noticed was a stack of Azov Battalion badges proudly displayed on the counter.

'Aren't they Nazis?' I asked the assistant.

'No!' he shot back. 'That's just Russian propaganda.'

I knew it wasn't. Formed in 2014, the notorious Azov Battalion has been fighting Russia since Putin's annexation of Crimea and were involved in the recapturing of Mariupol. The group, who use the Nazi Wolfsangel symbol as its emblem, was formed by the white supremacist Andriy Biletsky and has attracted neo-Nazis from Ukraine and abroad. Reports suggest that the group has increasingly been de-Nazified and depoliticised, but the attendant's claims that the Nazi roots of the regiment are a Russian fabrication simply isn't true.

'Do you like Nazis?' the attendant asked. It wasn't a question I was expecting in the giftshop of the Intercontinental Hotel. Before I could respond with 'Obviously not!', he had slid open a secret panel at the back of his shelves and pulled out a plastic folder full of German SS propaganda posters from World War II. I stood open-mouthed as he nonchalantly thumbed through rabidly antisemitic posters glorifying the Third Reich. He had seemed offended at my suggestion that the Azov Battalion included Nazis, but was seemingly unperturbed by selling posters of Hitler. He then opened a second folder, this one filled with Soviet Union propaganda. For him, it seemed that both Nazi and Soviet posters were simply historical curiosities, a way to make money during a time of war. My experience in the gift shop was an interesting window into the complex 20th-century history of Ukraine, one marred by both Soviet and Nazi rule. The end of the Ukrainian-Soviet war in 1921 saw most of its territories incorporated into the Ukrainian Soviet Socialist Republic, which was a founding member of the Union of Soviet Socialist Republics (USSR). Despite representing just 2.7 per cent of the land area of the USSR, it was home to 18 per cent of its population, generating nearly

17 per cent of its Gross National Product. This included 60 per cent of its coal reserves, a majority of its titanium and a vital 40 per cent of Soviet agricultural output by value.[26]

The importance of Ukraine to the Soviet Union was reflected in the fact that two of its leaders, Nikita Khrushchev and Leonid Brezhnev, both hailed from eastern Ukraine. The historian Tony Judt argues that 'for much of its history as a Soviet republic, Ukraine was treated as an internal colony: its natural resources exploited, its people kept under close surveillance (and, in the 1930s, exposed to a programme of punitive repression that amounted to near-genocide)'.[27]

The arrival of the Nazis in 1941 offered no respite. Erich Koch, the Reichscommissar for Ukraine, declared in Kyiv that he would 'get the last ounce out of this country. I have not come here to spread bliss. I have come here to help the Führer.'[28] While seen as liberators from Soviet rule by some Ukrainians, vast numbers faced persecution and death. On the eve of the Nazi invasion, the country was home to one of the largest Jewish populations on the continent. By the end of the war, 1.5 million Jews has been killed by the Nazis in Ukraine, often with the help of local collaborators.[29]

By the end of World War II, Kyiv 'was a smouldering ruin'[30] and Soviet rule returned. Despite not having fully recovered from the 'deliberate, punitive famine of the thirties', it once again faced mass starvation in the winter and spring of 1946–47.[31] Stalin's reign of terror followed and, by the time Khrushchev came to power, nearly half of all people languishing in gulags, labour camps or in exile had come from Ukraine.[32] The wounds caused by decades of Soviet occupation have yet to fully heal in the minds of many Ukrainians, resulting in some viewing the Nazi 'liberation' from Soviet rule in the 1940s in a dangerously positive light.

It was through this complex history, and the ongoing debates around it, that I first heard of the Ukrainian punk bank Beton. I saw an article on the *NME* website titled 'Billy Bragg and Beton speak out on Ukrainian band's use of Stepan Bandera imagery'. It explained how Bragg had issued a statement after images emerged of Beton members wearing Ramones-inspired T-shirts reading 'Banderas'.

'This is deeply troubling,' said Bragg. 'Stepan Bandera was a far-right Ukrainian politician who collaborated with the Nazis during the occupation of Ukraine and whose followers were complicit in the Holocaust . . . The knock-on effect of this has been to allow Putin to smear all those who want a democratic Ukraine, free from Russian influence, as neo-Nazis.'

In Ukraine, many view Bandera as a national hero, a liberator, and an especially attractive historical touchstone during the ongoing Russian war of conquest in Ukraine. But this has led some to downplay or ignore his own extreme politics. The Organisation of Ukrainian Nationalists (OUN), of which Bandera was head, collaborated with the Nazis due to their shared anti-communism and antisemitism, while its armed wing, the Ukrainian Insurgent Army, took part in the murder of Poles and Jews on a terrifying scale in Belarus, eastern Galicia and Volhynia.[33] During the Maidan protests of 2013–2014, some promoted a positive myth of Bandera and even called themselves 'banderivtsi'.[34] The historian Serhy Yekelchyk has explained that 'it can be argued that, in the course of the EuroMaidan Revolution, the image of Bandera acquired new meaning as a symbol of resistance to the corrupt, Russian-sponsored regime, quite apart from the historical Bandera's role as a purveyor of exclusivist ethno-nationalism'.[35] This adoption of a sanitised image of Bandera's is what Beton appeared to have done.

It is this combination of Ukrainian collaboration during World War II and the veneration of figures like Bandera by some that oppose Russian influence, further enhanced by the role of Nazis in units such as the Azov Battalion, that under-pinned Putin's absurd claims that his war of conquest was in fact an effort to 'denazify' Ukraine. In a TV address on the day of his bloody incursion, he explained that his goal was 'to protect the people that are subjected to abuse, genocide from the Kiev regime' and to 'demilitarize and denazify Ukraine'.[36] The claim was a transparent attempt to manipulate history, distort reality and manufacture a justification for his invasion. Ukraine undoubtably has a fascistic element within its society, but so too do all European states. Also, Putin's 'denazification' claim conveniently ignores the fact that president Volodymyr Zelensky is Jewish, lost family members in the Holocaust and was democratically elected. Putin isn't seeking to remove Nazism. He's trying to remove democracy.

The *NME* article explained that Beton and Bragg had spoken, prompting another statement from both parties. Beton's read:

We need a national debate about our history and contested memory – exactly the kind of debate that would be impossible in Putin's Russia. The invader is trapped by the past, seeing everything through the prism of Russia's imperial history. We in Ukraine are seeking to escape that prison and to take our place as a nation free to make our own democratic choices . . . This is the Ukraine that we are fighting for – a place where people of all races and creeds can work together to build a nation free from oppression.

Bragg clearly accepted Beton's explanation and published his own response following a conversation with Andriy Zholob.

'Beton,' he said, 'are an anti-fascist band and he [Andriy] asked me to help craft a statement that both apologised for the offence caused by the shirts and clarified the band's position.' The resulting apology seemed sincere and it is certainly true that many nations hammer out nuance and chip away controversies while sculpting the statues to their heroes. Some months later, when I was interviewing Bragg in Oxford, he told me: 'In the end, you either focus on their history or take them on face value, what they are playing and what they are trying to do, and I decided to take them on face value and what they were doing. And they're aware now that some people had issues with some of their symbols. They're aware of that now and, with that awareness, they will be cognisant of the way they go forward. But in their struggle to stand against an invader, I'm as much in solidarity with them as I was opposed to the Iraq War.'[37]

However, it was another element of the press coverage around the scandal that interested me most. Several pieces mentioned in passing that Andriy was a doctor working on the frontline and it was this that I wanted to speak with him about most. Safely out of the bitter wind and tucked up in my Kyiv hotel room, I called him via WhatsApp. He spoke with an endearing warmth; 'Hey Joe. Nice to meet you, man!' He was based in Kramatorsk, right in the thick of the fighting in the east, and was working as a military surgeon, operating on wounded servicemen brought back from the frontline. 'Almost every day we have some Russian missile shots here,' he explained as the line fuzzed and popped.

Beton had been a ska-punk band for thirteen years, but failed to make the impact they had hoped for. 'To be truthful, no one here in Ukraine needed ska-punk,' Andriy joked. It wasn't until they adopted a harder sound that they started to get some success. I asked him what music he listens to. 'I like very much, Killswitch Engage. I like very much, Death. A metal band that is called Death. Obituary. I like very much Biohazard, I like Slayer and so on.' Only a metal fan based on the frontline of a warzone would need to clarify he meant a band called Death, not death itself. I couldn't help but notice all his influences were named after an element or outcome of war.

At the outbreak of the full-scale invasion, all three members of Beton threw themselves into the war effort. As a father of three, Bohdan Hrynko didn't receive a call to arms, so instead crossed into Poland each week to bring back vehicles to be used in the war. Oleg Hula had a company that rented sound and stage equipment, so he converted his storage warehouses into volunteer stores for clothes, medicine and other materials. However, Andriy was called to serve and answered. 'I decided I am not one of those guys who will hide away from the opportunity to protect his land. I absolutely understand my place in the war. I do not shoot but I take care of the wounded.'

Remarkably, it seems that none of the band felt that the war would stop them playing, 'We had decided anyway that we will continue to play because musicians need to practise,' he explained. 'If we stop practising, then we stop our band.' For Andriy, this meant taking his guitar to war with him. 'When I went to the army, I brought my acoustic guitar here to the front. I'm playing here. I practise every day. And I create new songs. I record them on my phone camera and send them to my boys from the band. And they are doing rehearsals. I know the band is alive and we are working with new material.' I thought back to when I was in a band as a younger man and we would cancel rehearsals because we were simply hungover.

Andriy talked enthusiastically about the genesis of 'Kyiv Calling', the idea coming from a press officer of the Free

Ukraine Resistance Movement as a way to raise funds. Andriy worked up a demo of 'London Calling' with altered lyrics – 'one of the punk rock hymns', as he described it – and it was sent off to the remaining members of the Clash for their approval. To Beton's surprise and delight, they responded straight away, wishing them well. There was one caveat: 'Please just don't do harm to our song.'

The subsequent release garnered global media coverage and raised significant sums in donations. As we talked, however, it became clear that, for Andriy, punk rock could achieve much more than raising money for the war; it was an art form that could be weaponised. He felt that punk music was not separate from the war effort, but part of it. He has received letters from soldiers saying they listen to his songs on their way into battle. 'It brought me to tears,' he explained. 'My friends who are near me in the trenches, they are playing our music in their cars when they are going to positions. It's a very powerful thing for me. I have a feeling that we made something. We played some music that helps guys who are walking nearly to their death. It gives them some powerful feelings.

'Here on the battlefield, I absolutely understand that wounds, blood, mud and so on, is everywhere. And if we can somehow, for a little moment, clear it with our music, with our lyrics, I suppose it is a very powerful armour for somebody. Like a shield for somebody. And maybe it's also powerful. It's not a gun, but is something like a flag for someone going into battle.' He compared it to medieval soldiers marching to war with horns: 'Punk rock is battle music.'

Our conversation had inspired and upset me in equal measure. I was very aware that, in the following days, I would leave Kyiv and head home to London while he would still be in the trenches, dealing with unimaginable scenes of death and mutilation. I had a choice to go home. He didn't. But what would he do once the war was over?

'We are waiting for the victory because we absolutely believe that, after victory, we will make the greatest shows of our lives. We are dreaming about touring, about meeting friends, about finding new friends among musicians, meeting famous musicians. You know, I'm forty-two and I still say that when I grow up, I will be a punk rock musician. I want to play punk rock. And I want to live in a safe and normal world.'

—

With my trip nearly over, I had one last stop before the long train back to Lviv and then to the safety of Poland. I had been told that if I really wanted to understand what it meant for music to be used as a 'weapon' against Russia, I needed to visit the radio station on the frontline of the cultural war. Hidden away in a warehouse near the Dnipro River, I heard Gasoline Radio before I saw it. Too cold to walk, I took a taxi down into the Podil district of the city. To reach this low-lying part of Kyiv, the cab negotiated winding roads that offered panoramic views across the harbour, the bitter wind making the river violently jerk until it foamed white.

As I stepped out the car, I heard a faint, dampened repetitive thump. Like a radio being tuned, the music grew louder and crisper with each step towards it. I entered a shabby courtyard and followed my ear up a metal staircase. The door opened itself as I knocked, so I let myself in, walked along a short corridor and found the source of the music. Two DJs with their backs to me were broadcasting deafening techno from a set of decks. A woman approached me, looking completely unphased that I had let myself in. 'I'm looking for Oleksii,'

I offered. She nodded, walked me through to a small office with cases of vinyl records along one wall, gave me tea, and assured me he would be with me soon.

Oleksii Makarenko launched Gasoline Radio on 22 February 2022, just two days before the full-scale Russian invasion. The timing couldn't have been worse and, with the residents of Kyiv being forced into bomb shelters for the first months of the war, the broadcasts were paused until May. Since then, it has evolved into a central focal point for Ukrainian electronic and experimental music, as well as giving a platform to an eclectic mix of genres, ranging from traditional Ukrainian folk and classical to electronic, ambient, avant-garde and experimental music.

Oleksii came into the room, dropped his bag, shook my hand and said I could ask whatever I wanted. With his strong moustache and trendy clothes, he would look at home on the streets of Williamsburg in Brooklyn, but as he began to speak, there was a seriousness and intensity that made clear he took his music extremely seriously. Like everyone I spoke with on my trip, he found the early months of the war a painful challenge. 'On the first day after the full-scale war, I was thinking I should play some music to relax, but when I put my earphones on, I started to hear a phantom siren. It was a terrible feeling.' I asked him what it was like trying to launch a new radio station during such a difficult time. 'It was a nightmare, because we had nothing. Really nothing.' Yet he was philosophical about the situation, explaining that the circumstances required ingenuity. The struggle created energy and demanded commitment.

Gasoline Radio had a clear mission from the start: to provide a platform for new, alternative, young and, perhaps most importantly, Ukrainian artists. 'Before the war everyone was trying to be like a Berlin DJ, like a Berlin club, and no one spoke about Ukrainian culture.' Oleksii is part of a movement of musicians and artists who, affected by the war, are consciously trying to seek out, preserve, create and amplify Ukrainian art. 'We want to make a new image of Ukrainian culture, but it should be based on our history and our heritage.' This ethos is reflected in Gasoline Radio's varied broadcast schedule. 'That's why on one hand we are focusing on Ukrainian traditional music, some classical music, and on the other hand it's electronic music, experimental music, some new sounds of Ukraine.'

Importantly, this renewed focus on domestic and folk sounds isn't merely patriotism during war, but actually has a clear practical objective. Oleksii becomes animated as he dives into the history of hundreds of years of Russian dominance and its suffocating effect on Ukrainian culture – and thus, by extension, Ukrainian's sense of national identity. 'It's super important for different territories of Ukraine – Donbas, like Luhansk, like Kharkiv – because until now a lot of people haven't understood that they are living in Ukraine.' Oleksii explained how many who grew up in the Russian-speaking areas in the east of the country lacked an understanding of a distinct Ukrainian culture and identity. That changed with the Russian invasion, when people began to explore their own history and traditions, consciously seeking out their own roots. 'Finally, we started to look inside. All the artists, all the little scenes now focus on Ukrainian culture firstly.'

It is this project of rediscovery and cultural education that Gasoline Radio is part of. 'So now we are trying to find some songs, some folklore from these regions to show that they are historically Ukrainian territories. If you try to learn some music, folklore, you will see the difference between us and Russia.

And in that way, it is a real weapon.' Aleksii described it as 'putting up cultural borders'. The sentence jarred with me at first. Music and art have always been about tearing down borders, exploring human commonalities that can bring us together, not segregate us from each other. But what Oleksii was saying made sense. Putin has long asserted that Ukrainians and Russians are 'one people', while former Russian president Dmitry Medvedev described Ukrainians as 'people who do not have any stable self-identification'.[38]

In the eyes of many Russian nationalists, the thirteenth-century kingdom of Kievan Rus', which extended from the Carpathians to the Volga with Kyiv its capital, is an integral part of the identity of Russia and its empire. The notion that Ukraine is a constituent part of the Russian nation goes back to the founding myth of modern Russia, with Kyiv being seen as the 'mother of Russian cities'. The first Russian printed history textbook, dating from 1674, popularised this myth and, throughout the imperial period, many viewed Ukrainians as 'Little Russians'. This changed following the 1917 Bolshevik Revolution when a distinct Ukrainian culture was acknowledged, even if this didn't extend to political independence.[39]

This idea that Ukraine isn't a real country with its own histories, culture, folklore and traditions, but merely a part of Russia, has been a central justification for Putin's bloody war of expansion. What Oleksii means by 'putting up cultural borders' is actually a declaration of independence in the face of conquest. It's about rediscovering their own musical roots to find out what makes Ukraine a distinct nation. An external threat has made them look inwards. He mentioned a friend of his from Donbas who only recently realised that he had grown up in a Russian-dominated world. 'When he came to Kyiv, he said, "Fuck! I live in a Russian world. Russia on TV, Russia on the radio, Russia everywhere. For me, it's hard to understand why I am Ukrainian." So I showed him. "Just look at this. This is your traditional music from your region. These are your rituals from your region." And he went, "Wow, now I can form my Ukrainian identity."' This is what Olesksii meant when he said, 'For now, music is a weapon'. I finally understood it.

This conscious effort to uncover traditional Ukrainian folk traditions has taken numerous forms. The Gasoline Radio team have organised what Oleksii called 'expeditions', where he travels around Ukraine seeking out local folk music, hunting for arms for his cultural war. Interestingly, this mood of redis-covery has begun to change the sound of contemporary Ukrainian music. Before the war, most electronic musicians made music that would work on the dancefloor of a major European club, but now they make music for themselves, for Ukrainians. Freed from the expectations of the booking agents of Berlin nightclubs, there has been an explosion of variety within the music scene. 'Diversity in music is our resistance from now on,' Oleksii confirmed.

The most interesting trend is electronic musicians introdu-cing Ukrainian folk music and instruments into their compositions, rooting their contemporary music in the coun-try's past. This was something that Volodymyr Baranovskyi and Taras Clasps had also told me the night before. 'I'm starting to look inside the country's music,' Volodymyr had explained. 'I'm starting use more samples with traditional instruments. It's quite a simple way to bring deep roots and culture into electronic music.' He went as far as to argue that this fusion brought about by the war has led to the creation of a whole new genre of electronic music in Ukraine.

—

I caught a taxi back to Kyiv-Pasazhyrskyi station and looked up at the shattered blue glass of the Samsung skyscraper one last time. Just as when I arrived, the station pulsated with groups of soldiers buying snacks for their journeys to war. An elderly woman with a wind-aged craggy face, hair tucked tightly under a scarf, placed her hands tight on both sides of a soldier's face. Her child was off to war. They hugged, her holding on until he forced open her grasp. As he turned towards the platform, she made the sign of the cross repeatedly as the doors closed with a clunk. I knew I had the luxury of choosing to head west and not east, the very thing that the protestors at Maidan Square had been fighting for nearly a decade before.

When I got back to London, I dropped my bag and instantly walked over to my record player. At the end of my evening with Volodymyr in Kyiv, he presented me with a vinyl copy of his 'Distant Star' EP. I placed the record on the deck, flicked down the arm and listened as the familiar crackle of vinyl filled my flat. I sat on my sofa listening and thought back to one of the last things Volodymyr said to me before we parted: 'I don't feel that I can even collect vinyl at my home because I don't know if I will live here in one month. I was a huge fan of collecting everything, vinyl too, but now I don't know what to do with this stuff because nobody knows where you will be the next day.' I listened to the song, looked at my own record collection and properly realised how lucky I was to be safe in London.

Encore

WHEN I SET OUT on this journey to explore how music has been used as a form of resistance, I had one question in mind: Can music really change the world? As I have reached the end, I've decided that it can't. Not on its own, anyway. Music doesn't change the world; it's people that do that. But what I've realised is that for many millions of people, living at different times and places, it was music that made them feel that change was possible. When various regimes and systems of oppression consciously sought to dehumanise, de-individualise, break and oppress them, it was music that gave them the strength to go on.

While travelling through various countries seeking out these stories of resistance, I have been constantly reminded by the remarkable similarities I've found in such different places. The music itself often couldn't sound more varied, but our impulse to find comfort and strength in it seems universal. At first, like most people, my understanding of what counts as resistance music was limited to explicitly political protest songs. There's no doubt that there are countless remarkable examples of people writing songs that express their anger, highlight injustice and demand change with their words. But I've come to realise that it is much broader than that. I've come to understand that resistance music itself doesn't have to make any mention of politics at all. Sometimes just listening to something you are told you aren't allowed to is enough.

For those behind the Iron Curtain, the regime could be opposed by listening to love songs written by the Beatles. In Ukraine, I heard of people using instrumental music to assert their identity and difference in the face of attempts to erase them. In the case of movements like Two-Tone in Britain, it was a way to demonstrate our commonalities, a living blueprint of a multicultural society. In Congo Square in New Orleans, or on the streets of Johannesburg, slaves once gathered on their fleeting days of rest to play music. In the prison cells of Robben Island or the Fort Prison in South Africa, they sang to assert their humanness in the face of their inhuman treatment. In places as different as Dublin and Rio de Janeiro, they gathered around tables in pubs and bars to play songs that remind them of their history. While electronic music in Ukraine, Afrobeat in Nigeria and trad in Ireland sound totally different, all have been used to make people dance away their fears and feel alive. It seems that no matter what the music sounds like, it can be, and has been, used by people as a form of resistance.

In today's world, where authoritarian politics are on the rise and the politics of prejudice and hatred are still far from disappearing, where mass mobilisation will be required to meet the challenges posed by climate change and ever-growing inequality, and where unity and collectivism will be required to heal our ever more polarised societies in the digital age, we need resistance music as much now as ever.

I hope this book has reminded you that music can be a weapon in our arsenal in the fight for social justice, equality and freedom, and a way to unnerve, rattle and even scare those people, movements and regimes that seek to oppress and control us. Don't just pick up an instrument or put on a record next time you are happy or sad, in love or heartbroken, but also when you are angry. When you see something is unfair, unjust or just plain wrong, there will be a record out there that will make you feel that you have the power to do something about it. And if there isn't, try making one yourself.

I'm more convinced than ever that music is a central ingredient of what makes us human. Every society that has yet been discovered has found an outlet for our species' unavoidable response to rhythm. No other animal matches their body's movement to the beat, except for us who rely on it to find joy, love, sex or even a means to communicate with a god. This means it is a universal human impulse that unites us, giving it the power to inspire another fundamental impulse – freedom. Now is the time to look back and learn the lessons from those musical rebels who came before us, to get inspired to fight back and most importantly . . . to dance.

References

INTRODUCTION

1. Grattan Flood, *A History of Irish Music* (Dublin: Brown and Nolan, 1905), 1.

ONE – *The Tri-Coloured Ribbon*

1. 'Musical Metropolises: where to plug into the sound of a city', Lonely Planet, online, 18 July 2018
2. Dermot McLaughlin, 'This Glorious Instrument', *The Journal of Music*, online, 6 April 2015
3. Grattan Flood, *A History of Irish Music* (Dublin: Brown and Nolan, 1905), 30.
4. Stephen R. Millar, *Sounding Dissent: Rebel Songs, Resistance, and Irish Republicanism* (Ann Arbor: University of Michigan Press, 2020), 4.
5. Samuel Beckett quoted in: Rod Sharkey, 'Singing in the Last Ditch: Beckett's Irish Rebel Songs', Vol. 3, Intertexts in Beckett's Work / Intertextes de I' oeuvre de Beckett (1994), 67.
6. Georges Denis Zimmermann, *Irish Political Street Ballads and Rebel Songs: 1780-1900* (Geneve: Imprimerie La Siréne, 1966), 10.
7. Thomas Turino, *Music as Social Life: The Politics of Participation* (Chicago: University of Chicago Press, 2008), 33.
8. Quoted in Grattan Flood, 1.
9. Micheál Ó Siochrú, *God's Executioner: Oliver Cromwell and the Conquest of Ireland* (London: Faber and Faber, 2008), 2.
10. Quoted in J. C. Beckett, *The Making of Modern Ireland 1603–1923* (London: Faber and Faber, 1981), 13.
11. F. J. M. Madden, *The History of Ireland* (Abingdon: Teach Yourself, 2007), 25.

12. Ibid, 26–27.
13. S. J. Connolly, *Oxford Companion to Irish History* (Oxford: Oxford University Press, 2002), 135.
14. Beckett, 102.
15. Ó Siochrú, 1–2.
16. Ibid,1.
17. T. Crofton Croker, *The Historical Songs of Ireland* (London: Percy Society, 1841), quoted in Georges Denis Zimmermann, *Irish Political Street Ballads and Rebel Songs* (Geneva: Imprimeria La Sirene, 1966), 35.
18. Alvin Jackson, *Ireland, 1798–1998: Politics and War* (Oxford: Blackwell, 1999), 1.
19. Thomas Bartlett quoted in Jackson, 1.
20. 'The Declaration and Resolution of the Society of United Irishmen of Belfast', quoted in Jackson, 12.
21. Jackson, 17.
22. Millar, 22.
23. James McHenry quoted in Millar, 22.
24. Millar, 16.
25. Ibid, 16.
26. Song by Theobald Wolfe Tone, *Northern Star*, 18 July 1792, quoted in Millar, 17.
27. Robert Emmet, 'Speech from the Dock', 19 September 1803, quoted by encyclopedia.com
28. Millar, 20.
29. Robert Emmet quoted in Millar, 22.
30. Zimmermann, 9.
31. Ibid, 9
32. Ibid, 10.
33. *The Nation*, 14 January 1843, quoted in: Zimmermann, 10.
34. Thomas Davis, quoted in Millar, 35.
35. Zimmermann, 10.
36. *Irish Independent*, 10 July 1911, quoted in Bríona Nic Dhiarmada, *The 1916 Irish Rebellion* (Cork: Cork University Press, 2016), 5.
37. *Daily Telegraph*, 10 July 1911, quoted in Dhiarmada, 5.
38. J. C. Beckett, 435.
39. Beckett, 437.
40. *Songs and Poems of the Rebels Who Fought and Died for Ireland in Easter Week, 1916* (Dublin, c.1917).
41. The English-language version of 'La Carmagnole' taken from the singing of Frank Harte and Karen Casey, quoted in Nic Dhiarmada, 82.

42. 'Easter Rising 1916: Almost 500 people die in six days of fighting', BBC News, online, 24 March 2016.
43. James Connolly Heron, 'Foreword', in Mat Callahan (ed), *Songs of Freedom: The James Connolly Songbook* (Oakland: PM Press 2013), ix.
44. Theo Dorgan, 'Preface', Callahan, v.
45. James Connolly, *Songs of Freedom* (New York: J. E. C. Donnelly, 1907), 2, in Callahan, 14.
46. James Connolly, 'A Love Song', in Callahan, 21.
47. Nora Connolly quoted in James Connolly Heron, 'Foreword', in Callahan, x.
48. Richard Parfitt, *Musical Culture and the Spirit of Irish Nationalism, 1848–1972 (New York: Routledge, 2019).*
49. Ibid.
50. Jack Sheehan, 'Irish rebel music is more than an endorsement of the IRA, it is a way to connect with the past', *The Irish Times*, 28 May 2023.
51. Ibid.
52. Pádraig Mac Lochlainn, Twitter (@PadraigMacL, 7 September 2023).
53. Nick Reilly, 'The Wolfe Tones' rebel song 'Come Out Ye Black and Tans' tops UK and Ireland iTunes charts', *NME*, 9 January 2020.
54. Deirdre Falvey, 'Come Out Ye Black and Tans: Think you know what it's about? You probably don't', the *Irish Times*, 20 March 2019.
55. Paul Ainsworth, 'Wolfe Tones announce Dublin stadium gig after attracting record crowds at Electric Picnic festival', the *Irish News*, 6 September 2023.

TWO – *A Change is Gonna Come*

1. 'African American Spirituals', Library of Congress, online.
2. W. E. B. Du Bois, quoted in Reilan Rabaka, *Civil Rights Music: The Soundtrack of the Civil Rights Movement* (Lanham: Lexington Books, 2016), 53.
3. Lawrence Levine, 'Slave Songs and Slave Consciousness' in Stephen Duncombe, *Cultural Resistance Reader* (London: Verso, 2002), 217.
4. Ralph Ellison, *Shadow and Act* (New York: Random House, 1964), 247–248.
5. Francis Davis, *The History of the Blues: The Roots, the Music, the People* (Cambridge: Da Capo Press, 2003), 2.
6. Ted Gioia, *How to Listen to Jazz* (New York: Basic Books, 2016), 74–75.

7. Gioia, 95–96.
8. Steven Mintz, 'Historical Context: Facts about the Slave Trade and Slavery', The Gilder Lehrman Institute of American History, online.
9. 'How did the slave trade end in Britain?', Royal Museum Greenwich, online.
10. Thirteenth Amendment to the U.S. Constitution: Abolition of Slavery, 31 January 1865.
11. Bob Zeller, 'How Many Died in the American Civil War?', History.com, online, 23 August 2023.
12. Khushbu Shah and Juweek Adolphe, '400 years since slavery: a timeline of American history', the *Guardian*, 16 August 2019.
13. 'Black Codes', History.com, online, 1 June 2010 (updated 29 March 2023).
14. 'What Was Jim Crow?', JimCrowMuseum.ferris.edu, online.
15. Khushbu Shah and Juweek Adolphe, op cit.
16. Leonard Feather, quoted in David Margolick, *Strange Fruit: Billie Holiday, Café Society, and an Early Cry for Civil Rights* (New York: Ecco Press, 2001).
17. 'Our Legacy', tootsies.net, online.
18. Julian Bond quoted in 'The Civil Rights Movement: Grass Roots Perspectives', Franklin Humanities Institute at Duke University, online.
19. Horace Randall Williams and Ben Beard, *This Day in Civil Rights History* (Montgomery: NewSouth Books, 2009), vii.
20. Peter Guralnick, *Sweet Soul Music: Rhythm and Blues and the Southern Dream of Freedom* (New York: Harper & Row, 1986), 21.
21. Guralnick, 18.
22. Guralnick, 7.
23. 'Songs and the Civil Rights Movement', The Martin Luther King, Jr. Research and Education Institute, online.
24. Tom Taylor, 'When Sam Cooke sang Bob Dylan's "Blowin in the Wind" at the Copa', *Far Out*, online, 28 November 2021.
25. Jacob Uitti, 'Behind the Mysterious Death of Sam Cooke', *American Songwriter*, online, 2022.
26. Aretha Franklin and David Ritz, *Aretha: From These Roots* (New York: Villard Books, 1999), quoted in; Anna North, 'The political and cultural impact of Aretha Franklin's "Respect", explained', *Vox*, online, 17 Augst 2018.
27. Rochelle Riley, 'Jesse Jackson on Aretha Franklin's civil rights legacy: "She was the fountain of love"', *USA Today*, 16 August 2018.
28. B. B. King, quoted in Davis, 43.
29. Davis, 43.

30. Allyson Hobbs, 'The Lorraine Motel and Martin Luther King', *The New Yorker*, 18 January 2016.
31. Andria Lisle, 'I Know a Place', *Wax Poetics*, issue 11, Winter 2005.
32. Guralnick, 354–355.
33. Booker T Jones quoted in Guralnick, 355.
34. Isaac Hayes quoted in Guralnick, 355.
35. Paul Zollo, 'On the Saddest Song Ever Written, "Why (The King of Love is Dead)"', *American Songwriter*, 2020.
36. Guralnick, 10.
37. Andrew Reese, 'Soul Music and the Civil Rights Era: Breaking the Racial Barrier', *Facing Today*, online, 29 March 2015.
38. 'From Memphis to Muscle Shoals: Unity Rocked by Violent Tragedy' podcast, American Hit Network, 20 December 2016.
39. Reese, op cit.
40. 'Black Power', National Archives, archives.gov, online.
41. Sarah Pruitt, 'How the Black Power Movement Influenced the Civil Rights Movement', history.com, online, 27 July 2023.
42. Vann R. Newkirk II, 'King's Death Gave Birth to Hip-Hop', *The Atlantic*, online, 8 April 2018.

THREE – *Tropicália*

1. Gilles Peterson and Stuart Baker, *Bossa Nova: Bossa Nova and the rise of Brazilian Music in the 1960s* (London: Soul Jazz Records, 2010), 5.
2. 'Brazil: the collapse of the empire', Britannica.com, online.
3. Ibid.
4. '1954: Brazilian President Found Dead', BBC News, online.
5. Marcos Napolitano, 'The Brazilian Military Regime, 1964–1985', *Latin American History*, online, 26 April 2018.
6. Ibid.
7. John McEvoy, 'Britain's Hidden Hand in Brazil's 1964 Coup D'Etat', *Declassified UK*, online, 10 November 2021.
8. Tom Phillips and Caio Barretto Briso, 'Bolsonaro supporters fill Copacabana beach in yellow-shirted show of force', the *Guardian*, 8 September 2022.
9. Chris McGowan and Richard Pessanha, *The Brazilian Sound: Samba, Bossa Nova and the Popular Music of Brazil* (Philadelphia: Temple University Press, 1998), 21.
10. Angel Romero, 'Samba Brasileiro – A History', *World Music Central*, online, 1 July 2004.

11. Peterson and Baker, 5.
12. Caetano Veloso, *Tropical Truth: A Story of Music and Revolution in Brazil* (New York: Da Capo Press, 2003), 45.
13. 'The bossa's not so nova', *Melody Maker*, 17 November 1962, 7.
14. Max Jones, 'Bossa? It is Brazilian', *Melody Maker*, 1 December 1962, 10.
15. Tom Jobin quoted in Denis Milstein, 'Revival Currents and Innovation on the Path from Protest Bossa to Tropicália' in Caroline Bithell and Juniper Hill (eds), *The Oxford Handbook of Music Revival* (Oxford: Oxford University Press, 2014), 424.
16. Peterson and Baker, 8.
17. Veloso, 146.
18. Peterson and Baker, 7.
19. Veloso, 22.
20. Ibid, 24.
21. Peterson and Baker, 6.
22. Ibid, 10.
23. 'The bossa bandwagon Not for me! Says Paul Desmond', *Melody Maker*, 24 November 1962, 9.
24. Chris Richards, '"Jazz Samba", landmark album recorded in DC church, turns 50', the *Washington Post*, 19 April 2012.
25. 'Bossa nova's here!', *Melody Maker*, 1 December 1962, 1.
26. McGowan and Pessanha, 70.
27. Denis Milstein, 'Revival currents and innovation on the path from protest bossa to Tropicália' in Caroline and Hill, 425.
28. Peterson and Baker, 10.
29. Beatriz Miranda, 16/05/2023, 'Bossa nova pioneer Carlos Lyra at 90: "We wrote songs about our reality: the beach, sun and love stories"', the *Guardian*, 16 May 2023.
30. Ibid.
31. Ibid.
32. Veloso, 5.
33. Veloso, 6.
34. Stuart Baker, sleevenotes to *Tropicália: A Brazilian Revolution in Sound* (London: Soul Jazz Records, 2006).
35. Ibid.
36. Tárik de Souza, sleevenotes for *Grandes Nomes: Caetano*, quoted in McGowan and Pessanha, 84.
37. 'Paul Weller – What's in My Bag?', YouTube.
38. Baker, op cit.
39. 'The story of Hélio Oiticica and the Tropicália movement', *Tate*, online.
40. Veloso, 27.

41. McGowan and Pessanha, 84.
42. Christopher Dunn, *Brutality Garden: Tropicália and the Emergence of a Brazilian Counterculture* (Chapel Hill: The University of North Carolina Press, 2001), 3.
43. Veloso, 20.
44. Ibid, 7.
45. Ibid, 30.
46. 'The Story of Tropicália in 20 Albums', *Pitchfork*, online, 19 June 2017.
47. Dunn, 109.
48. 'The Story of Tropicália in 20 Albums', op cit.
49. Ibid.
50. Dunn, 73.
51. 'The Story of Tropicália in 20 Albums', op cit.
52. Caetano Veloso quoted in Dunn, 147.
53. Ibid, 147.
54. Dunn, 2.
55. Marisa Alves de Lima, 'Marginália: Arte e cultura na idade de pedrada,' O Cruzeiro, 14 December 1968. Cited in Dunn, *Brutality Garden*, 149.
56. 'The Story of Tropicália in 20 Albums', op cit.
57. Kamille Viola, 'Bohemia is Reborn: Famous for its music, Bip Bip plans to return to programming, *Veja Rio*, online, 18 October 2021.

FOUR – *Zombies!*

1. Alex Hannaford, 'He was in a godlike state', the *Guardian*, 25 July 2007.
2. All direct quotes in these last two paragraphs come from Fela Kuti, quoted in Carlos Moore, *Fela: This Bitch of a Life* (Chicago: Chicago Review Press, 2009), 243–244.
3. Toyin Falola and Matthew M. Heaton, *A History of Nigeria* (Cambridge: Cambridge University Press, 2014), 197–198.
4. Fela Kuti in *Sunday Punch*, 25 June 1978, quoted in Michael E. Veal, *Fela: The Life and Times of an African Musical Icon* (Philadelphia: Temple University Press, 2000), 167.
5. Guy Arnold, *Africa: A Modern History, 1945–2015* (London: Atlantic Books, 2017), 19.
6. Falola and Heaton, *A History of Nigeria*, 158.
7. Richard Bourne, *Nigeria: A New History of a Turbulent Century* (London: Zed Books, 2015), 97.
8. Tony Allen with Michael E. Veal, *Tony Allen: An Autobiography of the Master Drummer of Afrobeat* (London: Duke University Press, 2013), 11.
9. Ibid, 11.

10. Falola and Heaton, 158.
11. Arnold, 189.
12. Bourne, 121.
13. Arnold, 213.
14. Arnold, 399.
15. Ibid, 399.
16. Ibid, 398.
17. Ibid, 398.
18. Ibid, 401–402.
19. Ibid, 401.
20. Veal, 140.
21. Allen with Veal, 111.
22. Veal, 144.
23. Veal, 154.
24. Fela Kuti quoted in Moore, 137.
25. Allen with Veal, 114.
26. Fela Kuti quoted in Moore, 138.
27. Majemite Jaboro, *The Ikoyi Prison Narratives: The Spiritual and Political Philosophy of Fela Kuti* (self-published, 2012).
28. Fela Kuti in Moore, 138.
29. Ibid, 140.
30. Veal, 155.
31. Fela Kuti in Moore, 140.
32. 'Kalakuta Museum', felakuti.com
33. Paul McCartney, quoted in '"Band on the Run" Sessions in Lagos', the-paulmccartney-project.com
34. Paul McCartney interviewed by Rick Rubin in the documentary series *McCartney 3,2,1,* 2021.
35. John Collins, *Fela: Kalakuta Notes* (Middletown: Wesleyan University Press, 2009).

FIVE – *White Riot*

1. Ronán Hession in Niall McGuirk and Michael Murphy, *Punks Listen* (Dublin: Hope Publications, 2022), 203.
2. Robert Winder, *Bloody Foreigners: The Story of Immigration to Britain* (London: Little, Brown, 2004), 267.
3. Panikos Panayi, *Immigration, Ethnicity and Racism in Britain, 1815–1945* (Manchester: Manchester University Press, 1994), 10.

4. Ibid, 23.
5. Peter Hennessy, *Never Again: Britain 1945–51* (London: Jonathan Cape, 1992), 440.
6. Mike Phillips and Trevor Phillips, *Windrush: The Irresistible Rise of Multi-Racial Britain* (London: Harper Collins, 1998), 6.
7. Numbers from Winder, 270.
8. Winder, 272.
9. Winder, 265.
10. R. Donaldson, 'A Jamaican in London', *Checkers Magazine*, 1:1, July 1946, 23.
11. Ruth Glass, assisted by Harold Pollino, *Newcomers: The West Indians in London* (London: Centre for Urban Studies & George Allen & Unwin, 1960), 31.
12. Zig Layton-Henry, *The Politics of Immigration: Race and Race Relations in Postwar Britain*, (London: Wiley-Blackwell, 1992), 47.
13. Interview with Cecil Holness in Phillips and Phillips, 89.
14. Phillips and Phillips, 92.
15. Poll cited in Anthony Chater, *Race Relations in Britain* (London: Lawrence and Wishart, 1966), 7.
16. Sam Selvon, *The Lonely Londoners* (London: Penguin Books, 2006; first published Alan Wingate, 1956), 61.
17. Selvon, 20–21.
18. Layton-Henry, 37.
19. Dilip Hiro, *Black British, White British: A History of Race Relations in Britain* (London: Paladin, 1992), 36.
20. Edward Pilkington, *Beyond the Mother Country: West Indian and the Notting Hill White Riots* (London: I. B. Tauris, 1988), 106.
21. Ibid, 106-124.
22. Mark Olden, *Murder in Notting Hill* (Winchester: Zero Books, 2011), 26–27.
23. For further details on the riots in Notting Hill and Nottingham, see Pilkington, 106–124, and Olden, 26–36.
24. *Melody Maker*, 6 September 1958, cited in Rich Blackman, *Babylon's Burning: Music, Subcultures and Anti-Fascism in Britain, 1958–2020* (London: Bookmarks, 2021), 44–45.
25. Blackman, 44.
26. Blackman, 52.
27. Enoch Powell, 'Rivers of Blood' speech made at the Conservative Political Centre, Birmingham, UK, on 20 April 1968.

28. David Olusoga, *Black and British: A Forgotten History* (London: Pan Books, 2017), 513.
29. Figures from *Searchlight* magazine quoted in Richard Thurlow, *Fascism in Britain: From Oswald Mosley's Blackshirts to the National Front* (London: I. B. Tauris, 2009), 260.
30. Chris Sullivan, Review: '*White Riot* – Why We Need a New Rock Against Racism', *Byline Times*, online, 30 April 2020.
31. David Bowie interview in *Playboy*, September 1976.
32. Andrew Marzoni, 'The Fairest Soul Brother in England', *The Baffler*, online, 26 February 2019.
33. *NME*, 14 August 1976, 43.
34. Eric Clapton letter to *Sounds*, published in Daniel Rachel, *Walls Come Tumbling Down: The music and politics of Rock Against Racism, 2 Tone and Red Wedge* (London: Picador, 2016), 13.
35. Roger Huddle quoted in Rachel, 17.
36. Red Saunders quoted in Rachel, 17.
37. *Temporary Hoarding*, issue 1, 1977.
38. Ibid.
39. *Temporary Hoarding*, issue 4, Winter 1977.
40. Rich Blackman, 123.
41. Ibid, 135.
42. *Temporary Hoarding*, issue 4, Winter 1977.
43. David Renton, *Never Again: Rock Against Racism and the Anti-Nazi League, 1976–1982* (Abingdon: Routledge, 2019), 169.
44. Joe Strummer in *Temporary Hoarding*, issue 1, 1977.
45. Mick Jones in *Temporary Hoarding*, ibid.
46. Jonny Rotten in *Temporary Hoarding*, ibid.
47. Poly Styrene in *Temporary Hoarding*, issue 4, Winter 1977.
48. Tom Robinson in *Temporary Hoarding*, ibid.
49. David Childs, *Britain Since 1945: A Political History* (sixth edition), (London: Routledge, 2006), 216.
50. Pauline Black interview, 'The Two-Tone Movement' radio documentary, BBC Radio 6 Music, 29 May 2008.
51. Horace Panter, *Ska'd for Life: A Personal journey with the Specials* (London: Sidgwick and Jackson, 2007), 62.
52. Phill Jupitus, 'Foreword' in Panter, xi.
53. Interview with a fan, 'The Two-Tone Movement', op cit.
54. Adrian Thrills interview, 'The Two-Tone Movement', op cit.
55. Rankin Roger, interview, 'The Two-Tone Movement', op cit.

56. Pauline Black interview, 'The Two-Tone Movement', op cit.
57. Pauline Black interview, '2 Tone: The Sound of Coventry', BBC TV documentary, 30 September 2021;
58. Horace Panter interview, 'The Two-Tone Movement', op cit.
59. Alexis Petridis, 04/06/2020, 'The 100 Greatest UK No 1s: No 2, The Specials – "Ghost Town"', The *Guardian*, 4 June 2020.
60. Ibid.
61. Red Saunders quoted in: Blackman, 168.
62. Rachel, xxii.

SIX – *Back in the USSR*

1. Winston Churchill, 'Iron Curtain' speech, 5 March 1946.
2. Hugh Seton-Watson referenced in R. J. Crampton, *Eastern Europe in the Twentieth Century – And After* (Abingdon: Routledge, 2008), 211.
3. J. B. Borev quoted in Davide Dolce, 'Censoring Music in the Age of Stalin: Shostakovich and Stravinsky', *Calliope Arts Journal*, 2 April 2021.
4. Ibid.
5. Stephen Coates (ed), *Bone Music: Soviet X-Ray Audio* (London: Strange Attractor Press, 2022), 11.
6. Ibid, 11.
7. Ibid, 14.
8. Ibid, 24.
9. Maxim Gorky, *The Music of the Gross*, quoted in 'Totalitarian Jazz', x-rayaudio.com, online, 20 April 2018.
10. Coates, 14–15.
11. Ibid, 15.
12. Danny Lewis, 'When Rock Was Banned in the Soviet Union, Teens Took to Bootlegged Recordings on X-Rays', *Smithsonian Magazine*, online, 10 December 2015.
13. 'Stilyagi - Fashion, Youth Counterculture and Individuality in the Communist Soviet Union', *The Costume Society, online*.
14. Danielle Chiriguayo, 'Bone Music: '"Strange dusty records" give hope that change can come', krcw.com, 6 February 2023.
15. Coates, 51.
16. Ibid, 31.
17. Ibid, 50.
18. Mikhail Farafanov and Rudy Fuchs, quoted in Coates, 62.

19. Stephen Coates interview, 'X-Ray Audio: The Documentary', YouTube, 2016.
20. Synopsis, 'The Beatles: The Cavern Club – August 22, 1962': Synopsis', mubi.com
21. Leslie Woodhead, *How the Beatles Rocked the Kremlin: The Untold Story of a Noisy Revolution* (London: Bloomsbury, 2013), 11.
22. 'How the Beatles Rocked the Kremlin', BBC TV *Storyville* documentary, 2009.
23. Kolya Vasin in Woodhead, 76.
24. 'The Beatles Museum on Pushkinskaya, 10 has been sealed. The deceased Kolya Vasin left a note', Fontanka.ru, online, 2 September 2018.
25. Artemy Troitsky interview in 'How the Beatles Rocked the Kremlin', op cit.
26. Artemy Troitsky in Woodhead, 18.
27. Vladimir Pozner interview in 'How the Beatles Rocked the Kremlin', op cit.
28. William Jay Risch (ed.), *Youth and Rock in the Soviet Bloc: Youth Cultures, Music, and the State in Russia and Eastern Europe* (London: Lexington Books, 2015), 1.
29. Timothy W. Ryback, *Rock Around the Bloc: A History of Rock Music in Eastern Europe and the Soviet Union* (Oxford: Oxford University Press, 1990), 152.
30. Stas Namin, in Woodhead, 29.
31. Ryback, 153–154
32. Ryback, ibid, 153–154.
33. Ibid, 155.
34. Ibid, 155.
35. Ibid, 56.
36. Ibid, 96–97.
37. Ibid, 99–100.
38. Dan Stone, *Goodbye To All That?: The Story of Europe Since 1945* (Oxford: Oxford University Press, 2014), viii.
39. Ibid, ix.
40. Mary Craig, *The Crystal Spirit: Lech Walesa and His Poland* (London: Hodder & Stoughton, 1986), 128.
41. Crampton, 360.
42. Craig, 127.
43. Ibid, 130.

44. Kevin McDermott and Matthew Stibbe (eds), *Revolution and Resistance in Eastern Europe, Challenges to Communist Rule* (Oxford: Berg 2006), 125.
45. Geoffrey Swain and Nigel Swain, *Eastern Europe Since 1945* (London: Macmillan, 1998), 168.
46. McDermott and Stibbe, 125.
47. Craig, 179.
48. Swain and Swain, 169.
49. Crampton, 375.
50. Ryback, 181.
51. Exhibition film shown at the European Solidarity Centre, Gdansk, Poland.
52. Ibid.
53. Tom Junes, 'Facing the Music: How the Foundations of Socialism Were Rocked in Communist Poland', in William Jay Risch (ed.), *Youth and Rock in the Soviet Bloc: Youth Cultures, Music, and the State in Russia and Eastern Europe* (London: Lexington Books, 2015), 246.
54. Ibid, 246.
55. Ibid, 247.
56. Exhibition film shown at the European Solidarity Centre, Gdansk, Poland.
57. Ibid.
58. Crampton, 380
59. Jon Elster, Introduction, in Jon Elster (ed.), *The Roundtable Talks and the Breakdown of Communism* (Chicago: University of Chicago Press, 1996), 3.
60. Crampton, 391.
61. Swain and Swain, 176.

SEVEN – *Free Nelson Mandela*

1. 'The History Behind the Kaapse Klopse', *Cape Town Magazine*, 2021.
2. Guy Arnold, *Africa: A Modern History, 1945–2015* (London: Atlantic Books, 2017), 331–332.
3. David Welsh, *The Rise and Fall of Apartheid* (Jeppestown: Jonathan Ball, 2009), 2.
4. Ibid, 3.
5. Arnold, 330.
6. Ibid, 330.

7. Ibid, 330.
8. General Smuts in Arnold, 330–331.
9. Welsh, 7.
10. Ibid, 47.
11. Arnold, 332.
12. Welsh, 52.
13. Arnold, 334.
14. Ibid, 335.
15. Ibid, 335.
16. Sarah Roller, 'District Six', historyhot.com, 24 November 2020.
17. 'The History of Langarm: Is This Dance Culture Still Alive in Cape Town?', CapeTalk, online.
18 Welsh, 121.
19. Ibid, 121.
20. Arnold, 50.
21. Welsh, 121.
22. Colonel Pienaar quoted in Arnold, 50.
23. Arnold, 50.
24. Nelson Mandela, *The Illustrated Long Walk to Freedom: The Autobiography of Nelson Mandela* (London: Little, Brown, 2001), 80.
25. Dr Seme quoted in Heidi Holland, *100 Years of Struggle: Mandela's ANC* (Johannesburg: Penguin Books, 2012), 29.
26. Welsh, 122.
27. Ibid, 122.
28. Ibid, 73.
29. Mandela, 80.
30. Ibid, 80.
31. Ibid, 81.
32. Ibid, 89.
33. Welsh, 128.
34. 'Truth Commission: Special Report – Modise Phekonyane', SABC News, online.
35. Suthentira Govender, 'Joburg has the most dollar millionaires in Africa, report shows', TimesLive, online, 19 April 2023.
36. Nelson Mandela, quoted on: 'Historical Insight', mandelahouse.com
37. Arnold, 564.
38. Ibid, 565.
39. Welsh, 101.
40. Arnold, 595.

41. Ibid, 595.
42. Ibid, 565.
43. Sign in the Hector Pieterson Museum, Orlando, Soweto..
44. Anne Schumann, 'The Beat that Beat Apartheid: The Role of Music in the Resistance against Apartheid South Africa', *Stichproben – Vienna Journal of African Studies*, Nr. 14/2008, 8. Jg., 20.
45. Ibid, 22.
46. Reyaaz Scharneck, '"Wathint' abafazi, wathint' imbokodo" (You Strike a woman, You Strike a Rock) – the battle cry of South African women', Community of Democracies, online.
47. Schumann, 23.
48. Ibid, 23.
49. Miriam Makeba with James Hall, *Makeba: My Story* (London: Bloomsbury, 1988), 1.
50. Makeba with Hall, 1.
51. Makeba with Hall, 98.
52. Nelson Mandela, 'Message from Mr Nelson Mandela on the passing of Miriam Makeba', Nelson Mandela Foundation, online, 8 November 2008.
53. Nelson Mandela quoted in Schumann, 23.
54. Welsh, 269.
55. Ibid, 269.
56. Lloyd Ross, 'The Rise, Fall and Resurrection of Shifty Records', shifty. co.za, December 2008.
57. Laura Brink, 'Voëlvry: South African's Rock 'n' Roll Revolution', Cherwell.org, 15 February 2023.
58. Ibid.
59. Ben Forrest, 'Louis Moholo: the leader of avant-garde jazz fighting against apartheid', *Far Out*, online, 10 January 2024.
60. 'Soul in Exile', *NME*, 18 June 1988, 25.
61. Ibid.
62. Ibid.
63. Ibid.
64. 'South Africa's Academic and Cultural Boycott', South African History Online, online.
65. Joe Taysom, 29/07/2020, 'When Gram Parsons Left the Byrds After Refusing to Perform for Segregated Audiences in South Africa', *Far Out*, online, 29 July 2020.
66. UN Declaration quoted in 'South Africa's Academic and Cultural Boycott', op cit.

67. Kelly Scanlon, 'Every Artist That Broke the Cultural Boycott of Apartheid in South Africa', *Far Out*, online, 8 October 2023.
68. Tim Jarvin, 'Taking the Art Out of Apartheid', *NME*, 28 June 1986, 11.
69. Daniel Martin, 'Paul Simon Has 'No Regrets' Over 'Graceland' Controversy', *NME*, 27 April 2012.
70. Robin Denselow, 'Paul Simon's Graceland: the acclaim and the outrage', the *Guardian*, 19 April 2012.
71. Ibid.
72. George Michael interview in Tony McGee, 'Mein Whampf!: George Michael and the Decline of Western Civilisation', *NME*, 28 June 1986, 9.
73. Arnold, 329.
74. Ibid, 339.
75. 'Thatcher, the Commonwealth and Apartheid South Africa, blogs.lse.ac.uk, 9 April 2013.
76. Jarvin, 11.
77. Alan Jackson, 'Pressure Groups . . . 100,000 Demand Trade Embargo!', *NME*, 5 July 1986, 45.
78. Peter Elman, 'Nelson Mandela 70th Birthday Tribute', reproduced at tonyhollingsworth.com.
79. *Sounds*, 18 July 1988, 5.
80. 'Cry Freedom', *NME,* 18 June 1988, 3.
81. *Sounds*, 18 July 1988, 5.
82. Elman, op cit.
83. 'Address by Nelson Mandela at Wembley Stadium Concert, London', mandela.gov.za.
84. Welsh, 273.
85. Ibid, 274.

EIGHT – *Kyiv Calling*

1. Pavlo Zibrov, 'I Want to Go Home so Much (Я так хочу додому)', YouTube.
2. Google translation of the lyrics.
3. Serhii Plokhy, *The Gates of Europe: A History of Ukraine* (London: Penguin Books, 2016), xxi.
4. Ibid, xxi.
5. Ibid, 333–334.
6. Ibid, 334.
7. Ibid, 335.

8. 'Q&A: Ukraine Presidential Election', BBC News, online, 7 February 2010.
9. David Kirichenko, 'The Overlooked Presidency of Yushchenko', Euromaidan Press, online, 20 January 2023.
10. Tony Judt, *Postwar: A History of Europe Since 1945* (London: Vintage, 2010), 753.
11. Ibid, 753.
12. *Winter on Fire: Ukraine's Fight for Freedom*, Netflix documentary.
13. Ibid.
14. Ibid.
15. Ibid.
16. Figures taken from Plokhy, 353.
17. Plokhy, 339.
18. *Winter on Fire: Ukraine's Fight for Freedom*, op cit.
19. 'Russia's invasion plan could see military take nine routes into Ukraine, hitting Kyiv's doorstep within two days – reports', Sky News, online, 11 February 2022.
20. 'An Update From Community Fund', K41Community.fund, online, 26 January 2023.
21. Torsten Landsberg, 'Kyiv's K41 club staff find refuge in Berlin', DW News, online, 18 March 2022.
22. Illia Ponomarenko, 'Even if Russia attacks, Ukraine's fall is not predestined, 15 February 2022, quoted in *War Diary of the Ukrainian Resistance: The Kyiv Independent* (Cheltenham: FLINT, 2023), 27.
23. *War Diary of the Ukrainian Resistance: The Kyiv Independent* (Cheltenham: FLINT, 2023), 64.
24. 'Ukraine: Russian Forces' Trail of Death in Bucha', Human Rights Watch, online, 21 April 2022.
25. Scott Neuman, 19/02/2023, 'After a year of war in Ukraine, all signs point to more misery with no end in sight', National Public Radio, online, 19 February 2023.
26. Judt, 648.
27. Ibid.
28. Erich Koch quoted in R. J. Crampton, *Eastern Europe in the Twentieth Century – and After* (London: Routledge, 1997), 182.
29. Dan Stone, *The Holocaust: An Unfinished History* (London: Pelican Books, 2023), 141.
30. Judt, 16.
31. Ibid, 166.

32. Ibid, 423.
33. Stone, 155.
34. Andrii Portnov, 'Bandera Mythologies and Their Traps for Ukraine', openDemocracy, online, 22 June 2016.
35. Ibid.
36. Olivia B. Waxman, 'Historians on What Putin Gets Wrong About "Denazification" in Ukraine', *Time*, 3 March 2022.
37. Interview with author.
38. Andrew Wilson, 'Russia and Ukraine: "One People" as Putin Claims?', Royal United Services Institute, online, 23 December 2021.
39. Plokhy, 350.

Acknowledgements

This book is packed with stories of remarkable and inspirational people who often risked their lives to make the world a better place. We would live in an even darker age without their bravery and music. My first thanks are, of course, to them, especially those who kindly gave up their time to speak to me for this book.

I am also deeply indebted to my agent Kay Peddle, without whom this book would have never made it to print. Her guidance, advice and patience are extremely appreciated. I must also thank my editor Fritha Saunders and all at Footnote Press for taking on this project and being such a pleasure to work with.

A book like this relies heavily on the scholarship of numerous academics, researchers and journalists who have produced necessary and fascinating work. I hope my truncated overviews do not exploit or misrepresent their work. The endnotes of this book show where my countless debts lie, and I hope I represent their work fairly.

I must also thank those who kindly accompanied me on some of the trips abroad that made this book possible, namely Matthew Walker, Sian Cain and Sam Dulieu, who came to Ireland; Duncan Stoddard, who travelled across the United States with me; and my dad, who kindly accompanied me to Ukraine.

I owe a huge debt to those friends who have offered thoughts on various sections, including Ali Horn and Rob Powell. A special thanks must go to Ciaran Cummins, who offered detailed feedback throughout. Your honest criticism, ideas and recommendations have been a great help and improved this text significantly. Without our joint trips to the British Library, I'm not sure I would ever have got this finished.

I also want to thank my friends, colleagues and comrades at HOPE not hate for their patience and support, especially Nick Lowles.

Finally, I want to acknowledge my family. Endless love and thanks to Mum, Dad, Philip, Kelly, Rich and Elliot.

Index